Holte Enders in

We few, we happy few, we band of
he that sheds his blood with me today shall be my brother....'

Ray Barnes,

Steve Barnes,

Paul 'Beebo' Beard,

Pete Bishop,

Malcolm 'Coke' Costello,

Patrick 'Black Pat' Edwards,

Gary Exton,

Des Gallagher,

David Garner,

Steve Groves,

John Haynes,

Gary Harwood,

Chris Hassan,

Paul 'Paulie' Heath,

Andy Kitson,

Gary Lyttle,

Kevin '2 Stone' Maloney,

Andy 'Spike' McGachie,

Gary Morgan,

Dave Moore,

Kevin Murphy,

Simon 'Simmo' Hanley,

Steve Norton,

Steve Powell,

Adam Powers,

David Rammell,

David Ravenhall,

Luke Reid,

Mickey Rivers,

Barry Sheery,

Michael 'Spoon' Somers,

Dougie Thompson,

'Bunny' Weir,

Paul 'F-Man' Yates

REST IN PEACE

1

Acknowledgements

The authors would like to thank the following people in the compilation of this book: Aaron, Aggie, Alcoholic Andy, Alex, Allen, Asda Gary, Banbury Boys, Bash, Bayo, Barry Peck, Biddle, Big Brett, Big Dave Smith, Big Dean, Big Irish Jim & John Paul, Big Paddy, Big Paul & Terri, Big Simon, Big Trev, Big Tony, Billy, Blockhead, Bob, Boot, Botch, Bourney, Brick, Brett Clarke, Brillo, Broffy, Bruno, Bungle, Burkey, Cana, Carl and Russell C, Carl M, Carl Salter, Casey, Charlton, Chemical Chris, Chester Phil, Chris D, Chris W, Clinchy, Clive, Cookie, Craig B, Craig Fowler, Crazy Steve, Cridgey, Crooky, Dave Nealon, Dandy, Danny Hutton, Danny O, Dave Brown, Daz, Deakin, Dean Garrington, Dec, Denzil, Derby Paul, Dino, Dog, Dominic, Don, Duncan, Eddie the Bluenose, Eddie Norton, Farmer, Fat Wayne, Fleety, Gav, Gaz C, Geoff, Ginge, Greenie, Gregg, Gypsy Terry, Handsy, Harold, Ian and Mark C, Jake, Jamie Wellings, Jason R, Jason W, Jez, Big Jimmy, Joe Jordan, Johnny Moo, Jonesy, Justin, Kasim, Kev J, Keeny, Kitty, Lewis, Liam McCarron, Linnie, Little Gaz, Little Jay, Liz, Louis, Loz, Mac, Mad Andy, Mark Baker, Fordey, Mark Hammond, Matty, Melvin, Millsy, Moggo, Nacker, Neil McEwan & Brian 'The Lion' Bailey, Neville from Nechells, Nobby, Nostrils, Oldy, Oz, Paddy, Page, Palm, Panic, Paul H, Paul M, Pembo, Pete, Pete Mc, Phil, Pip, Postman, Powelly, Ray, Reidy, Richie S, Rob S, Roly, Ross, Russell O, Sally, Scooby, Scraggy, Screwdriver, Sedge and Dave, Seth, Shrek, Skinhead Neil, Snake, Solo, Spenna, Stan, Steamy, Steeley & Blounty, Andy, Pat, Buzz and Kung Fu Billy, Steve Baker, Steven Murtagh, Steve White-Jeans, Stickman, Shanna, Spiky Dave, Steff, Stokesy, Suntan-Sam, Swiggsy, Sweeney, Tate, The Brothers Grim, The General, The Loon, The Webb Brothers, The Worcester Lads, Tic, Timmy L, Tom, Tucker, Little Tucker, Two-Man, Victor, Wattsy, Waz, Wilf, Wilson, Yowey, Yob, Youngy, Young Ginge, Young Clarkey, Young Greg, Zak, Zack, Trudy Lutwyche, Ray Scrivens and family, Jan Reid, Simon, Terri, Ian and anyone who we forgot.

Special thanks to Mr Bob Busby.

Photography by Simeon Thaw.
Additional photographs supplied by Danny Hutton and Michael Lutwyche.

Introduction

We are Villa 'Hardcore', Aston Villa Football Club's hardcore support. We are football hooligans. Thugs, yobs, scum, hooligans, whatever labels you, the police or the press have seen fit to attach to us. Those labels haven't deterred us, they simply made us endeavour to go one better. I don't care what people call us. If any of us cared about public opinion we wouldn't have done what we've done over the past 15 years. It is fighting for fighting's sake. The approval of our peers has always been preferable to the opinions of the press or the public at large.

Since the early 1990s Aston Villa Hardcore has been arguably the most prolific football hooligan gangs in the UK. Described by police as one of the worst two hooligan gangs on the England international scene. There are currently 80 Villa Hardcore members subject to football banning orders. Sentences totalling over 80 years have been handed out to participants in a series of high profile incidents involving Aston Villa's Hardcore. Amongst these hard men who have relentlessly taken on the top firms of other football clubs one man's name stands out. He is Steven Fowler, who has been described by police and judges as a 'hardcore 'Category C' hooligan leader'. The police identify football supporters in three categories, A, B and C. Category A supporters are normal fans who attend football matches with no intention of causing any problems. Category B supporters are people the police identify as people who may be prone to disorder on certain occasions especially when alcohol is involved. Category C fans are people who attend football matches with the sole intent of causing trouble usually in organised gangs. Fowler's rise to prominence both nationally and worldwide has been meteoric. Known to police forces the world over Fowler first came to the notice of the world media when he was thrown out of France during the World Cup in 1998. He has since been denied entry into numerous countries during major football tournaments which were being staged there. He is now subject to one of the longest banning orders in British football.

In this book we explain how as Villa Hardcore, we developed our own matchless culture and how we became one of the most highly organised football firms in the country. You will read how we exported our own particular brand of football hooliganism to Europe and the rest of the World. We cover a series of incidents which include clashes with the cream of English footballs hooligan elite. You will find out how other gangs on the England scene reacted when we erupted onto the international scene and took them by shock and storm, and how they had to join forces to deal with us. Fowler's boys took on everyone, from West Ham's Inter-City Firm, Birmingham City's Zulu Warriors, Chelsea's Head-Hunters to Middlesbrough's Frontline. All of them were notorious as some of the hardest hooligan gangs in English football, but we as Villa Hardcore showed them neither respect nor fear.

You will read about the triumphs, the losses and the disasters - because this is not a book like so many hooligan books which pretend that there were no losses. This is an honest book and we do not shirk from admitting to some uncomfortable facts. We'll explain how and why we took on the press. How they attacked us and labelled us. How we reacted. How we stayed one step ahead of them and played them at their own game. And we'll tell you how we took football rivalry with our local rivals Birmingham City to a new level by initiating and maintaining this attack on the ground, in the press, on the airwaves and in cyber-space.

We will reveal our constant battle of wits with the police and particularly the football intelligence officers. Discover why we were targeted by anti-terrorist police. Discover how the exposure of being in the media spotlight and plastered across every national and international newspapers affected some of us. You will read about false allegations, dawn raids, high-profile court cases and lengthy prison sentences - you will find out how all that happening to an individual actually felt. We were labelled scum and jailed as real criminals but in our eyes and minds we are ordinary hard working men who only fought others of the same mind.

Steve Fowler and I decided to write this book because we wanted people to know the truth. We wanted what has occurred to be recorded as honestly and as accurately as possible by ourselves rather than leaving it for people to rely on lies written about us in other books or the press.

Over the last decade football hooligan books have become quite common. Another common denominator has been that, in the main, the authors or the teams in question have never been done. They've never been run. They've taken mobs of 400 plus everywhere and generally taken the piss wherever they have gone. This book will be different. It will not be about bragging and pretending. It will be about reality.

As Villa Hardcore we adapted to the challenges of the 90s. We operated in smaller numbers than was the case in the 80s. Some people say the 80s was 'when it mattered' my answer to that is it always matters, circumstances just change. Also to read a lot of these books you would be forgiven for thinking

Aston Villa fans are not a group to be taken seriously. They pretend that we're nothing, and that you can come to Villa Park and stroll round the place like you own If that was the case isn't it strange that Steve Fowler and the Hardcore are mentioned in most of these books? Why would that be if we're nothing of consequence?

The truth of the matter is we've upset a lot of people. We are no respecters of reputation. We took everyone at face value. If they earned our respect they got it. If they were found wanting they were treated with contempt and scorn. We've upset them and it still hurts them - so much so that they refuse to give us any credit. We turned up with sometimes low numbers and we called it on. We would get into pubs and defy the opposition to remove us. Then we exploded onto the England international scene in 1996. Rightly or wrongly we treated the established England hooligan hierarchy with utter contempt. Respect was given when it was earned not just because someone happened to support a certain team.

What you won't find in this book is any pictures of us shaking hands with any criminals, B-list celebrities, ex-boxers or washed-up footballers. None of us want celebrity or notoriety. We're not suddenly going to be calling ourselves 'hooliologists'. We do not want fame or infamy. A couple of years ago we were asked to feature on Bravo Televisions 'Real Football Factory.' There was no chance of us even entertaining the idea. We told them to sling their hook. We don't seek any notoriety or gangster image. We will disappear back into obscurity once we have had our say. We are what we are, a football firm. We're not gangsters. None of us are into any sort of organised crime other than following our football club. We're not into drugs. We're not into protection or extortion. We don't steal. We are not, in our eyes, criminals. We're hard working family men. It is simply a football thing with us, a Saturday thing.

So why are we Villa Hardcore? To understand us you need to know who we are. Aston Villa Football Club was formed in 1874. Aston was then just outside Birmingham but since 1911 it has been an important industrial part of the biggest city in the West Midlands of England. Birmingham is the UK's 'second city'. It is a city built on industry, manufacturing and the blood sweat and tears of its inhabitants over hundreds of years. Birmingham was once known as the 'Workshop of the World' or the 'City of a Thousand Trades.' This was due to the numerous manufactured goods made in the city which found their way all over the world. Birmingham although not technically inside the boundaries has always been considered as the central hub of the

'Black Country', an area to the west and north of Birmingham. It runs from Dudley in the south to Cannock in the north and from Wolverhampton in the west to West Bromwich in the east. The Black Country was the birthplace and became the heart of the Industrial Revolution in the UK. It supplied our forefathers with the tools with which to build an empire. We are proud, tough and determined working-class people - people with a strong identity of which we are rightly proud of. We are people who have never shied away from hard work or getting our hands dirty - rough and ready, spit and sawdust people who accept the harsh and often dirty realities of life. We are proud Mercian's who value our roots.

People from Birmingham are known as 'Brummies'. We are historically very proud of our city and our identity. Birmingham, known as 'Brum' or 'Brummagem' to its inhabitants, is a heavily industrialised city and as such has suffered from an image problem. For years Brum was seen as a dirty city, with factories and warehouses in close proximity to the city-centre. Its image problem wasn't helped by large scale slum clearance of the inner city in the 1960s and 70s. They left the factories in situ and replaced the old terraced housing and streets with a sprawling concrete jungle and mass of imposing, characterless tower blocks. They ravaged the city-centre with concrete monstrosities and unwelcoming subways and walkways. They built a ring-road which Captain Cook would've found hard to navigate.

The people of Birmingham were never consulted about these changes or asked if they wanted to be involved in this huge social engineering and building experiment. It was touted as 'transformation' and 'improvement.' It turned inner-city Birmingham into a series of high-rise ghetto's and its people suffered for decades as a result. They turned the old slums, which had character and community spirit, into newer slums but without the character of the old and left people remote and disenfranchised. Through determination and endeavour the people of Birmingham have turned the city round. We were left with the damage after the architects who nearly ripped the soul out of the city had long since gone. Experiments are fine, but you should not plough ahead wholesale until you have some conclusion to the consequences it creates. That is the mistake they made, they created a monster. Things however have changed dramatically over the last 15 years or so with a massive re-building programme. Birmingham has made vast strides forward with its city-centre now one of the most pleasant and safest to visit in the country.

Why, then, did some young working-class Brummies become involved in football violence? Why did we do it all? Why was it so important to us? The answer is simply - we are working-class people, from working-class areas. These areas have their own rules. We are traditionally hard people who lead hard lives. We have an inherent aggression. We have an inbuilt pride. I am proud of my roots. I am proud of who I am and where I am from. It's a tribal mentality especially engendered in a proud island race. Aston Villa is my local club. I identify with my club - it represents my background. Football played a very important part in my life as I was growing up. Aston Villa for me represents the City of Birmingham and I am a proud Brummie. If someone affronts Aston Villa they are affronting me because I am Aston Villa. We are the club - we are the people. It doesn't matter who owns it, whoever is playing for it, we the fans are the constant. It is our club. It is my club, my identity.

In our eyes if you are fighting at a football ground or on the streets around a stadium you are fighting for your club. You are fighting under the banner of Aston Villa. You are fighting for your city. For a lot of people simply the confrontation across a fence is enough. For others though there is a need to get in amongst them and show them who is boss. As an away supporter you are on the offensive. We're Brummies and we're here. We can do what we like, when we like. What are you going to do about it? It is that sort of mentality. The public in general don't understand that mentality, or they'll kid you they don't. They're normally the ones straining, standing on tip-toes to get a better look at the action when it's kicking off inside a ground. It's inherent in us all. Since hooliganisms heyday in the 80s successive governments have introduced laws to clamp down on football violence. When it has suited them in the past they have been thankful for our aggression.

Football has always attracted violence. From its conception before organised leagues came into being, football was frequently used to settle grudges. Be it the players or the fans, scores were settled at football matches. Violence has always been part of the game. Football violence is not a new phenomenon it has been going on for centuries in this country. The risks are bigger now than ever before. Ten year bans and restrictions on your movements are now being handed out on top of lengthy prison sentences. Even with these penalties people still fight at and over football matches. Get arrested at a football match now and you are treated more severely than a lot of criminals. This country places more restrictions on football hooligans than it does sex offenders.

We as working-class people with our own traditions and way of life feel that we are now surplus to requirements. The days of manual mass manufacturing have gone. We have become an embarrassment to the Guardian-reading chattering classes. They have discarded us. They have produced an underclass. They have neglected our education for decades. Bungled and ill-thought out education experiments which they often reverse belatedly after kids start leaving school unable to read and write properly. Is it accidental that standards have fallen? Were the mistakes of the experiments made with good intentions or purposely? The purpose in my opinion was to produce an under-educated, apathetic mass dependant on benefits, tax or child credits. It produces people who are reliant on the government. The result is a subservient mob, guided by the media (who are complicit) and which is easier to control. When they improved education standards en-masse in this country they produced a dangerous thing, working-class people with broader horizons. People who wanted to better themselves. They created people who organised themselves to fight for better standards. Better standards of living and better standards in the workplace. By the 1970s the masses in this country were not passive anymore. We demonstrated and voiced our opinions on countless issues. We became politically aware - you could say we had too much democracy. We abused our new found power. The people who claimed to represent us through various trades unions cared little for their members and more for some warped left-wing political ideal. The ruling elite sought to limit our participation in politics - in effect they decided to dumb us down.

We are the enemy now. No longer with modern hi-tech warfare do they need us to answer the rallying call and die in our hundreds of thousands fighting their wars. All we are lacking is a modern day Kitchener screaming down from bill posters - 'Your country does not need you'. We are dinosaurs in a modern age. Dinosaurs that refuse to become extinct. We are spit and sawdust, working-class folk. We are honest people who have been fooled time and time again. We have been fooled either by the establishment and the ruling elite, or politically motivated trades-unions that lied to us when they claimed to represent our best interests.

For hundreds of years we have been bred to feel a pride in our nation and bred to fight. Born to fight on foreign shores and shed our blood whilst other more fortunate classes benefited from our sacrifices. We have been encouraged to be proud of our flag and our monarchy. We are proud of our rich tapestry of culture, heritage and history. Now the mass voting middle-classes are ashamed to fly the Union Flag or the Cross of St George. They wish to be ashamed of our past and expect us to do likewise. They expect us to display the same capricious behaviour they are so prone to. They have sought to hijack our culture because they have none of their own. They've infiltrated into every aspect of working-class life and attempted to take it over.

How do they achieve this? The answer is simple, they vote. The under-educated, apathetic working-classes are now more likely to vote for a television phone-in than they are in choosing who runs the country. We have become an easily malleable ignorant mass that they can control through fear. They're currently ruining English football which they commandeered during European Championships held in England in 1996. Obviously the whole Sky television package and now Setanta has facilitated this even further. All nicely packaged for the conforming nonchalant masses. No swearing, no standing, no banter, no fighting, no smoking, the list is endless. Again they expect us to fit in with their narrow-minded liberalism. Paint your face and blow a fucking bugle. Fit in or fuck off.

Football was an outlet. It was an outlet for long dreary hours in a job going nowhere but senility, a pension and the scrapheap. Football was a safety valve for working-class men who worked hard during the week and liked to let off steam on a Saturday afternoon. We're no longer the pet project of the middle-classes. The cheery, cheeky, chirpy working-class stereotype has long gone. They tired of that long ago. They now view us with a mixture of disgust and disdain. We've served our purpose. They now import their labour if they want low-wage, low-skilled mass production. They import all our goods. They have destroyed our manufacturing base. We have no skills to fall back on anymore. No apprenticeships anymore, people are quickly and shoddily trained and leave places of learning under-educated and under-skilled. In the past if this country was ever threatened we fell back on our manufacturing and our skills. From the longbow to the Spitfire - we could adapt to any challenge. Those days are sadly gone. They think if they stamp down hard on us that they can then move on and worry about far more important things like fighting Zionism or seeking to solve global warming from the safety of their semi-detached suburban ideal. Saving someone else's culture whilst destroying ours.

We are currently engaged in a class-war in this country. The trouble is the working-classes are too indifferent to even notice let alone organise themselves and fight back anymore. Perhaps there is a reason as football hooligans we are targeted so vehemently by the establishment? Organisation is a keyword in all this. Our organisation as football firms is second to none. The police are constantly playing catch up. We have a loyalty and a devotion to the cause and each other which is seldom matched. We do it for the sake of it. They can't understand that mentality so they struggle to contain it. Our organisation and keeping one step ahead of the police is taken for granted. Our organisation is what scares the establishment. We are the last bastion of organised working-class resistance.

If you doubt this take a look at what happened when the Balkans exploded into civil war during the 1990s. Football firms were at the forefront of the guerrilla warfare which ensued. Infamous Serbian fighter Zeljko 'Arkan' Raznatovic formed the Serb Volunteer Guard also known as the Tigers. This group was primarily made up of football hooligans from Red Star Belgrade. They travelled the former Yugoslavia and had a massive impact on the troubles there. Other hooligan gangs in other parts of the former Yugoslavia did likewise. If you think that went unnoticed by the powers that be in the UK then you are very naive. As a football firm we can get 100+ lads undetected into any town or city-centre regardless of CCTV or police presence. They fear us. We, as British football hooligans, are the last bulwark of defiance of a defeated people.

It is our organisation they fear the most. They seek to control us with bans from football and constraints on passports and travel. Bans for offences committed at football matches or civil bans for associating with certain people who have committed offences at football matches. They seek to contain us with travel restrictions when the England team is playing abroad. This year the European Championships were held in Austria and Switzerland. No British team qualified for the tournament. Yet still the authorities insisted that football fans who were on bans that prevented them from travelling abroad at certain times still handed their passports in. None of the home nations were playing in the tournament. What other group of people would they get away with doing that to? Truth of the matter is the football bans and travel restrictions has become an industry now in its own right and we and our rights as per usual are expendable. It is the process of ironing out any defiance we may still have in us.

All this wasn't clear to me in the 1970s when I first started attending matches regularly. The Villa were down on their luck and playing in the old Third Division of the English Football League. It was the 70s, a dark chapter in Britain's history. It was a decade of industrial and civil unrest, three day working weeks and power cuts. At every football ground in the country football hooliganism had exploded onto the terraces. The onset of post-war cheap public transport saw young mainly working-class males travelling the country following their respective football teams. They were clashing, sometimes violently, with the supporters of opposing teams at and around the football grounds or the transport network.

Football has always been the game of the British working-classes. Violence has always played a large part in British working-class life. Tough men who aren't afraid to use their fists have always been respected within those communities. This obviously transferred easily onto the football terraces. Violence is and always has been a quintessential part of working-class life. Working-class men the length and breadth of the country have usually favoured sorting differences or local rivalries out with their fists. There has always been a certain honour attached to sorting out disagreements man to man and 'losing face' is something which had to be avoided at all costs.

The main thing I noticed about football violence when I was growing up was that when the fighting started, everyone, and I mean everyone (including the players at times) in the ground would switch their attention from the game and focus on the trouble. If the violence was bad enough it made the television and radio news. These hooligans, these ordinary working-class men like I would be one day, were the centre of attention. They were watched in awe or disgust by 40k+ people. They were the stars for however long it took the police to quell the trouble. Gangs such as the Steamers, the C-Crew and the Villa Youth emerged from back-street working-class areas and took prominence. Although these gangs would fight any other gang in the country our main and bitter rivals were and are Birmingham City. Known as the Blues, they have perennially under achieved and won nothing of note since forming in 1875. From the 1980s a racial divide developed between Birmingham's two football clubs. It was a divide which lasted for nearly two decades. I would be cheating if I allowed it to pass unexplained. To explain it I have to give the reader some background information.

Birmingham is a multi-cultural city which has had large influxes of immigrants over the years. In the 1980s Birmingham suffered two large scale riots. The disturbances in 1981 were centred in the Lozells Road area of Handsworth in Birmingham. Handsworth has a large West Indian community who settled here in the 50s and 60s because it contained a lot of large houses in a once affluent area. These had been turned into flats and rooms to accommodate the large number of immigrants who post-war were invited to settle and make new lives for themselves in the UK.

At the turn of the 80s the Black community suffered from higher than average unemployment. Tough laws had been brought in to combat high street crime levels in certain areas of the country. These were stop and search powers granted to the police. They would be commonly known as the 'suss laws.' In Brixton, London in the April of 1981 a large-scale riot had erupted. The police were seen as the common enemy and were attacked. Buildings were looted and burnt to the ground. This was followed by a riot occurring in Toxteth, Liverpool, on the 5th of July for similar reasons.

Five days later, on July 10th, Handsworth in Birmingham exploded. A young black man was stopped by the police close to the Acapulco Café on the Lozells Road. Local people intervened and the police called for back up. It wasn't long before the whole area erupted into an orgy of violence and destruction. It was mainly disaffected, disenfranchised black youths with little or no prospects venting their anger at the police and especially the despised SPG (Special Patrol Group). The West Indian community felt ignored and at the same time singled out by the draconian clampdown on street crime. These weren't race-riots, white people took an active role, but it was mainly West Indian people against a virtually totally white police force.

Black people saw the police or the Babylon as they called them, as a symbol of oppression. As their identity evolved they began to explore Black-British culture which in turn embraced a new sort of music from the USA. Hip-hop had originated from the 'block parties' of New York especially the Bronx, which had a large West Indian immigrant population. Huge sound systems with massive speakers would blast out music at open air parties held in urban areas. Residents would speak over the music - it evolved into rapping or toasting. The West Indian community of the UK identified with this music and greeted it with open arms. One of Hip-hop's leading protagonists was Afrika Bambaattaa - real name Kevin Donovan. Bambaattaa had been a gang member in New York. Following a life changing visit to Africa, he had changed his name to Afrika Bambaattaa Aasim, in honour of a Zulu chief Bhambatha, who had led an armed rebellion in South Africa during the early 1900s. Bambaattaa led the Soul Sonic Force a group which toured the world in 1982 making its music more accessible. Black youths identified with this image. At around the same time a film entitled Zulu Dawn appeared on television which showed the British army being defeated at Isandlwana by the Zulu's in 1879. The chant 'Zulu!' could be heard continually throughout the film.

The content of the film obviously resonated with Birmingham's disaffiliated black youth. At some clubs in Birmingham city-centre, especially clubs like The Powerhouse, where hip-hop nights were running, the chant 'Zulu!' could be heard following the films screening on television. At around this time Birmingham City's hooligan following started calling themselves the 'Zulu Warriors'. To read their book it appears it just came out of no-where at Manchester City on the 20th November 1982. It didn't, it came from Birmingham's night-clubs.

The Zulu's became notorious throughout the country. They attracted a lot of Birmingham's Black youth to the fold in the early to mid 80s. Some of them were involved in large scale shoplifting and robbery which they conducted as they travelled the country following Birmingham City. It became fashionable to follow Birmingham City in that atmosphere of riot and public disorder. Many people associated themselves with the Zulu Warriors simply for that. A lot of them didn't care about Birmingham City, just about the Zulu's. This had the effect of polarising both sets of fans. Blues became Birmingham's multi-racial firm where as Villa's mob became predominantly white.

We had black lads with us at the Villa, some very good ones, but a lot were attracted by what was going on at the Blues. It was amazing really, looking back at how it turned out. Before then Blues and their Tilton Skins or the lads from the Happy Trooper on Chelmsley Wood were always the racist supporters in our city. Villa always had a large second generation Irish support, so right-wing extremism was never really going to prosper at Villa Park. As the two Birmingham firms polarised into virtually a racial divide a small racist element did come into it, briefly it must be said. Some lads sympathised with right-wing issues. As the Villa Youth developed and began taking on the Zulu's we were being attacked and beaten by a mainly Black firm week in week out. It is probably surprising more didn't end up developing right-wing sympathies.

It suits some people however to keep this right-wing tag around our necks. It suits them because we are easily bracketed then. Are we a racist firm? No. That is simply not the case. We have been predominantly white but that is for the reasons stated above. I defy anyone to grow up in Birmingham and be truly racist, there will always be a minority of racists but that can be said on both sides of the coin. We received negative publicity from the press. They accused us of being right-wing fascists and the Zulu's used that to their advantage. They would ring round telling people the BNP or Combat 18 were in town as Villa Hardcore, and so sometimes we were fighting the whole of the town not just other football fans.

The key thing about the Hardcore was that we were not an exclusive group. We didn't look down on other Villa fans. We are all Villa fans. We were Villa's 'hardcore' support and most importantly we were and still are all mates. We have people in our group who haven't got a fight in them. They're no less important than the people who have. They all contribute in their own particular way. We're all mates. People always have a take on football violence; everyone talks a good fight in the pub. One thing I can safely say about the Hardcore is we put ourselves in there amongst it. We walked where others feared to tread. We would turn up in places, no matter what our number and make the necessary calls. We'd always turn up. We'd always let the opposition know where we were. It was up to them then to stop us. Either shift us or stop us walking round taking the piss.

Villa Hardcore emerged in the early 1990s. As will be explained later, football violence had a lull during the rave years of 1988-91. In the early formative years we were a very loose-knit collective. People would have their own little circle of friends and we'd bump into old acquaintances and make new ones within their circle of friends. People would talk to mutual acquaintances and the firm came together that way. It should not be understated what role Garry Tucker played in all of this. He will talk to anyone and he would often organise coaches which the core of the Hardcore would travel upon in the early days.

In our minds we represented Aston Villa. We also represented Aston Villa at international level. Our world is not a politically correct world. We may not fit most people's expectations of good citizens but all of our lads are working, paying tax and a lot of them have mortgages, decent jobs and prospects. We're not the scum we are made out to be, we've been men doing what men have done for millennia, and this is our story.

Chapter One: Villa Youth

Football hooliganism started to become a problem in the late sixties. Violence had always been associated with football - from its early days as the mass participant football matches which pitted village against village - disagreements and old grudges have always been settled at football matches. The evolution of football in England - especially since the inception of the Football League in 1888 - has always been shadowed by social disorder. The late 19th century and the birth of the Football Association saw teams sprang up all over the country. Locals identified with the team in their particular district. In the early days unruliness at football matches rarely merited much column space in the national or local press. When it did occur it was ignored or seen as the more exuberant or unruly of the working-classes letting off steam. The word hooligan first appeared in 1898 and it quickly came into common and widespread use, before then offenders were usually termed 'ruffians' or 'street Arabs'. When football related violence did get a mention in the popular press, it was usually a large-scale riot involving thousands or resulting in deaths. Unless it spilled out of the stands on to the pitch or into the streets it went largely unreported.

Following the Second World War Britain saw some major changes. Social and economic conditions improved even for the lower echelons of society. People experienced low unemployment and a rising standard of living. Also for the first time youth sub-cultures started to emerge. There have always been gangs in this country, we are a tribal people. Victorian gangs such as Birmingham's 'Peaky Blinders', the 'Scuttlers' of Manchester or the High Rippers from Liverpool would clash with other gangs locally at music halls or suchlike or nationally at venues such as race courses. Of course these facts have largely been whitewashed from the collective memory by people who wish to convince us all you could leave your back-door open then, when it was all fields round here.

The post-war years saw the rise of the first real youth culture, the Teddy Boys. The Teds as they were known, cared how they looked, appearance was everything. They had taken to a new fashion of the time which was based on an Edwardian style. After this group came to prominence Edward was soon shortened to 'Ted' by the press and the movement had a name. They formed gangs and clashed with other Teddy Boy gangs, again usually at music halls. The Teddy Boys really hit the headlines when large numbers of Teds helped swell the numbers of groups of white youths who participated in race riots in the Notting Hill area of London throughout August and September of 1958.

The Teds of the 50s evolved into the Rockers of the 60s who were set to clash with another sub-culture which would appear, the Mods. The term Mod comes from the word modernist, which many young people had used to describe the new sub-culture which was sweeping the country. They looked down on the traditional British forms of dress and music and adopted a classic Italian tailored dress code and also appropriated Italian motor-scooters which were obviously a contrast with the motorbikes favoured by the Rockers. Gangs would often clash over territory or when they accidentally came into contact with each other. The rivalry between the two was jumped upon by the press when gangs of Mods and rockers clashed at seaside resorts in Britain during the Easter Bank Holiday of April 1964. Further clashes, again at seaside resorts, continued throughout the summer.

In the 50s and particularly the 60s the working-classes started to find a bit more money in their pockets. Also affordable travel for the masses meant that young men began to travel the country watching their team.

Bob: The 1957 FA Cup Final at Wembley was my first match. My Father was always a Villa fan. He took me to the final. I loved it. I became a Villa supporter. We were Witton Enders. The Witton End was also the end which the away fans used to gather. You always used to get away fans. You would get more when we played Midlands clubs. The away fans being there meant the banter was always better in the Witton End than the Holte End. The banter was always friendly. The Holte End was always Villa's end of the ground. We used to try and sneak round to the Trinity Road Stand at half-time. The pies were always better over there. It was where the directors sat. The stand had terracing underneath the seats. Sometimes they'd leave the gates open and we'd be able to sneak in and sit upstairs.

Our support has always traditionally been from North Birmingham and beyond. There were always coaches arriving, packed with Villa fans, from places like Lichfield. There was always banter between various Villa supporters on the Witton End. We had a lot from the Black Country who used to stand there. We'd ask them where they'd parked their horse and carts while the match was on. It was friendly banter. It made you feel part of it all. You would sometimes get trouble in the Witton End during the late 60s, especially when we played Birmingham City. We've always hated each other. In my opinion, in those days it was down to success. They always resented us. We were by far the more successful of the two clubs.

The Villa nearly went bump in the late 60s. My Father bought shares which were offered for sale to save the club. Villa shouldn't have been in that position. We were

having big crowds. The money went somewhere. One of the directors used to live two doors away from us. You'd see him come out of his house and get into a taxi on match days. He used to have his black trilby and big black overcoat on as he walked to get into the taxi. It was all part of the image of course. This was in the days when virtually no-one caught a taxi, you couldn't afford to! My Father never spoke to him and he always ignored my Father. My Father loved the club. He didn't like what was happening to it. He bought the shares and they were put into a drawer upstairs. When my Father died they passed to my Mother. I was reading the paper years later and I saw an article saying that Villa shares were now worth £400 each. I said to my Mother that we should think about selling them. We knew someone connected to the club and they asked Doug Ellis, who was then Chairman, whether we should sell them. He said to hold on to them they would increase further. Not long after that they slumped and were virtually worthless.

Another important factor in the rise of football hooliganism which can't be ignored is the fact that in the mid 60s football was televised regularly for the first time. Clashes which occurred inside football stadiums were now broadcast to people nationwide some of whom had possibly never attended a football match. The violence obviously horrified a large section of the general public. At the same time I have no doubt, it also excited a large proportion of the young men of this country and they flocked to football grounds in search of 'aggro'. The mod movement of the early to mid 60s developed into the Rude Boy or Skinhead subculture. They adopted a harder working-class image than the Mods. Their image was increasingly based on violence and they evolved into the Suede-heads or Boot-Boys of the 70s. The Suede-heads continued the fashion of the cropped headed skinhead but the Boot-Boys had longer hair and adopted the more modern of fashions. Violence at football hit unprecedented levels and thanks to television cameras being a more frequent sight at football grounds it would only escalate and attract more combatants to the fold. One thing the media did was unite all the violent sections of local sub-cultures. They merged and congregated at football grounds because the press had informed them that was where the local 'action' could be found.

Up to the late 60s and early 70s gangs at Villa Park always came from individual neighbourhoods. The main mobs were from Erdington, Kingstanding and Quinton. These were areas in the north and west of Birmingham which had sprung up at the end of World War II. Inner-city areas were bulldozed due to bomb damage and the desire for slum clearance. The residents of Birmingham's inner-city were moved wholesale to these new developments. They became huge sprawling council-housing estates. These new estates carried on growing for up to twenty years and developed their own identities. Even up to the present day localised gangs still travel independently from both Kingstanding and Erdington to watch Aston Villa. They are traditional Aston Villa supporting areas. It is also an interesting fact that these areas go against the racial demographics of Birmingham. At the time of the census in 2001, both areas had white populations of around 89%. This figure went against the rest of Birmingham's demography where the figure was nearer 70%. Villa had fans from all over Birmingham and the Black Country, but these were the areas who could summon the larger of the gangs.

Pongo: I remember the old Quinton mob from the 1970s and 80s. In those days Quinton was regarded as pure Villa but things change. The Quinton Mob were Quinton first and Villa second. They used to carry red and black scarves as well as Villa ones to identify each other when trouble kicked off. I remember they had the one enormous skinhead who used have a piece of black masking tape across his forehead - as if he didn't stand out enough already! His job appeared to be to stand on the highest ground around so the QM could rally around him. I spent my teenage years in the south of the city. The only hassle I had off Blues in those days was from their National Front contingent. Blues then were notorious for their National Front support and I got loads of 'nigger lover' insults from them and the occasional dig from them for being Villa.

The first organised gang at Aston Villa which boasted members from all over the city was called The Steamers. They were from all parts of Birmingham but predominantly the south of the city. In the 1970s the Steamers travelled the country taking on anyone who wanted it. In the dark days of the early 70s Villa were in Division Three. In 1968 after suffering relegation Villa found themselves faced with relegation from the old Second Division. The fans held a protest meeting at Digbeth Civic Hall and the board resigned en masse and the club was bought by a London financier and solicitor Pat Mathews. Mathews was the chairman of the Birmingham Industrial trust so obviously had interests in the area. He installed Tommy Docherty as manager. Crowds boomed, jumping from 13,000 against Charlton to 42,000 for the next match against Cardiff City. By the end of the season Villa had crowds approaching 60,000. Matthews installed Doug Ellis - a Birmingham based travel agent as Chairman. Villa were saved from relegation that season but the euphoria quickly wore off and they were relegated the next season for the first time in their history to Division Three. Villa's support boomed while we were in the Third Division. We had bigger attendances than a lot of teams in the top flight. Television programmes were made about Villa's fanatical support. We were a famous, old, big club and when we visited places in the Third Division it would usually be our opponent's biggest game of the season. This ensured a large turn-out of locals and the Steamers were more than happy to take them on. Villa started to claw their way back to the top flight with Vic Crowe (an ex-Villa player) at the helm. Crowe was aided and abetted by Villa's devoted and numerous support. Crowe managed to get Villa out of the Third Division but couldn't attain the last step, promotion to the First Division, especially in 1974 which was Villa's centenary year. Crowe was sacked and tough-talking Ron Saunders was appointed as manager. Saunders soon became the Messiah to the fans as he took Villa to promotion and League Cup success in 1975. The good times were back. After an absence of eight years Villa were back where they belonged, the top flight of English football.

When I was in my early teens, Villa's hooligan following was known as the C-Crew. I started going to matches with lads from school and the Great Barr area of Birmingham where I was born. Villa were going from strength to strength on the pitch and the buzz around Villa at the time was amazing. 'Hail Saunders! Hail the Villa!' was the cry of local BRMB radio DJ Tony Butler, especially when Villa were playing in Europe. Fashion had started to play a part in terrace culture during the late 60s Now there was a new look sweeping the terraces. It was always crew-cuts and Doc Martens or the like before then, your typical 'bovver boy' image. We called ourselves 'Trendies.' We had wedge haircuts. MA1 green flying jackets, leather safari coats or puffer jackets were accompanied by tight jumbo corduroys or jeans. There was no Lycra then or stretch-denim, the jeans almost cut you in half. Everyone seemed to be wearing Patrick cagoules. Fila made an appearance helped by the Wimbledon successes of Bjorn Borg. We wore cycling shirts and yes, hands up ski-jumpers. We had white Kio moon boots or trainers, usually Adidas or Puma. Pretty soon we latched onto proper labels which most of the general public were still ignorant of. I thought I was the height of fashion in my Lacoste polo shirt and Lyle and Scot or Pringle jumper. For the next couple of years I alternated between tennis pro look or looking like an off-duty golfer.

Neville: The C-Crew really became an active firm at the start of the championship winning season of 1980-81. The firm originated from a group of younger lads who had

been organising themselves with varying degrees of success in the previous two seasons.

Two well known and popular lads, Paul "Billy" Brittle and Andy Browne began organising coaches for away games. At a home match against Everton in September 1980 the firm was beginning to be referred to as the C-Crew. There are various theories for where the name came from. The most popular being the 'C' stood for corner i.e. Corner Crew or that the 'C' was an abbreviation of 'Sea' i.e. Sea Crew. As I recall at the time of the Everton game most of the crew were watching games from the top left of the Holte End, not the bottom right-hand corner. It was not until after Christmas of that season that people began to stand down there in any numbers. The most likely explanation for the name is that the week before the Everton game, a coach-load of Villa had headed to Great Yarmouth after an away game at Ipswich. At some stage they were referred to as the 'Sea Crew' by people on board a coach that was heading straight back to Birmingham. Wherever the name originated from, it was without doubt a good time to be following Aston Villa. A league title was followed up with a European Cup triumph the following season. The C-Crew became involved in high profile incidents both on the domestic scene and abroad.

The C-Crew peaked at a European Cup semi-final in Brussels against Anderlecht. There was widespread rioting before, during and after the game. Villa fans inside the end reserved for the home support started fighting and fans from other parts of the stadium scaled fences to join them. Fans ran onto the pitch and the match was halted for a while. There was major fall-out politically following the fixture. Football hooliganism was labelled the English disease. Villa were threatened with being thrown out of the competition. At this point I thought we had it made. We were the best team in Europe and had also been labelled the worst fans. It couldn't get any better than that for me. Little did I know what was in store for us and the club in the next few years.

Reidy: All the older Villa lot from my area were involved in the C-Crew. We started travelling as a proper firm. We were from all parts of Birmingham. I was in Brussels for the infamous riot. I drove over in my car with a couple of mates. We met up with the rest of the C-Crew once we were over there. We couldn't get tickets for the Villa end of the ground. There must've been 6-7000 Villa there. We went in the Anderlecht section. We were at war at the time over the Falklands. They started singing 'Argentina'. They were also throwing bread at us. I think there was a bread strike on at the time. We waded into them. Riot police then waded into the crowd trying to separate us. It was going off everywhere all the way through the game.

Neville: Sadly, as the 1982-83 season saw the demise of a great team on the pitch it also heralded the end of the C-Crew. Times were different back then and jobs were not as easy to come by compared to nowadays. Needs must and many lads had started to become involved in money-making activities. These took priority over football and the crew suffered for it. A new firm was about to emerge, the 'Villa Youth.' Some of the old C-Crew boys were still about but this new firm mainly consisted of new kids on the block. The C-Crew disappeared as quickly as it had started but not without leaving its mark. Friendships that were forged in those days have endured the decades and still exist today.

When I finally graduated into the hooligan ranks at Villa Park the C-Crew had virtually disappeared as a group. Most of them were still floating about here and there but they were in smaller groups. Most of them were doing their own thing. There was a small group of us around my age. Villa didn't have an organised firm. We couldn't guarantee we'd have a decent turn out every week. We had no trouble for the big matches or the local derbies. Week in week out however was a different story. Most of Villa's hooligan support was centred on the Crown and Cushion in Perry Barr, the Bagot and the Norton pubs in Erdington and the Windsor, a pub in the city-centre. I started travelling away to matches with the Crown lads. A lad called Cheque-book Nigel used to run coaches regularly. He was aided and abetted by a lad called Ginger Pat. I was still young but the older lads used to look out for the younger lads. I met Villa legends such as Joey the Bat, Wilko and the Haines brothers. Forget the players. To me these were the legends. I became friends with them all. Fashion still played a major part in it all. During this time the look changed. We started calling ourselves 'Dressers.' The 'wedge' haircut was still de-rigueur, now accompanied by Lacoste or Armani shirts, Fila BJ, Tacchini or Ellesse tracksuits. Sabre jumpers or the blue and white or green and white rugby tops with Benetton across the front were popular. Adidas shoes and trainers were sought after. Burberry Jackets, anything which you had to go out of your way to get. Some of the older lads still held on to the bovver boy image, but in the main lads started to care about how they dressed. Fashion wise we followed lads like Steve 'Rat' Eades who personified the look of the time. Lads started sitting in the seating areas of grounds. It was all part of setting ourselves aside, apart from the normal support. We started carrying little umbrellas. They had a rock-hard solid plastic handle. It was part of the look but the handles did come in useful when applied with some force to someone's head. We also used to carry little Jif lemon bottles. Supposedly you would put ammonia in them but if you couldn't access industrial strength ammonia, bleach or any noxious substance would be put in. Weapons such as knives were rare with us. Some people carried them, but in my experience not many, apart from the Scousers or Londoners.

I got to know a lad called Dave Harrison from the Villa. You got to know people seeing them week in week out. Dave, who was called Chas, and I became good mates. We started knocking about with each other during the week. He was from Witton. Witton is the area which encompasses Villa Park. I started to spend more and more time in Witton and Aston. I made a lot of new friends. It was a harder environment than the area I had grew up in. I learned a lot. I became more street-wise. I hardened up. There was a gang of us who used the Witton Arms. We started calling ourselves The Witton Firm. We did the odd bit of graffiti around the area. We'd hit Witton train station. I remember we daubed 'Villa Skins kick to kill' on a few walls. We weren't skinheads. Neil, one of the lads said it made the area look grimmer when visitors got off the trains. We were kids and it was a laugh. A lot of the TWF were ex or current Villa lads. One of them, Gary Exton had been very well known at Villa Park. Others like Mark, Paul and Dave Casey, Fats and Victor still attend matches to this day. Proper good lads, they're the heart and soul of Aston Villa, local lads following their local team. We drank in all the pubs around the area but especially The Witton Arms. The Holte pub nearby had a room to the rear which was called the Florida Rooms. They'd have discos and functions there which we'd always try and gatecrash. It would normally go off outside the Florida Rooms at the end of the night and the Witton boys would normally be involved. They were all products of Birmingham's harsh inner-city environment. I learnt to fight. I also learnt it wasn't so much being able to fight; it was more having the courage to stand your ground and never leaving your mates which gained you the most kudos. You never left your mates, never ever, no matter what.

The Witton Arms became a pub which had a bad reputation. Around 1983 we'd take a small mob to Villa matches. Our little firm would meet up with lads from Kingstanding or the Bromford. A lad from Bromford called Geoff started running coaches. We had nothing organised during this time. We'd just travel in small groups to away matches and it would be hit and miss whether you'd meet up with more. August 1983 saw an article appear in 'The Face' magazine during the close season. It had documented the rise of the 'casual phenomenon'. People had latched onto this and everyone at the football had started to dress. You couldn't move for bleached Lois jeans. We had generally moved onto other labels. Cerruti became popular as did Aquascutum. On match-days we had a little firm in that bottom right of the Holte End. Lads had taken to standing at the bottom of the stand. It wasn't the done thing anymore to stand at the back of the stands with a scarf tied round each wrist. Standing down the bottom right of the Holte End had its practicalities also. You were always the first people infiltrating away fans would meet as they entered the ground. Not that many teams did attempt to infiltrate the Holte End however due to its sheer size. You'd have singing at that bottom right hand corner. Away fans would sometimes come into the Witton Lane seats and we'd sometimes be exchanging missiles with them during the match. They put a net up to stop that happening but if they did come in those seats we'd still clash directly outside following the match anyway. We were nothing special at this time but any teams who came looking for it would be challenged to some degree.

Blues started to have the upper hand in our city. We'd sometimes have up to 200 of them waiting for us to get off the train at New Street station following away matches. They have always hated us. It's bitterness. They envy our success and they envy our support. What they did was more than football though, it was bullying in the end really. We hadn't got the numbers, except on derby-day, to combat them. They'd steam into us and nine times out of ten the majority of us would scatter. If they caught you, they'd beat you senseless. They would then rob you or strip you of any decent clothing you might have been wearing. A lot of them were black, most of us were white. It was the start of the racial divide between the fans of the two clubs. However the black lads who were with us seemed to suffer worse if they were caught. I remember Blues especially used to hate Victor. He used to take it to them in town. He wasn't that much older than me but to me he never seemed scared of them. They terrorised us for a few years. It wasn't just match-days either. You could be up town with a girlfriend in the week for instance, they would identify you as Villa and attack you. It hardened us up looking back. It engendered a hatred for them in us. They'd pay for it one day.

Jonesy: Around 1985 we would have a firm going into town after Villa matches. We weren't necessarily looking for Blues. We were just off up town for a drink or some were heading home. I really became aware of the Zulu's at this point. A lot of black lads used to hang around the Bull Ring and wait for Villa lads. They weren't all Birmingham City supporters. A lot of them were what we called 'Townies.' I think they hated us because of where we came from, better areas, rather than the Villa. They all

became Villa haters. They would prey on small numbers of Villa fans in the city-centre. We played Liverpool away last match of the season in 1985. It was the day of the Blues-Leeds riot at St Andrews. I remember I was planning to travel up to the match by train. New St Station was full of Blues waiting for Leeds to get off the train and that was about 9am. I was standing outside when a coach went past. It was the Norton Flyers. I knew a few of them. They were a great bunch of lads, they were mad Villa fans. They would drink in the King Edward before home matches. They were from Pype Hayes and Erdington mainly. They stopped by the Rotunda to pick a couple of people up. I jumped on the coach. They were mainly old skinheads, rough and ready types. Blues paid a bit of an interest but weren't too keen. They started to come out of the station. Some of the Norton Flyers got off the coach to front them. Blues main lad was standing there and he clapped the coach. One of the lads thought he was taking the piss and went over and fronted him. He didn't want to know. After a couple of years of Blues having the upper hand that was the day I realised, Villa had lads just the same as them. We had just as many good lads than they did. It was amazing really, you had lads like the Norton, the lads from the Bagot and the lads from the Crown and Cushion and yet we were still coming off second best against Blues most of the time in the city-centre. The thing is in those days a lot of Villa drank in Sutton Coldfield. Sutton town-centre in those days, in my opinion, was much rougher than Birmingham city-centre. There was one night-club, called Park Avenue. You'd have lads from Pype Hayes, Castle Vale, Falcon Lodge, Kingstanding, Erdington and Great Barr in there. Everyone knew each other but no-one liked each other. I started knocking about with lads like Gez Barron, Smooth and Darren Morris. I started drinking up town with them. We started growing up. We got more streetwise. A lot of Blues came from Highgate at the time. They were closer to town than us. If you were from Erdington you didn't want to mess about going up to town and then back out to get home. It was different for them and they also had the relationship with the townies. They and the townies were one and the same at one point. They weren't football fans; they were just Villa-haters. It became trendy to be a Zulu so that's what they all did. They used it as an excuse to go out shoplifting.

There were still a few older C-Crew lads knocking about. Brittle, Static, Garry Lyttle, Gez, Eamonn, Scouse Martin, Macca, Black Roger, Fordy, Joycey, the Hamilton's, Clancy, Kitty, Keeny, Joe Carol and a few more. They were lads who had been in with the C-Crew and they were our mainstay for that period really, until some of us were ready to make the step up. Dave Ravenhall was coming on to the scene at this time. He was slightly older than us. Dave was from Kingstanding. He was an ex-amateur boxer who had won a couple of national titles. Dave was probably one of Villa's main lads at the time even though he was relatively young. Dave is sadly no longer with us. Dave was always with another lad called H. Around 1984 things started to change. We had a large number of younger lads join our ranks which resulted in the emergence of the Villa Youth. The Youth was something we all became part of. It started in Kingstanding and Witton. The common link was Cardinal Wiseman School in Kingstanding. Most of these younger lads attended that school. The group I knocked about with, Chas, Crumpton, Spencer, Arnott, Bondy and Duncan, were all slightly older than these lads. We started knocking about with them. A chip-shop in Kingstanding followed by the Crown and Cushion in Perry Barr became our meeting places. The Crown has always been a meeting place for Villa lads. Our profile was raised by a widespread graffiti campaign across the city.

The name 'Villa Youth' came on the number 11 bus after a night game at West Bromwich Albion. A lad from Witton called Johnsy came up with it. We'd been knocking around getting small young firms for matches. We needed a name to get some momentum. After the name was agreed everything just spiralled. We could have numbers of 40+ for some matches. We travelled to Stoke on the 27th August 1984.

This match was only memorable as it was I think the first time the Villa Youth travelled together, and the first time the Villa Youth made the papers. Villa won the match 3-1. After the match the police found there were too may people on the coach. They told us some of us had to get off and catch the train back. No-one volunteered. They left us there on the coach-park to decide. The driver disappeared. Smiffy from the Bromford noticed that the keys had been left in the ignition. He took them from the ignition and threw them into a river or brook which ran alongside the car-park. The police went mad, especially when they realised most of the coach passengers were under 16. They organised their own transport, two dilapidated old coaches. They searched us all and took us back to Birmingham at 30mph. They dropped us off at the Crown in Perry Barr. It made the papers the next day. Most of us were thrilled. That started the ball rolling, the exposure we received from that.

We were wearing our hair shorter. Crew neck jumpers, button down shirts and flared corduroys or jeans. Adidas Trimm-Trabb or Munchen trainers were popular. We used to get our flares from a place called International Stock on the Dudley Road in Birmingham. We'd get these jeans for about two quid a pair. No-one was wearing flared trousers at that time apart from football lads. The older lads who didn't know the look was progressing laughed at us younger lads with our flares. I had a pair of 38inch bell bottom Levi's which on reflection was taking it a little too far. They made a noise as I ran. A few of us were wearing Harris Tweed jackets. We adopted a scruffy look. Everyone had latched onto the labels. We never called ourselves casuals, we were dressers. We stayed one step ahead. Football lads have stopped doing that. We used to lead and others would follow. Now we have stalled fashion wise. People re-discovered Stone Island in the 90s and then ran out of ideas. Now its retro stuff if you want to be different. I always used to laugh at the old Teddy-Boys who you'd see as a kid. Middle-aged blokes dressing like teenagers with a quiff, a bootlace tie and a pair of brothel creepers. You see it now but these days its normally balding, red-faced, beer bellied forty-something's, who should know better. You see them bouncing down the road in Stone Island jackets which are two sizes too small for them.

We were all young. We were mainly kids turning out week after week to fight men. I was one of the oldest at 18-19. Word was spreading however and lads from all over the city were joining our ranks. Tucker appeared on the scene with his mate Mark. We started taking it to a number of more established firms all over the country with varying results. We would march into town after home matches. We'd get run or done most of the time but we were having a go. In late 1985 we had marched into town after a Saturday game. We had been slowly getting better numbers. We met Blues at the Fire Station in town. They liked to ambush us there when they could. It was their mob, the Zulu's. We outnumbered them and we ran them. We found out it could be done. They weren't invincible. That day was a turning point. We'd take mobs into town regularly looking for them after that day. Our successes encouraged a lot of older lads to come back into the fray.

We didn't always go to the games. We couldn't always afford to. We'd sit in Maurice's or Aldo's Cafés on Witton Island having a laugh while the game was on. New Years Day 1986 was memorable. We encountered another youth firm for the first time. It was Manchester City's Young Guvnor's. A lot of them hadn't paid into the match and were just hanging round up by the ground. We had running battles them while the game was on. They played Walsall a few days later in the FA Cup. A big mob of us met up in Perry Barr and travelled to Walsall to try and bump into them again. The police caught hold of us on our way to the ground and escorted us back to the train station. We played Arsenal in the League Cup in 1986. One of the lads who I knew from Witton was an Arsenal fan. His name was Geoff, he used to travel to London regularly to see them play and he knew some of their lads. It was arranged that Geoff would lead the Arsenals lads round to Aston Park after the match. Few teams have ever come to that side of the ground. Arsenal were always game in those days. After the match ended we all made our way to the top of Aston Park. We stood at the top of the hill waiting. We watched the crowds heading home. All of a sudden a shout went up and Arsenal were there, at the bottom of the park. We flooded down the hill towards them. In the light of the floodlights from Villa Park I could see there were hundreds of us. We were all running towards them at the bottom of the hill. They fired a flare at us. They also had ammonia. We flew into them. A few of them tried to make a stand. They were forced back down Nelson Road. Some of them were trying to hold it together but there were Villa firing into them from all angles. It was dark and it was confused. The police started arriving in numbers. People just disappeared into the night. We were on our way back. Just as the Zulu Warriors bandwagon had attracted lads to their ranks, the reputation of our young Villa Youth firm attracted more and more young lads from all over Birmingham, and more importantly had enticed some of the older lads out of retirement. We always travelled in convoys of cars, or minibuses to away matches. We always got into a place undetected that way. We took a number of pubs like that. We had a few coaches but those trips traditionally with the Youth used to end in tears, or with the coach ablaze. We got into places early and stayed there. It was then up to the locals to shift us. We got to matches anyway we could. Kevin Coyle and I hitch-hiked to Scunthorpe. I travelled to Leeds for a League Cup match with Wayne Crumpton and a Vespa scooter - it took us 6 hours and we got there late missing the match!

Even in the close season we would still meet each other at one of the Crown's on Saturdays. I had started knocking around with a couple of the older Crown lads. I would attend matches with Ian Haines, Gary Hamilton or his brother Trevor, Grovesy and Joycey, even Black Pat, all good proper game lads. We would drink in the Old Crown and Cushion until last orders at 3-30. We would then head up to the Review Bar on Soho Road. The Review Bar was a private club so ignored the old licensing laws. It was a strip-club. We'd also use the Monte-Carlo Club further on down Soho Road, the music was always good there, old style reggae and they threw in chicken in a basket for the admission money. When the pubs re-opened we'd usually then head into town for the evening. We were using both the Crowns during the week off and on. It made us more close-knit. You could land at either of the Crowns at anytime and find someone in there that you could easily spend the night drinking with. It was a good atmosphere and good people - it was full of colourful characters.

On the pitch things had really gone downhill. After the European Cup triumph of 1982 manager Tony Barton had left and had been replaced by a young up and coming manager Graham Turner from Shrewsbury. The cup winning team was dismantled. At the time everyone blamed Turner but in hindsight it is clear that it was Doug Ellis who was intent on wiping any memory of the European Cup win from the memory as it was won in his absence from the club. He shipped out the heroes of our European Cup triumph and treated them dreadfully. The club had no direction and started to struggle. At the start of the 86-87 season we were hammered at Nottingham Forest 5-0 and Turner was sacked. Villa fans didn't stop singing from start to finish of that match in Nottingham. Brian Clough ran halfway across the pitch and applauded us. That is one of my enduring memories from my years following the Villa. The great Brian Clough acknowledging our loyal support. I followed the Villa everywhere that season. It is the one season where I attended every match. Villa were in trouble - I felt they needed me more than ever. I answered the call.

   Villa were relegated in 1987. We had trouble with varying degrees of success virtually everywhere we went. At the end of the season we played Manchester United at Old Trafford. Villa were already relegated. We met at the café over the road from the Crown that morning. I was with two Witton lads, Spoon and Punk. We had no tickets Villa had sold out. Someone who had just come from Villa Park said Villa had been given another 400 tickets. We raced down there and everyone managed to get a ticket. We travelled up to Manchester. Away fans used to stand behind the goal at Old Trafford. We had tickets for the seats to the left of the travelling Villa fans in the seats. There were about 50 of us in the seats who you could've classed as football lads. We had nothing to play for and just treated the day as a bit of a party. We were vocal. Villa lost the match 3-1. We saw Villa score a goal away from home. We celebrated like it was a winning goal in a cup final. At the end of the match we emerged from the ground. United's lads were waiting for us in the tunnel outside. Spoon was one of the first out and he was clattered straight away. He charged back out and was hit again, this time by a copper. Punk and I couldn't stop laughing. Brittle one of the older lads was urging us to fight our way out. We steamed outside and everything was confused. I saw a Villa fan in front of me take a blow from a United fan. I hit the Manc in return and was clattered by blows from all around me. We got out onto the main concourse by the club shop. There were thousands of them. They saw it going off in the tunnel and had just waited till we emerged. We were in a loose group and they hit us from all sides. People were shouting 'stick together Villa!' but we had no choice. We were forced into a small group. They were hitting us from all sides. The police came flying in. They got horses in between us. United were flying in between or even underneath the horses to get at us. There seemed like thousands of them. We couldn't have run if we had wanted to. The police managed to get a decent line in between us and them and eventually dispersed them. We were just laughing about it afterwards. I think it was relief, we couldn't believe we'd got out alive.

We had a formidable firm once more, old and young. We were taking it to a lot of clubs. Graham Taylor was installed as manager when Turners replacement Billy McNeill left the club following relegation. A lot of Villa lads will tell you the season 87-88 in the Second Division was one of our best. Villa were in trouble but we all pulled together off the pitch. We were organised. We were taking on all-comers. We went to Stoke, plotted up in one of their main pubs and they couldn't shift us. We went to Huddersfield twice. It was that good when we visited them in the September that we returned there after a match at Barnsley in the following January. At Barnsley Trevor, Joycey and I had fronted about 40 Barnsley close to a pub full of Villa. We had run towards them expecting the rest of the Villa to empty the pub and follow. They were mostly normal fans and didn't budge. We did however manage to hold them off for a while. We took a firm of 300+ to Millwall. We took big mobs to Leeds United twice in that season. We took the Brunswick pub in Manchester and Man City couldn't shift us. We had trouble wherever we went. We were a relatively big club for the division and the other gamer clubs would turn out for us in numbers.

Birmingham City Vs Aston Villa Division 2 12th December 1987

We met that morning at the Crown. We numbered around two hundred. We caught the train to Duddeston from Perry Barr. We planned to walk to the ground from there. Garry Lyttle was organising things. Gaz was one of the older lads who sadly passed away a few years later. Everyone of all ages knew, liked and respected Gaz. A few more met us when we got off the train at Duddeston. We marched towards Digbeth and onto the High Street. We came out just by the Old Crown pub. It is one of the oldest pubs in Birmingham, built in 1368. It was built to last obviously. When we hit it that day it was touch and go whether it would survive. Skinhead Neil and another lad went up to the door and opened it. The pub was packed. As the door opened the windows of the pub were smashed. 'Come on! We're fucking Villa!' Blues were shocked to see us appear and scrambled to shut the door and keep us out. CS gas was sprayed into the place. Missiles were flying in and out of the shattered windows. Neil had given up at the door and was now trying to get in through the windows. The police arrived. As they landed we moved on up the road. Blues came out of the pub and this started fresh exchanges in the road. The police managed to get in between us. We headed towards the Clements, the next pub in line.

We swarmed round the Clements trying to get in. The police caught up. We headed towards the ground. We were forced by the police towards the away end. We were penned in there by a police cordon and horses. We were in a massive queue, waiting to enter the ground. Blues appeared and charged into us. They surprised us and the police. They were obviously pissed off at what we'd done earlier. That's the thing with them, when they were on top, 83-87 they didn't do anything at Villa Park except turn up. When we started to fight back we would make sure they knew we had paid a visit. People scattered and we were fighting with them. The police got a grip and a small group of us found ourselves being forced towards the home turnstiles. Blues were all around us and it was time to keep quiet not try and reason with the police. A lot of Villa fans now arriving saw the queue and compared it with the queue for the home section. A lot of Villa thought 'stuff it' and went into the home section. A few black cabs pulled up, it was the Bagot. They saw the queue for the away end and paid straight into the home section. We could hardly make it obvious we were Villa. We were all split up. We didn't plan this. As far I was concerned it was get onto the terraces, get to the front, get on the pitch and then the safety of the Villa end. The section nearest the Villa fans was packed. It was full of Blues lads. I recognised one of our older lads, standing near the fence. He had a scarf around his face. We were looking for any opportunity to get out of our current situation. I noticed a few more faces in the crowd. Villa had two sections of the Tilton Road end behind the goal. There was an empty section and then the Birmingham fans were in the final section. Slowly but surely the two of us grew in number. We had hundreds of their lads around us. Our only hope was to get onto the pitch or over the fence. Some of the Villa in the away end spotted us. They started calling then they started to surge towards the fence. It was the last thing we needed to be honest. Some of the home fans around us clocked it. They started to take an interest in our group then just steamed into us. We were forced towards the fence and I was slammed into it. People were falling over each other. Lads in the Villa section could see what was happening. A shower of coins rained down into the section we were in. As I half stood against the fence I noticed a dark shadow above me. Villa fans had scaled their fence and were coming to help us. A gap developed. Hundreds of Villa fans were flying over. The cavalry had turned up. Blues still had a fearsome reputation at this point but they came regardless. We were getting slaughtered and they came to help some Villa in trouble. The Police were trying desperately to restore order. Villa fans piled into the middle and fighting was going on through and over the fence. 'Youth! Youth! It now seemed we had the upper hand. They were forced completely back into the Spion Kop section of the ground by us and the police. Some order was restored with Villa fans entrenched in the whole of the Tilton End. Blues continually made attempts to get at us and reclaim the lost ground but the police were now established well enough to prevent them even attempting it. More and more police were continually streaming in to the ground during the game as reinforcements were called. The situation became more inflamed as Garry Thompson scored the only goal of the game for Villa to enable us to win 1-0. I walked back to Aston with Ian Haines and a few of the Crown lads. There were about eight of us, we were spread out. I'd had enough by this point. I was battered and bruised and I just wanted to get back to the Crown and nearer home. As we walked up Lawley Middleway a group of about 40 lads came out of a side road. They were Blues. For some reason they paid us no attention. They just carried on into town. It helped we were spread out I suppose - we didn't look like a mob. To say I was relieved is an understatement. There were incidents in and around the city-centre after the match and well into the night. That was our day. After years of coming second best we had taken it to them and won. Things would never be the same again.

It was around this time the rave scene started to take off. It all started innocuously enough with the Acid-House scene. The Hummingbird was the first place in Birmingham to have acid-house nights on a Thursday. The Hummingbird was our club. We had few recognised pubs in Birmingham city-centre before the Youth. The last bastion of Villa resistance, The Windsor had gone. We always drank in town regularly, especially at weekends. The Old Contemptibles, The Cabin, Le pub and Cagneys were regular haunts. Our night-club was Top Cats on Newhall Street. All of these venues were on the north side of the city centre. Blues still had hold of the John Bright St part of town.

We started to frequent the Kipper Club at the Hummingbird every weekend. Blues claim they used to go to the Hummingbird. They didn't. We didn't mix on any level at that time. Blues came in once. They were in a group of about

10-15 and kicked off. Brendan McCann, one of the Youth's main-lads at the time, was having it with them on the dance floor. I steamed in and was promptly knocked spark out by one of them. I came round just in time to see them running for the exit. A number of lads, Fat Stan included, were steaming into them. According to them, they walked round like they owned the place. It never happened. The whole rave and warehouse party scene then took off. Combined with the ecstasy a lot of lads found they'd rather be attending these than fighting at football matches. Villa had a great season after promotion to Division 1 in 1988. We took loads on the last day of the season to Everton when we finished second in the old Division One. We took thousands and virtually took over Goodison Park.

The whole football violence scene died a death for a couple of years. You literally went to a football match for the football and a drink. On the rave scene a few Villa lads found themselves dealing with the opposition. A lot of boundaries were crossed which wouldn't have been before. At the time I remember thinking that was it, it was all over. I didn't realise that football hooliganism was about to make a dramatic comeback and as Aston Villa Hardcore we would be at the forefront.

Chapter Two: Villa Hardcore. Plotting Up

There was a hardcore bunch of us who had kept it going. We were still 'football lads.' We weren't ravers. We didn't want to know about the rave scene. We were football. We still dressed like football lads. Fashion was still important. One obvious change was our jeans had got baggier, the flares had gone. Diesel, C17, Armani and Stone Island were the preferred brands for denim along with Hugo Boss. These were accompanied by the compulsory Lacoste polo or dress shirts. Ralph Lauren, Chipie, Burberry, Aquascutum, Gio Goi, Best Company, Stone Island and Chevignon were all sought after. We were mostly still wearing Timberland shoes or boots. Trainers were as popular as always. Adidas Gazelle and Superstars were common along with Reebok. A few of us had Schott leather jackets or their classic bombers. Napapjiri along with gore-tex jackets such as Berghaus.

Danny Hutton: The only place you could get Stone Island in Birmingham was a shop called Autograph just off New Street. For Armani and Boss we used a shop called Clothes Out. Capolito Roma was still going from the 80s. They supplied Timberland and Henry Lloyd. Eltex by the Oasis Market supplied Valentino and Rackhams also on Corporation Street always stocked Aquascutum, Marco Polo, Barbour and Lacoste.

We were simply Villa's boys. A lot of us were the older generation who had been involved with the Villa Youth in the early 80s. People like Skinhead Neil. Neil had been front page news all over the world in the summer of 1988. He had featured on the front of the New York Times during the European Championships in Germany. Neil always seemed to be in court over one thing or another then. It was mostly football and he got a bit of a name for himself nationally. There was Jonesy who I travelled everywhere with then. I had known him years and we used to socialise together as well. The Clintons, the Salter's and the Jeenes brothers were also regulars. The Scott Arms pub provided quite a few lads, as did the Leopard in Erdington.

Jonesy: We started to get more successful under Big Ron Atkinson. We had about 30-40 lads at the time. People like Neil, Luddy and the Clintons. We started drinking in the Adventurers, a pub half a mile away from the ground. A few other lads from Erdington and Castle Vale came onto the scene. Tucker reappeared. We started to become more organised.

There was a small mob from the Scott's. Russell and Carl were two brothers who were always there. There was Dog and Yob, whose name did exactly what it said on the tin. Big Dave Smith a mountain of a bloke. You then had the South Birmingham lot. Pete Mc, Nobby, Botch and others were lads who had been around since the Youth days. Pete and Harold reappeared with Johnny Moo and some more lads from the Leopard in Erdington. Other lads were still travelling independently in localised groups. The Bagot always had someone travelling. Our group were from all over the city. We had lads drift in and out. The Crown and the Youth would still turn out for big matches. A few familiar faces started popping up. Gary Reid was someone who I hadn't seen in years. I got to know Reidy through Stan. Reidy is one of those people you don't even have to check if he's standing you can take it as read that he is. He's also very funny and constantly taking the piss. To be fair he can take it as well as give it out. Reidy only has one ear. Reidys ear or lack of it has given us a lot of laughs over the years. He has a false one. His false ear has been found in various locations, from the top of someone's pint to some bird's handbag. One thing I've never got over is the blokes got 4 of these false ears, all different colours for different times of the year when he's got various tans.

Reidy: Blues played Villa in December 1987. We had been fighting Blues before and during the game in the corner of the Tilton. At Midnight the same day, I was standing side by side with a Blues fan fighting Leicester's firm. They had passed through Birmingham and had thought they could slag off Brummies. About 12-15 of them were drinking in town. My mate, who was Blues and I were talking to a couple of them. I went to the toilet and when I came back they were getting shirty with him. We were outnumbered. I knew we were going to get a kicking, but I still went for gold. During the ensuing row my ear was bitten off by one of them. When it was bitten off everything seemed to stop. The rest of them stopped fighting and I battered the lad who had just bitten me. The police turned up and neither of us wanted to press charges. That's just how it goes sometimes. I went home but had to eventually go to hospital. I was in for five days and I now have a synthetic rubber ear.

Tucker also reappeared after a few years absence from Villa Park. Also other lads I already knew Dominic Byrne and Dave Rammell. In their group was a lad in his early 20s called Fowler. Fowler came to prominence after a game at Sunderland. Things were happening again. Fowler rapidly became the driving force. We hadn't become stale as such, but we weren't exactly brimming with ideas either. He had a new outlook. He didn't ask what others teams were like.

He took everyone at face value, including us. He judged people from his own experience. A lot of people my age didn't like it. They resented Fowler. They weren't doing anything of note so why should Fowler be? He was one of the lads straight away. He would always be having banter with someone. Thing about Fowler is, he can take it as well as give it out. When he meets someone he'll sound them out with a bit of banter. If they give him some in return he'll laugh. It builds a team spirit. Our main lads have always been approachable by anyone. Fowler was always, 'Why can't we do that? Who the fucking hell are they? We're just as good as them!' He always took people how he found them. He was no respecter of reputations. Fowler has this way about him. He'll say something or challenge you to do something with him. If you hesitate he will just look at you, deadpan and ask, 'Are you scared?' It always has the desired effect. You'd do stuff for Fowler that other people couldn't encourage you to do. You know he'd do it for you and he wouldn't ask you to do anything he wouldn't do himself.

Jonesy: Fowler stood out because he was so game when there was any trouble. He was younger than us. He gained a reputation in a very short space of time. Most lads take five or six years to build up a reputation. He achieved that in the space of about 12 months. We'd meet at the Adventurers after the match. Sometimes we'd travel into the city centre to drink or to have a pop at Blues. The 1994 Coca-Cola cup win pulled a lot of people into the club. We gained a few more lads that way. We started to have bigger and better numbers out.

My first memory of Aston Villa was my father, or the old man as I called him in later life, taking me as a small child. When I was young and growing up you didn't seem to have many kids supporting teams outside of the West Midlands. In Great Barr it was mostly Villa, the rest were West Bromwich Albion with the odd Birmingham City fan. No-one at school really supported the big clubs at the time. There were I remember a couple of Leeds United fans, but these were people who didn't really know about football. They'd just chosen Leeds because they were successful at the time. The old man used to attend Villa Park one week and the Hawthorns, the home of West Bromwich Albion, the next. He did this for years, right up until 1959. He stopped after a local derby between the two clubs. Villa needed a win to stay in the old 1st Division. Albion had nothing to play for. A late Ronnie Allen goal meant Villa were relegated. From that day on the old man chose the Villa. He chose the loser on the day, the under-dog. In today's society obsessed with success I wonder if the same decision would be made. Then our culture was intrinsically linked with backing the under-dog. The old man stood in the Witton End of the ground. It used to be an open terrace. It seemed huge. It was only dwarfed by the huge terracing at the other end of the ground which was called The Holte End. The Witton End was a swaying mass of people. It always appeared dark to me, although it had no roof. It was the crowds that did it, I was only small. I used to take a small stool or crate to stand on to compensate, a lot of kids did that. Everyone seemed to know each other. They'd all stood in the same spot for years. On reflection most probably didn't even know the others name, but they'd discuss the match like old friends.

I used to love the big games with the big crowds. The Witton End had a grass bank at the back. I remember rolling down it with loads of other kids while the match was on. The first match I can really remember was a night-match. I think it was against Norwich City. I couldn't tell you the result. I only remember it because someone scaled the floodlights and it caused a commotion as the police attempted to get them down. When my memory really kicks in is the mid 70s. In 1975 and after an absence of six years, Villa under the uncompromising Ron Saunders were promoted to Division 1. They also lifted the League Cup at Wembley Stadium. I can remember the League Cup Final. Villa beat Norwich City with a Ray Graydon penalty. We didn't go to the final. I listened to it on the radio. Then I watched the highlights on Star Soccer on the Sunday afternoon. Things were looking up at Villa Park. Then the club committed the cardinal sin of demolishing the old Witton End of the ground. They replaced it with what they called the North Stand. It was and still is a horrible square shaped monstrosity. It was seats with some terracing at the bottom. The terracing at the bottom was usually half visiting fans and half home support. For the bigger teams the whole end would be handed over to the visitors. Segregation had now come into football. It was seen of a way to lessen the chances of opposing fans clashing during the match. The seating above was always given to home supporters. The seating was too far away from the pitch. It always seemed removed from the whole atmosphere of the ground. The old man continued to take me onto the terracing at the bottom of the Witton End. Even when the whole end was given to away support we would go and stand on there. In his eyes he had always stood in the same place. Neither the club of any visiting fans were going to stop him doing what he had done for years. When I was small they had been difficult times for Villa, but it never came across like that to me. Successive relegations should've killed the club off but it didn't, people rallied round. People supported them more because they were going through a difficult spell. Tommy Docherty had famously said, 'If you put eleven Villa shirts on a washing-line you would have 20 thousand people turn up to watch them dry.' There was a buzz about the club. A newspaper called The Villa Times would come out on a Friday. I would always look forward to getting it. I became obsessed with football and Aston Villa.

The first time I really remember seeing any trouble at the football was a match against Port Vale. The North Stand was not open, but they'd opened the terracing at the bottom and we were standing on there. A group of Port Vale fans were standing in the middle of the terracing. They seemed to be led by this big bloke with a beard. He was wearing a big black and white top hat. They were loud and trouble kicked off. I remember people seemed to come from everywhere and they were kicked all over the place. Gaps appeared where the fighting was erupting and the crowd swayed and surged to compensate. I was scared but the old man told me to just stand there. He said if we stood still we'd come to no harm and we didn't. He would sometimes point out the trouble-makers to me while we stood in the ground. He would say, 'Here you go, watch that bloke there. There'll be trouble in a minute!' Nine times out of ten there was. He was always very aware. He always seemed to know what was going on. When it did kick off in the ground everyone on the terraces would stop watching the match and watch the trouble. It seemed part of the entertainment at times. No-one used to be really shocked when it happened, it was just accepted. The people who were fighting became the stars. For a brief moment they were more important to a lot of the spectators than the match itself. The police would then wade in. The old man would be giving me a running commentary. There were no riot shields or protective clothing for the police in those days. They just waded in and tried and sort it all out. At some matches trouble would be occurring throughout the game. The Old Man was fearless. He was from a large family in Kingstanding. He was ex-REME and had boxed in the Army. His father had died when he was very young. His mother took it badly and my father and the younger of the children were virtually brought up by his sister Kath. They were unbelievably poor. He had escaped into the Army aged sixteen. He forged his birth certificate to get into the Army, that's how desperate he was to escape his situation. He'd then send his mother so much out of his wages every week to help the situation at home. He saw active service during the Suez Crisis in the early 50s. He was a good man. He was a hard man. He wasn't the type of bloke to back down with anyone, although he wouldn't seek confrontation. He always taught me it was better to walk away from a confrontation and never taught me to fight. I also never heard him

Lads running to meet Leicester in Birmingham city centre.

Villa and Leicester meet.

Goodbye Leicester!

Reidy and Fowler, who's number 1?

Villa Hardcore landing in Manchester city centre.

Drinking in Manchester.

Villa Hardcore having the run of Manchester.

Manchesters only firm of the day show.

Looking for Coventry in Birmingham city centre.

Still looking for Cov at Villa Park.

Dave Moore never forgotten, rest in peace.

Dave Rammell never forgotten, rest in peace.

Late kick-offs 'leading to too much drinking'

POLICE WARN AS DRUNKEN FANS IN CLASH

A POLICE chief called for a crackdown on matches kicking off late after hundreds of fans clashed before the Coca-Cola cup final.

The 5pm start at Wembley meant that fans had more time to spend drinking, said Commander John Purnell of the Metropolitan Police.

Mr Purnell, head of operations for the game, called for an end to late kick-offs for important fixtures.

Supporters clashed in pubs and outside the ground before yesterday's game, marring Aston Villa's victory over Leeds.

Around 200 people were involved in a battle at one Wembley pub.

Police made 50 arrests, raising fresh fears about hooliganism in the runup to the European soccer championships.

Mr Purnell said today: "An evening kick-off enables a large quantity of fans to spend the build-up to the game drinking and arriving at the stadium ready for trouble."

He said there had a major disturbance at a pub in Wembley before the match, involving about 200 fans.

Match report — Page 58

Around 30,000 Villa fans travelled from the Midlands to watch the game.

Scotland Yard said a total of 50 fans were arrested — half Leeds, half Villa.

Most have been charged with drink-related public order offences and a few with possession of drugs.

They have been bailed to appear before Brent magistrates on April 24 and 30.

More than 77,000 fans watched Villa's victory, which has booked the team a place in next season's EUFA Cup.

Villa won the Coca-Cola Cup two years ago and have now equalled the record for five wins in the competition.

CUP FANS RAMPAGE IN CITY HOTEL BAR

FOOTBALL thugs transformed a peaceful Birmingham city centre bar into a battleground.

Windows in the Prince Hotel bar were smashed and ammonia was sprayed as supporters gathered before last night's Coca-Cola Cup match between Aston Villa and Wolves.

Hooligans burst into the hotel in Station Street, outside New Street station, after Wolves fans gathered for a drink.

They smashed furniture and fittings and fought. Bar licensee and hotel deputy manager Anthony Shelvington, aged 57, became sandwiched between rival gangs as he unsuccessfully tried to bolt doors.

By CAROL HASSALL

Mr Shelvington said: "One minute these people were peacefully enjoying a couple of drinks, and the next they were animals.

"There were about 30 Wolves fans here. They weren't drunk.

"Most were on about their second pint when the windows smashed and ammonia was sprayed.

"Then it just turned into a battleground. They picked up chairs and smashed them around. It was a miracle no-one was hurt."

Mr Shelvington added: "I made sure regulars and staff were safe and the police response was very quick."

The bar would be open as usual tonight, he said.

Supt Tony Garbett, of Steelhouse Lane police station, said that officers were investigating whether the attack could have been planned.

But the cup tie itself had attracted less trouble than expected, he added.

Nineteen people were arrested outside Villa Park for public order offences.

Second pint

The thugs threw a fire extinguisher through the window of a car and damaged a police van, then ran off as officers arrived in force.

Three men were arrested at the scene.

Similar outbreak

● Up to 40 Asian youths were involved in skirmishes in Witton Lane and Bevington Road, Aston, at about 6.30pm and again at 8pm.

No-one was injured and two arrests were made.

Police had stepped up patrols in the area because of the match at Villa Park and because of a similar outbreak of violence between Asian gangs last Sunday night. Twenty-two people were arrested.

■ HAVOC: Anthony Shelvington assesses the damage to his bar

■ CLEARING UP: A motorist sweeps broken glass from his damaged car outside the Prince Hotel after Wolves and Villa fans clashed. Pictures: PATRICK NEAME

Violence flares as fans fight on the streets

Villa fans on rampage

RIVAL football hooligans fought running battles in the streets os Sheffield as the new season kicked off yesterday.

Aston Villa and Sheffield Wednesday supporters clashed before their teams' 'grudge' match in the street's around Wednesday's Hillsborough stadium.

After the game, 100 Villa fans surrounded a car parked in a side street and smashed all the windows with house bricks.

Police made 27 arrests — 13 home and 14 away fans — for public order offences. A police spokesman said: "Most of the fighting took place before the match.

"But a large group of Villa supporters decided to smash up a car after the game for no apparent reason."

The match saw Villa manager Ron Atkinson returning to Sheffield Wednesday for the first time since he quit the club in the summer.

He was given a police escort to the match, booed and greeted with chants of 'Judas' when he walked on the pitch to the dug-out. Villa won the game 3-2.

EXCLUSIVE
by **Adam Smith**
News Reporter

Riot police tell residents to stay in their homes

Gangs of stick-wielding hooligans fought pitch-battles through the streets of Perry Barr when football violence spiralled out of control after an Aston Villa match.

Police in riot gear were forced to keep fighting fans apart as innocent bystanders and motorists were caught up in the violence.

The fighting erupted at 9pm for half-an-hour after the end of Sunday night's FA Cup match between Aston Villa and Manchester United.

Rival sections of fans charged at each other at Witton island, then police escorted Villa fans along Aston Lane but violence flared up again around Perry Barr island.

The opposing fans grabbed sticks, bottles and bricks to attack each other and several eyewitnesses described a gang with sticks in a white van targeting Villa fans.

The Crown and Cushion pub closed its doors early after staff feared the pub would be targeted by the hooligans.

Assistant manager Simon Horsewell said: "We decided to close the pub when we were getting text messages and calls from regulars outside the ground describing how bad the fighting was, it just wasn't worth it.

"The pub lost a lot of money, 7pm was a stupid time

> **'I couldn't believe my eyes at all. You don't expect to see that type of thing on a Sunday night'**

to kick off, everyone was drunk and we had to employ bouncers not to let away fans in, which is something we never do for Villa games."

Aston Lane resident Mary Davis was shocked at what she saw on Sunday night.

Mrs Davis said: "I opened my door and police in riot gear were running up the street towards the Crown and Cushion telling everybody to get indoors.

"I couldn't believe my eyes,

you don't expect to see th type of thing on a Sund night and ten minutes lat they all came back again the number 11 bus."

Simon James, who lives North Road, also witness the fighting.

"It was complete mayhe I've never seen so ma people fighting in my life, t police told us to go son where safe."

There were 7,000 away fa almost double the amou permitted in a league ga and the match being televised.

Police had an estimated men on duty and made arrests in and around ground,

---

swear. He always wore a shirt and tie, even to the match. When I went to senior school I started having problems. I got involved in a gang for the first time. Great Barr School was huge. It was one of the biggest schools in the UK. It had over two thousand pupils. In my class there were four or five local lads who I had gone to junior school with. We were mostly all Villa fans. We started knocking about together. I still see the odd one or two now following Villa, lads like Dave Nokes who I saw recently for the first time in what must be 20 years. Our behaviour at school got gradually worse. We started to hang around together out of school. Pete's Café in Great Barr became a meeting place. Also Jean and Ron's chip shop next door. We'd mix with other local kids of differing ages. Jean and Ron's became even more popular when they installed the first Space Invaders machine in there. We would all flock round playing or watching others try and beat high scores. We were as unruly out of school as we were in school. A few of the lads were older and already going into the local pub, the Drakes Drum. The rest of us who weren't old enough and didn't appear old enough would socialise in the café and the chip-shop. We'd stand there and laugh as we'd take it in turns to flick our used chewing gum into the curry sauce which was kept warm nearby. As we reached the end of school we started attending matches together. I was allowed to go to matches on my own from the age of about 15. We would catch the number 46 bus and we would get off at Perry Barr and walk down Aston Lane toward Villa Park soaking up the atmosphere. The atmosphere would intensify the closer you got the ground. We would take our places at the back of the Holte End. I had migrated to the Holte End as soon as I started attending matches alone. My old man followed suit a few years later. The back of the Holte was where the clubs hooligan support congregated. I used to stand on the right-side of the Holte End at the back with the lads from school.

There was a bit of a pre-match ritual at the back of the Holte End in those days. Nearly always a flag or scarf of the opposing team would be tied to the rafters and burnt. People were still in the main wearing scarves to matches in those days. The item going up in flames had obviously been taken from a visiting supporter. The Holte was a massive terrace. In the late 70s it had been divided into two halves. At that time it held about 28 thousand people. When they split it into two halves people started choosing which side at the back to stand. Lads from certain areas had their preferred places where they stood. A rivalry between the two sections started. The chanting of one side or the other and fighting would break out during dull matches. It was exciting and we'd get involved on the fringes. I was aware of the C-Crew being the gang at Villa Park at the time. I also became aware of a new fashion which seemed to be taking off. Lads were starting to shed the bovver boy image. I switched from spectator to active hooligan. I was of course only on the fringes at first. I'd run to and fro with everyone else. It started to matter to me what the outcome was. It's always been a Birmingham thing with me. Coming from Birmingham and being a Brummie is a source of pride. I like turning up and showing people that Brummies are as game as anyone else. Probably one of the best nights for the clubs hooligan following was the riot in Brussels in April 1982. Villa were playing the second leg of the European Cup semi-final against Anderlecht. Villa held on for a 0-0 draw. They had won the home-leg of the match 1-0 and a draw would be enough to send them through. We listened to the match in Jean and Ron's and celebrated wildly when we got through to the final. I was allowed to go to the final by the old man as long as I went on the official supporters club transport. I went with one of the local lads, Gary Cooper. He was one of four brothers from Great Barr. They all followed the Villa, the two eldest, Kev and Clive were people we looked up to as kids. They also had another brother, Mark who was my age. Eamonn Byrne was one lad from Great Barr who we looked up to. He was as game as anything and just a year or so older than us. We travelled by coach and ferry to Rotterdam. The match was being played in the main stadium which was the home of Feyenoord. We were on the uppermost tier. A memorable day was capped by a Peter Withe goal. Aston Villa, from Birmingham in the West Midlands of England became Champions of all Europe. It was an amazing experience.

Fowler: I was born in Hockley in Birmingham in 1969. When I was six months old my folks moved to a house on Castle Vale. At that time the Vale was a new housing estate. It was constructed as an overspill area for Birmingham. The inner-city slums of Aston, Hockley and Nechells were cleared in the 60s and a lot of people from there moved to Castle Vale. It was the largest tower block estate in the city. It had 34 high-rise multi-storey tower blocks. It was built on the site of an old airfield. Many of the streets and buildings have aeronautical themes. I've always lived on Castle Vale. In the late 70s Castle Vale began to decline. The area began to be synonymous with crime, especially car theft and joyriding. A quarter of its residents were unemployed and by the 1980s the Vale had been identified as one of the most crime-ridden estates in the country. Castle Vale is roughly about a mile long by half a mile wide. It's not that big and it's cut off from the rest of Birmingham. There is no area which connects directly to Castle Vale, no boundary connections. Pype Hayes is next to it, it's not connected. You have Chelmsley Wood the other side but there are fields in between it and Castle

Vale. The other side is the Bromford estate but you have to go over a bridge to get between the two estates. At the top of the Vale you've got Minworth but there's a stretch of road, Park Lane, with factories on it which marks the boundary. None of it is connected it is an estate on its own, it has major roads ringing it. When we were kids we were proud to come from the Vale, it had a feared reputation. There were alleyways everywhere and we knew them like the back of our hand. You used to get cars squeezing down the narrow alleyways trying to get away from the police. Recently they've closed a lot of the alleyways off barring people of the escape routes. It's still a close-knit community. You've got your areas like Erdington and Kingstanding, they're massive areas but the Vale in comparison was small. No firms used to come on to the Vale simply because it was getting off which was the problem. We used to have trouble with each other of course that was always sorted out one way or another. Some people at the top end wouldn't know much about people from the bottom end of the Vale. I know it sounds mad but that's just how it was.

We were always playing football as kids. As soon as school finished we'd all be out with a football. Fighting was always a part of growing up on the Vale. There were 5 schools on the Vale. They were Castle Vale Comprehensive, St Gerard's, Pegasus, Topcliffe and Chivnor. I went to St Gerard's Junior School and we'd fight with the other schools. Castle Vale was a hard estate there were always fights and you had to learn how to fight. We lived in the middle of the Vale, the Watton Green part. There were lots of gangs on the Vale. My gang was called The Faces. We all had small smiley type faces tattooed on our legs. I shared a bedroom with my brother. He was always away at Borstal. He had a bottle of Indian ink. I used to borrow this and the other lads and I would use it to tattoo ourselves. When I was around the age of five, my brother had a Birmingham City kit. I don't know why he had this kit. He suddenly became a Birmingham City fan. Seeing that, I became a Birmingham City fan myself, as you do at that age. You see your older brother doing something and you think it's cool. So when we had the faces tattoos I also had a small BC tattooed on my leg. My mother and father were never into football, they simply didn't like it. When say the World Cup was on television they wouldn't watch it. I'd have to sit in the kitchen watching it on a little old black and white television. My father was a hard man, he was a fighter. He used to do the doors of pubs on Castle Vale. He always worked on the motorways. They were building a lot of motorways at the time. He was always away a lot, especially in the summer when there was more light for them to work longer hours. My brother was two years older than me. He was always fighting at school. He was expelled from school and no other school in the area would take him. He had to attend an approved school. He also went to Borstal. You always look up to your older brother. I remember when he was due to be released from Borstal I'd be standing at the bus stop waiting for him to come home. We used to fight each other and he'd always win. We had nothing when we were kids. I went to a Catholic senior school. It was St Edmund Campion in Erdington which was a few miles away. My old man is a Paddy. He came over here when he was 15 from Ireland. He worked in London for a while then went home. Then he returned and came to Birmingham working on the motorways. My mom was introduced to him by a friend. He wanted his kids to go to a Catholic school. I wanted to go to Castle Vale Comprehensive where all my mates went. I didn't want to mess about catching a bus to school in the freezing cold. Attending school in Erdington, I made friends with a lot of Erdington lads. Erdington, Kingstanding and Great Barr, for anyone who doesn't know Birmingham, are staunch Villa areas. I had pals from the Vale and Erdington, lads like Dominic and Craig who were well into the Villa. Everyone was mad into the Villa. A lot of the kids at school were what we called Plastic Paddies, they considered themselves Irish. I am English, my dad is Irish. I was born here and have grown up here. I consider myself English not Irish. Me and my mates we all considered ourselves English, we weren't into that Irish stuff.

When I was starting school my brother had just been expelled so I had his uniform. That's what it was like, we had nothing. The first day at school I got absolutely leathered by the headmaster. I'd met a kid called Tommy Kelly and we were messing about in assembly. In the afternoon the headmaster, Mr Brennan, came into our class. He said he wanted a word with Kelly and Fowler outside. He was a hard man our headmaster, hard as nails. He battered us. I was 11. I'd had the slipper at my old school but he knocked the living daylights out of us. He literally beat us up. He'd hit you in the chest so there were no bruises. He kept on saying, 'do you want to be like your brother do you?' I didn't want to be like my brother. He was probably the reason I lasted till the fifth year at school. He was always going away to Borstal, I didn't want that life. If you ask my mom now she will say I was no trouble as a kid. I think that is mainly because she compares me with my brother. Compared to him whatever trouble I got into as a kid was nothing. I have never liked people telling me what to do. I got into a lot of trouble at school over that. I got into fights. Fights were nothing to me. I had a brother at home who could kick the shit out of me. Whatever I received in a fight was nothing compared to that. I got into the usual trouble kids used to get into on the Vale. I stole cars, we all did. I was also done for breaking into the Drome Café which is on the A38 which passes Castle Vale. I was about 12 at the time. We were little fuckers to be honest. The first pub we started going into, we were 15 at the time, was the Residents Association Club. I remember at the time in there mild was 52p a pint. We used to go in there and have four pints for £2-08. Then we went from the residents club to the Lancaster, a pub which is no longer there. The hardest pub on the Vale used to be the Artful Dodger. That was the main pub on Castle Vale. We used to fight Chelmsley Wood, which was a neighbouring estate. At the back of the Vale you used to have the old aircraft hangers. By the hangers was an old iron bridge over the river

Tame, we used to meet the Chelmsley Wood lot there. You would sometimes have 200 Vale and 200 Chelmsley running at each other. It was thrilling for us as kids.

When I got to about 13 one of my mates was a lad called Brad. He and his dad were Villa fans. They were Villa mad. I started to go to the Villa with them. I started attending Villa matches regularly and became a Villa fan. My first Villa game was at home to Stoke in 1979 and I watched Villa win 2-1. I remember Stoke were getting relegated, they had a really small following about 30 or so fans. My first away match was Leicester City. I was about 14. I remember coming out of the ground afterwards and there was fighting everywhere. They were steaming into each other and I was open-mouthed watching it all. At around fifteen Brad and I stopped going with his old man. We started going with other lads from the Vale. There would be a group of us who would attend matches together.

I've only ever been to one Birmingham City match. That was the infamous game in 1985 against Leeds United. I went with all the Villa lads my age from school. Villa were playing away at Liverpool that day. We couldn't afford to go to Liverpool to watch the Villa so we all went to that match. We'd heard that Leeds were coming to Brum. We'd heard they were all neo-Nazis and they were coming to do Blues. We caught the bus into town and walked toward the ground. There were coaches coming past with windows broken and Leeds fans hanging out of them. We watched the riot. We were standing at the back of the Kop watching it all. To us it was brilliant. That game, I reckon every hooligan in Birmingham that wasn't at another match was there that day. People knew it was going to go off and every thug from estates all over Brum went to that match. It wasn't just Blues, you had allsorts there. Blues like to say 'Oh Fowler was a Blues fan,' well yeah if that's what they want to say, let them. I went to one Blues game as a kid and it was that match.

I was 16 and I went to work in London for a bloke who is now a good friend of mine, Ian Reid. I was due to start a plumbing course at the UCE in Perry Barr. I didn't want to go down the road my brother went down, I wanted a trade. I went to a friend's uncle's house and Ian was there. He offered me a job during the holidays before I started my plumbing course. I started working for him. I enjoyed working for Ian and didn't start my plumbing course. I started working for him full-time. I went to London to work and returned at weekends. From the age of 16-19 I didn't go to many matches. I used to go to the odd game if Villa were playing in London. I remember the one time in London, Villa were playing Chelsea in the Rumbelows Cup. I decided to go to this game and travelled across London from Peckham where I was staying to Stamford Bridge. I was on my own. I was sitting on the tube with all the Chelsea fans. I got off the tube and walked to Stamford Bridge. I could not, for some reason, find the away end. I went up to a copper and asked quietly if he could direct me towards the away end. He replied in the loudest voice possible, 'Oh! You want the away end do you?' and proceeded to tell me in a loud voice how to get there, I thought I was going to get killed. When I got inside there was only 200 Villa fans there. The old away end at Stamford Bridge was massive and we were in this little section in the middle. The game went into extra-time and we lost and were knocked out of the cup. I was on about £60 a week then. After the weekend I would have roughly £15 to last me the week in London. I couldn't always afford to go to matches. I was working on the Isle of Dogs. I was working on the new headquarters of the Daily Telegraph. I was terrible really, I had an attitude. As far as I was concerned I worked for Ian, he was my boss. If anyone else told me what to do I'd tell them to fuck off. I got into a few fights down there. It was wrong looking back now. I have some young lads working for me now and if they were like it I wouldn't stand for it. I was tolerated because I worked. I was there every Monday morning without fail. That went in my favour, I was a grafter. We had a flat in the middle of Peckham which we used to stay at. Peckham was grim, even in those days. It made rough areas of Birmingham seem like paradise.

When I was about 19 I returned to Birmingham. I used to drink in the Rose and Crown and the Yenton pubs in Erdington. I used to drink with kids from school that were into the football, such as Dominic Burne and Craig Bull. We got to know other lads who went to the football from the Yenton, lads like Dave Rammel. The one year, the 90/91 season, I didn't miss a single match. There would be around ten or twelve of us. Football had died a bit of a death, not many people were going at that time really. One night after closing time there was a fight outside the Yenton. I chinned this one bloke. There were a few people fighting. One of the geezers was glassed but I didn't know it at the time. A few days later, I was working in London and my Mom told me that CID had been round to speak to me. I rang them up on a number they had left. They told me they wanted to tie up a few loose ends regarding a fight I had been involved in. When I attended the police station I was arrested and charged with GBH. They thought it was me who had glassed the kid. I knew by this time it was Dominic who had done it. They showed me pictures of the guy's injuries and to be honest they were pretty bad. All the witnesses had identified me as the one who had glassed him. I wasn't going to grass up my mate so I kept quiet. When I got out I rang Dom and told him what had happened. He said he wasn't having that and went into the police station and told them it was him, not me who had done it. You can't knock that.

We started drinking in the Adventurers after matches. It was around 1992 and we used to drink in the bar by the pool table. We met Tucker around this time. Tucker is the type who will talk to anyone. He used to come into chat to us. Then we went to Sunderland on a coach and we were arrested. That is where I really came to the notice of the main Villa lads. It's not something I am proud of. We were all steaming drunk and we were attacking everyone, not just football fans or lads. When we looked at the depositions afterwards there were so many people who were hurt we were shocked. It started over some idiot wearing a Blues shirt as we walked into the pub. I'm not ashamed of it but I do regret it. That person who went to that pub wearing a Birmingham City shirt, the shirt of our hated local rivals should take some of the blame. He knew Sunderland were playing Aston Villa. Why did he think it was wise to wear a Birmingham City top? We never found out why, but he was cut badly. I regret it but I don't feel bad about it. It happened. We were locked up for nine to ten weeks. When I came out of prison I started going back down the Villa. We were drinking in the Adventurers after one game and Tucker came in to speak to us. He told us he was running a coach to Grimsby for a cup-tie. We had a minibus arranged but we arranged to meet Tucker and his lot up there. We had trouble there and we all enjoyed it. We had the makings of a firm and we all started travelling together. When I came onto the scene proper, Villa had lads, but no organisation. We had a decent firm but we'd all drink together for a while then go and do our separate things. When I was arrested in Sunderland people were saying to me when I came out 'come on Fowler you should put yourself up for leading it all,' so I thought bollocks I will. You had better lads than me, but they were coming to the end of their time. They didn't want to take it on. I was 23. I was up and coming. Some people are just as game as me, but they don't always have the front. They won't stand on a chair in a pub and shout, 'Right drink your fucking drinks now! We're going!' Some people are just not up for that. They're probably as game as me when they come out to fight but they just struggle with the front it takes to lead a firm.

I've always had this mad thing in my head about Villa I have. It's about people thinking we're mugs. I know, I have always known, we are as good as anyone. On our day we can take on and beat the best. I've always been determined that no-one will ever mug us off. All the times I heard Villa haven't got a firm, after the Villa Youth stopped. I just wouldn't have it. I put myself forward, everyone knows me now. Nearly every football violence book you pick up mentions me and Villa Hardcore. We achieved what we set out to do. Everyone mentions us now. There might not have been many of us at times, but wherever we went we let them know we were there, and where we were. I was always on the phone to everyone. 'Yeah this is Fowler, we're Villa Hardcore, we've landed on your manor' that sort of thing. Wolverhampton town centre, right in the middle, 50 of us, no problem. Everywhere we went I told them 'We're here!' Another match, Leicester away, we went to Hinckley. Fuck the match. We went into Leicester city-centre while it was being played. We got on the phone to Leicester, boom, we've landed, get your arses down here. Everywhere we went, it didn't matter where. Our lads used to say, 'Fucking hell Fowl there's only 30 of us!' So fucking what? I can look round at what I've got next to me and think nah no problem. They aren't even going to get through the door. I look around at some of our lads. They might not be the hardest but I know, I know for a fact, they're not going anywhere. I'm not leaving them and they will not leave me, it's a bond. I'm not stupid, I'm not psychotic. We were never done that badly, but we did get done. We're the first to put our hands up to that when it has happened. Firms of 80-100 are great to have, but the effect goes with those numbers. They may be nice kids, all of them, but half of them are going to be taking a backward step before anything happens. That's football hooliganism. There are loads who talk a good fight. 90% of football hooligans talk about it in the pub afterwards when they've done nothing. I can't stand lads who drone on about it in pubs. I like to get in there and do it, not talk about it afterwards. People like me and that nucleus of Villa Hardcore. We acted. We got in there and got involved, that's the difference.

For me it's all about the buzz. I don't know many football hooligans who are not working. We work hard five days a week then on Saturday it's our day. You get up in the morning, get ready, put your clobber on and you look forward to the day. It isn't just the fighting; it's also the banter between our lads.

People say I got the Villa together again. I don't believe that. For me, it was Tucker who got us all together. He would talk to anyone and we all started to know each other through Tucker. I sometimes used to look around in the Adventurers and think these lads they'd take anyone. We just had no leadership. Throughout school I'd always been a leader, someone who had the mouth. I knew we could do something. I started to tell people to drink up and that we were going. Everyone looks for a leader. We needed someone who could just lead.

When I was growing up Blues were undisputed top-dogs in Birmingham from 83-87. I was looking at our lads, like the Black Country or the Brownhills lot, they could all fight. When I went to Blues in 1993 with the Villa firm from the Ben Jonson, it was awesome. I watched Blues run from it before they even met it. The firm stretched for a quarter of a mile at least. We were at the front. We were running at Blues and I could see some of them standing and thinking, 'It's only Villa.' They'd look round and their mates had gone, run away. We clattered them. We smashed everything and everyone that night and Blues know it.

They ask me why I fight at football matches. I don't know. It's like asking why we used to fight as kids. It is just the natural thing to do. It happens to varying degrees in all walks of life.

We were very active on the England scene. That was our scene. It was all about showing the rest of the country what we could turn out. We had big turnouts on a number of occasions. I don't care what people say, but for a while, from 1993 no-one could touch us away with England. Yes we didn't go about some things the right way, but most of the trouble with other England fans was them taking us too lightly. They were too dismissive of Villa and I can't have anyone saying Villa haven't got a firm. I can't go to games with a bunch of lads who I think have got so much heart and balls and then go to say, Amsterdam the next week with England and listen while someone says 'Villa haven't got a firm.' I just have to say something. Truth of the matter is when we started attending England matches as Villa Hardcore some people didn't respect us. In reciprocation we didn't respect them, and trouble occurred. It was never about me. It was never Fowlers firm, like you read in some of the books. We were Villa Hardcore. We hit the scene, we didn't give a fuck. We had the attitude that it started then, no history about who had what in the 80s. Don't tell me, like West Ham tried to, that Villa haven't got a firm, when we've landed on their manor calling it on. Let's see what you've got. It was that sort of attitude. I've been to many places since and I've had different firms kissing my arse. In Liverpool when England were playing Finland, I had lads from different mobs coming over and buying me drinks. Phone calls from other firms, 'Alright Fowler, two of our lads are in the same pub as you. Is it alright for them to come over and say hello?' Don't tell me Villa aren't rated now when you have firms, and these were respected firms, coming over and buying me drinks. They were showing me and Villa Hardcore respect. People ask me who I respect. The truth of the matter is I don't know many of the other main lads. I have spoken to them on the phone, but I couldn't tell you what they look like or anything else really. The one exception is Sunderland. People like Steve McGeorge, a great bloke who we have become friends with. We were rowing with them one day and we had respect for the way they conducted themselves. We stayed in touch and sometimes we go up there to visit. They look after us and we return the favour. They're a good bunch of lads.

Mobile phones have made things easier. People have no excuse anymore to say, 'Oh you just landed on us!' We'll say, 'Well we told you we were landing.' It's no excuse. I remember the 80s. You had mobs of 300 clashing with similar numbers of opposing fans. How many out of that lot are going to have a decent scrap. With us and the lower numbers we all had to get stuck in. I prefer lower numbers of 50ish. I've led big firms of 300 plus. I've looked round and looked at most of them and thought, I don't want them here. I just wanted the 50 or so lads I could rely on. With that 50 we could go through most firms. Most of the lads in a big firm like that will be ready on their toes if it goes tits up. It's like a herd of antelope or something when they see a lion, once one starts running they all do. With my 50 I knew none of them would leave me. I used to say to them, 'If you're going to run don't bother coming!' How many people have you heard of getting seriously injured at the football? Very few I would say. What's the worst you will get at the football, a punch on the nose or a kick up the arse? So what? I've seen more serious injuries as a result of fights in pubs on Castle Vale. If you want to be a hooligan, get involved. Don't fuck about running up and down the road. Get stuck into them. Don't wear the Armani coat and the Armani cap and look the part when you have no intention of getting stuck in. You see them in the pubs after rows, 'Oh we did this, and we did that!' I'm standing there thinking, no you didn't! We had the one row in town with Blues. They were mostly all big black lads. They were all shouting my name. They wanted Fowler. I was rowing with them and when I looked half of our firm had disappeared! After that I was angrier with my firm for leaving me than I was with Blues. I walked into a pub afterwards and they were all sitting there, looking at the floor. If any of them had said anything I'd have killed them. I was that angry. I have to think sometimes though, hang on, they aren't all like me. I have to take that into account, but at the time I was fuming. I'm not saying I'm the hardest, but they haven't all got the same mentality as me. When we were in that pub and Blues came in pulling out tools and stuff it was too heavy for some of them, I have to take that into account.

We have been accused of being racist. That is simply not true. Some of our best lads, Kasim, Victor, Big Tony and Jason are black. I would stand side by side with them anytime. They're all good kids. The racist rumours started with an article in the Daily Mirror in 1998. An article accusing England fans of racism featured two Villa Fans. Basically it accused them of being members of Combat 18. Combat 18 in those days was big news. It was mentioned virtually every time football and racism was in the news. Blues got hold of this article and suddenly they were saying we were all Combat 18. Because they were Zulu's we were now all racist and we were all Combat 18. One day a lad who worked for me, who is a Blues fan came to my house after a match. He had this poster with him he had been given at the Blues. It had a picture of me with 'WANTED DEAD OR ALIVE - COMBAT 18' across it. They were handing these out at the Blues. They turned it into a racist thing, not us. Then it wasn't about football it was about racism. When we were up town and they wanted a pop at us but hadn't got the numbers, they'd ring around telling people that the racists were drinking up town. Not Villa fans but the NF or something like that. They had to do it because they hadn't got the numbers otherwise. We were fighting them up town and 80% of them would be black. They turned it into the racist thing. Then our black or Asian lads would get stick, they'd be asked why they were hanging around with the racists. If you want to talk about racism look at their name. They chose the Zulu Warriors. Now traditionally the Zulu's fought the British. Can you honestly tell me there was no racism involved in choosing that name? Some of our older lot, some of them black, started to believe it. Now I don't mind it off Blues but when our own lads started to believe it, it upset me. I have done a lot of jail for the Villa. I expect Blues to come out with bullshit about me. I don't expect our own lads to come out with it or believe it. I didn't do all those nights in prison then to come out and have people on our own side saying, 'Oh that Fowler, he's racist.' I'll take it off Small Heath but not my own. I get on with the majority of the older lot. When I was growing up it was Brittle who was Villa's main man. Also people like Andy Browne, Jimmy Coley or Clarkie, they're great lads. They're proper lads. I don't want them believing all the bullshit about me. As for the Villa Youth, we have a lot of ex-Villa Youth in our ranks. We mix frequently with them these days.

47

When the Youth ended after a few years a lot of people came back onto the scene. We planted the seed for it to happen. As for The Bagot, well they're just The Bagot aren't they? They could've come with the Villa Hardcore but they've always preferred to do their own thing. They're good kids, good lads. They're always there and you can rely on them.

Football to me is, I work hard all week, I don't thieve. I learnt a trade, I work hard and then on Saturday I let my hair down. I meet my pals and we have a laugh at the football. It's as simple as that. That's why I got so wound up when the judge at the Uplands trial was calling us all scum. You stand there and you think why am I the scum of the earth? I work hard. I have my own house. I don't bother people who don't bother me. When I was a kid I always used to see my older brother in and out of jail. On our estate there were two paths, become a villain or learn a skill and work your way up. I always wanted to learn something and get a trade. I was never clever enough to go to University so I went for a skill. I went to London for three years to learn my trade and I got way from the Vale. When I came back, my mates were still robbing cars but I had my trade and I could earn money that way.

Reidy: I was born in 1960 in Phillips Street, Aston. I went to Thomas St Infants School. We moved Yardley Wood in 1966. There were a lot of self-build schemes going on at that time and my Father took advantage of one of these to build his own house. All my family supported Blues bar one Uncle who was a Villa fan. He started to take me to Villa Park. The Youth Cup Final between Villa and Birmingham City in 1969 was my first game. Brian Little was playing for the Villa and Trevor Francis for the Blues. My first real Villa game was against Bournemouth in the early 70s. Villa won 2-1 and I remember it was on Match of the Day that evening which was rare for a Third Division game. I went to Highters Heath Junior School and then onto Maypole Senior School. All my mates at school were Blues really. 80% of the school and area was Blues.

I started going to Villa matches on my own aged about 13. Villa were in the old Second Division. I used to go with a group of around 25 or 30 of us all from the Yardley Wood and Maypole area's of Brum. They called me Junior because I was the youngest of the group. We would stand in the middle of the Holte End towards the back. The first real punch up I witnessed was in 1976. Villa were playing away at Leicester. Chris Nichol scored two goals for us and two own-goals for them. The visiting end was rammed. There was a little fence separating the two sets of fans. Everyone piled over into the Leicester section and they ran out. We had the whole end to ourselves. The first time I got into trouble was in Liverpool. I still remember the date; it was the 5th of November 1977. I'd gone with Andy Browne who was a mate of mine. In those days there was no real segregation and the Scousers used to mingle in with the away support. I had a scarf round my neck and there was a bit of a ding-dong in front of me.

The coppers came in and grabbed me. They marched me round the pitch and threw me out at the Kop End of the ground. There I was with my Villa scarf surrounded by Scousers who were milling about outside. I managed to run back up to the Villa end and pay back into the ground. They've always had 'Scallies' up there, Stanley-knife Park we used to call it.

Villa and Blues have always fought each other for as long as I can remember. It used to be a big punch-up and then was all forgotten. There wasn't the hatred that is involved now. In 1975 we were promoted and played Birmingham at Villa Park in the September. We beat them 2-1 and there was nearly 54000 people at the match. That was my first real derby game. I remember they had most of the old Witton End. I also remember a match at Villa Park against Albion around this time. There was a bus strike and everybody had to get the train to the game. It was the first time I saw Pete the Greek. He was kneeling on the platform in New Street Station head-butting the floor. I remember trouble against Everton in 1978. The Witton End had a little standing section at the bottom now they had built the North Stand. There was now segregation with just a fence dividing the two sets of fans. They introduced a no-mans land section after that, with a good 20 yards distance between the two sets of fans.

In 1980 I met Joe Jordan and started going to matches with him. The next time I was arrested was the day of the stabbings in Birmingham. We were playing Liverpool. We had a bit of a thing going on with them at that time. We had heard they were bringing down a big firm for the match. We met early in the morning at The Windsor in Birmingham city-centre. We had scouts out looking for them and waiting for their arrival at New Street station. Some trouble had happened already and some Liverpool fans had been stabbed. We left the Windsor, a good mob of us around 200 strong. We bumped into a mob of Scousers by Colmore Row in Birmingham. They had roughly the same numbers as us and it went off for ages. When we got to Villa Park we started to hear about the stabbings. It was all rather vague and there was a rumour that Villa fans had been stabbed. After the match we all headed down to Witton Station. There were hundreds of us and we were hitting them from all angles. We battered any we could find. The police grabbed me and I was arrested. They charged me with threatening behaviour and affray. The affray charge was dropped. I was found guilty of the threatening words and behaviour charge and I was fined £600, which was a lot in those days. I also had to sign on every Saturday for a year. They did that, the magistrate said, to stop me going to cricket matches and causing trouble there!

I remember the game at Arsenal when we won the League Championship. I went to Highbury on the C-Crew coach. We parked up round the corner from the ground. We walked towards the North Bank, towards the Arsenal end of the ground. There was a big ding-dong as we neared their end. It was going off everywhere that day. There were 26000 Brummies there, it was bound to. Villa had the whole of Clock End of the ground. We also had about a quarter of both sides of the ground. During the game Arsenal fans walked down from the North Bank and it went off down the side to our left. Villa were chased out of there and ran into the Clock End. The few who weren't chased out had to keep quiet for the rest of the match. A few months later we played Walsall at Fellows Park in a friendly match. We stood along the side of the pitch in with the Walsall fans. We got involved in a punch-up and I was arrested again for threatening words and behaviour.

In reflection 1982 was the end of that era. Villa were on a downer after lifting European footballs most glittering prize. I remember a home game against Southampton. We had around 8000 fans there. It was a depressing time really. There was a lot of unemployment. I started playing football for the Gladiator. It was my local. I still went to the big games but not so regularly. In 1984 I started doing door work and became a doorman at The Duck Inn on the Hagley Road. In 1988 Villa were relegated to Division 2. I started going again. In fact I only missed one game that season. I missed it because I had my ear bitten off the week before. I wanted to visit grounds I hadn't been to before. We had the Youth then. The older lot myself included had no organised firm then but everyone seemed to know everyone. I was still going with a few lads from over my side of town. People like Andy O'Keefe and Fat Stan. I always took a minibus or van to games. We used to drink in the Adventurers and we'd often bump into lads like Luddy or Skinhead Neil and we'd drink with them. The Adventurers became a bit of a meeting point for a number of years. The people who drank in there were part of different firms but eventually we all came together to form the Hardcore.

Tucker: When I was born my parents lived in Longbridge. When I was two years old they moved to Chelmsley Wood. The first match I attended was against Bristol City I think. My uncle took me. My father worked away a lot in those days. I didn't go to anymore matches for a few years and then my father started to take me regularly to matches. The first real trouble I saw was against Tottenham at Villa Park. Some Spurs had got onto the top of the Holte End but there weren't enough of them. They were kicked from the top to the bottom. In 1983 I started attending matches on my own with lads from school. I went to Simon Digby School on the Wood. Chelmsley Wood is thought of as a Blues area but there always has been quite a few Villa fans living there. I went with the lads from school for a year but I was always attracted by the violence. I started to mix with other lads around my age, people like Luddy, Skinhead Neil and Big Tony. My mate Mark Hammond was always with me in those days. He still comes now and again but he often drifts in and out of the scene.

I started knocking around with the Villa Youth. We used to drink at the Crown in Perry Barr. Even when the Youth died a death I still went to the Villa. I used to go on my own and meet up with some of the lads who still went to matches. We used to go down towards Witton after matches. That was where the away fans went. When the violence virtually stopped for a season or two we started heading the other way and stopping off in the Adventurers. That's how we all got together. I started talking to Fowler and his lot. I got them involved. I did start the Hardcore rolling really. I was never the hardest but I always spoke to a lot of people. I would be ringing round during the week asking people if they were going to such and such at the weekend. I'd make all the arrangements and I would also run coaches and minibuses.

Jez: I was born in Quinton. I moved to Streetly in North Birmingham aged 11. When I moved there I got to know a few lads in the area. They were all Villa fans. I first went down the Villa around 1986. I used to attend matches with lads from school. They were lads from Streetly and Kingstanding. I knew Dandy from school. He was three years older than me. He stuck out at school because he was six feet tall had a skinhead and used to wear skin-tight jeans and Doc Martens. We all knocked about together and attended matches at Villa Park. I started attending matches home and away at around 14. Dandy knew Stan. Stan was a lot older than us. We were travelling to matches on EJH Coaches by this time. Stan had heard we'd had a few fights at away matches. He told Dandy that if we fancied ourselves we should start drinking in the Adventurers and meet the older lads. We started drinking in the Adventurers and we got to know a few people. We played Man City in 1993. It was the last game of that season I think. There was a mob of us and we bumped into some Man City at Witton Station. We had it with them under the bridge. I remember Luddy picking up a bin and throwing it at the Mancs. A load of bottles fell out and they started throwing them at us! Fowler picked up one of the bottles and put it over one of their heads. Trouble was the bottle he'd picked up was plastic. We disappeared as the police arrived and walked up the backstreets back to the Ads. On the way back I got talking to the lads. Fowler was talking to Dandy. He said 'fair play to your little fat mate, he's game.' From that moment on I was one of the lads.

Jonesy: My father's side of the family were always West Bromwich Albion fans. My mother was from Aston. Her family were all Villa fans. My father took me to a few Albion games and to a few Villa games. We went to one match between the two teams on Boxing Day in 1974. I was around 8 years old. Villa lost the match two nil. The Albion fans were calling the Villa goalkeeper Jimmy Cumbes 'Butter-fingers.' From that day on I became a Villa supporter. We moved down to Wales and lived near Tenby. It was called Little England beyond Wales, that area of Pembrokeshire. I would still come back to Birmingham for holidays and stayed with relations. I had a good upbringing from my parents to be honest. I had a lot of trouble at secondary school because I was English. I became very passionate about being English and being a

Brummie. The first international match I went to was Wales versus England at Ninian Park. I went on a coach from Tenby. Half of the coach was English and half of the coach was Welsh. England won the match 1-0 with Tony Currie scoring the winning goal. There was lots of trouble that day. I remember most of the English seemed to be from London. Fighting was happening all through the game. I remember being really aware of it and interested in it. I remember the next day at school. It was all we were all talking about. 'Did you see that bloke do this,' and so on. My parents weren't aware of it of course. I learned how to look after myself. I was doing two paper rounds and using the money to travel with a friend up to Birmingham on a coach to watch the Villa play. I was never on a tight leash but I became very single minded about what I wanted to do, and that was watch the Villa. The year we won the League Championship, out of 21 home matches, I managed to see 13 of them and that was aged 15 living in Wales. The first time I remember witnessing any trouble at the football was in 1980. Villa had drawn West Ham in the Quarter Finals of the FA Cup. The match was played in East London. West Ham didn't have big crowds, they averaged about 20 thousand at home matches. There were 30 odd thousand people there for this game and Villa had taken around ten thousand fans. There was fighting in all parts of the ground. I wasn't fully aware of what was going on but I got the general idea.

I came back to Brum when I was 16. I started going to the Villa with even more regularity. I started working and had money and started drinking in the pubs before the games. The first time I was arrested was at Everton in 1985. It was the first leg of a League Cup semi-final. I went on a coach from the Brookhill, a pub in Alum Rock. My behaviour had been on a downward spiral at home and I had gone to stay with an uncle of mine in Alum Rock. It was supposed to straighten me out I think. It had the reverse effect as they were all mad drinkers. I heard that a coach was going from the Brookhill. It was leaving around lunchtime. I started drinking at 12 and was having bottles of beer on the way up. I was with a cousin and the lads on the coach were mostly locals. Before the match we went in a pub called The Blue House close to the Everton ground. The pub was really divided into two halves, one Villa, the other side was Everton. There was a bit of singing and trouble erupted. I got involved a bit that day I was throwing chairs around and stuff. The police arrived and we flooded out of the pub. I was arrested, luckily only for being drunk and disorderly. I started getting more and more into the whole scene. I started travelling away regularly and drinking in the Witton Arms and the Crown and Cushion. I was working in the Wholesale Markets in Birmingham. I was drinking in the city-centre. We had a few pubs which were Villa at that time, Le Pub, Cagneys, The Windsor, The Old Contemptibles and the Cabin. We didn't really go into the Windsor that was more the older lads. They didn't have much time for us in those days and weren't very friendly towards us. I remember on Christmas Eve every year we'd always go up town for a drink. We would do it and

Blues would do it. There would always be trouble. They'd come up to us or we'd go down to John Bright Street where they drank. The social side of things at the football is one of the things I've always liked. I could go out alone and meet up with a variety of people. While I was banned from football Villa were promoted to the old Division One. I was at the game in Swindon. I was on News at Ten celebrating on the pitch with the Villa players. If you breached a banning order, the consequences weren't as bad in those days. If it was now I'd have been inside. I was getting in quite a bit of trouble at that time. I had three cases on the go at one point. I had been arrested at Barnsley, Huddersfield and against Birmingham. I was still a Villa fan primarily. I was always one of the first in the ground. The violence was all part and parcel of the whole day. We got more confident. We even waited for Blues to come off the train the one night. We wanted to turn the tables on them. We'd come a long way and we'd taken a few kicking's along the way. We were normally outnumbered up town against them. I received my first football banning order in 1987 against Blues at Villa Park. It was one of the first banning orders to be handed out in this country. We had been drinking offside at a pub called the Brookvale just off Spaghetti Junction. We had marched through the Brookvale estate and past a pub called the Yew Tree on Brookvale Road. We bumped into some of Blues main lot. We outnumbered them. There was about 80 of us and about 40 of them. I was hit over the head with a plank of wood. We ran them after a while. One of them was run over by a double-decker bus. We got towards the ground. There were loads of Blues milling around as we walked up Witton Lane. It went off and I ran over and hit one of them. Someone then hit me, before I knew what was happening I was arrested. I was charged with affray. I received a £500 fine and a years banning order. I grew up a lot in a short space of time.

Pete Mc: One of the first games I attended was Everton in the League Cup Final in 1977. My father took me. Most of my family are Villa fans. It was the natural thing to do, to support the Villa. I first witnessed football violence whilst on holiday as a nipper in Torquay. It was Plymouth or Pompey I think. They were playing Torquay and they had just smashed up an arcade. I remember thinking it was like something off the television.

Dandy: I was born in Great Barr. We then moved to Streetly. My first match was in 1976. Villa were playing Leeds United at Villa Park. I first attended matches with my father, Jim, and my older brother Ian. I have held a season ticket at Aston Villa for 24 years. The first trouble I ever witnessed was against Stoke City at Villa Park in the early 80s. Stoke came into the Trinity Road Stand where we were sitting. There was fighting during the game. Stoke actually invaded the pitch at one point. After the match there was trouble outside the ground on Trinity Road. Flares were being fired.

I remember, as a kid I found it really exciting.

Big Tony: I was born in Aston. I have always been a Villa fan. My first match was against Leeds United in the 70s. I used to stand at the back of the Holte End. The first time I was arrested at the football was when I was aged 13. It was against Sunderland. A van load of them suddenly screeched to a halt near the Villa Leisure Centre and they all piled out. I steamed into them and I was arrested. I have supported the Villa all my life. It is a big part of my life. I'm no longer involved with any trouble but if it comes I'm not the kind of person to back down as Burnley found out to their cost a few years ago.

Kas: I was born in the Lozells area of Birmingham. Lozells borders Aston and Handsworth. Villa was my local club. My brother used to be a massive Villa fan and he also worked for the club. I used to get free tickets and used to attend matches. I became hooked.

EJH Coaches

One of the groups which eventually merged to form the Hardcore originally travelled to matches with EJH Coaches. Casey, Cookie, Dandy, Danny O, Fat Wayne, Jason R, Jez, Crazy Steve, Danny Hutton, Steff and Snake all used to travel on this coach. EJH was run by a bloke called Chris Hill. Chris was in his 50s, a larger than life character.

Snake: I looked in the Sports Argus for a coach to travel up to Sunderland on. I saw one 'EJH Luxury Coach Travel.' The price included a video and a complimentary drink. We got to Birmingham city-centre for the pick up. There were a few boneheads waiting for it. Boarding the coach I was met by Chris Hill. 'Hello sweetie, do ya want to suck mah penis?' he said, as he handed me a can of lager. The video for this trip was Chubby Brown. Although on future trips the entertainment included classics such as Anal Dwarves, and Fisted Sisters.

Dandy: Chris Hill was 6 feet tall and covered in tattoos. He had a pair of eyes tattooed on his backside. He could usually be found baring his arse out of one of the windows at passing motorists. There was just a small mob of lads on the coach regularly. We were often joined by normal people. They had obviously seen his advert in the Argus but they were always 'new' normal people. He'd be fine at the start of the day but he'd get steadily drunk. He'd usually walk down the aisle with his cock out on the return journey. Normal people didn't usually make a second trip with EJH. On one trip to Bolton he was that bladdered that he nearly missed his own coach home. It was lucky for him that we passed him on the street as we'd given up on him.

Danny Hutton: They advertised in the paper next to the established supporters clubs coaches but let's say it differed from those sorts of coaches in many ways. There were always crates of Diamond White cider on board. Video facilities were available. Family films like Toilet Tarts or Fisting Fiona were shown. Chris Hill who organised it all was always pissed and he would normally fall asleep or miss the game. Once at Selhurst Park he was slumped over a crush barrier in the ground fast asleep. If you had read the adverts you would've believed it was a respectable family-friendly coach. You had the odd family, men, women and kids on there. They would only come once and they'd never come back. One of Chris's trademarks was, as soon as we neared a ground he would start shouting, 'Right! No singing yow wankers. If yow sing yow will all bay banned!' He would do this, screaming right in the faces of everyone including the women and kids. Then he'd crack open another can and start singing to himself. He would often walk up and down the aisle putting his cock into peoples' faces. There were some right characters on there when I think about it. Stuttering Martin from Lichfield, he came complete with mullet and moustache - he was the Ying to Chris Hills Yang. Semtex Sam and Fenian Phil, as we christened them. They were two Irish piss-head brothers from Sparkbrook who followed the Villa everywhere. Des, who was from Chelmsley Wood. He was a right Villa old boy. He came with songs and stories from the old Division Three days.

Dandy: Des from Chelmsley came with his mate John, he was once so drunk at Everton he pissed himself whilst waiting in the queue at the turnstiles. He was promptly arrested and missed the match.

Danny Hutton: We stopped off after one match in some backwater pub in Nottinghamshire. A wedding reception was taking place. Everyone at the reception was pissed. The bride, bridesmaids and wedding guests were floating in between bars. Chris Hill noticed the bride and said 'hello sweetie, yow look luv-lay.' He then tripped over the veil and his pint went all over her. He totally ruined the happiest day of her life. She was in tears and everyone got lairy. We were told to leave by the pub staff. Chris Hill topped the day off by pissing all over his own coach on the way home. Nice!

Dandy: In the end, the coach was stopped one day by police. The old bill found a load of ale, filthy porn and a bunch of well buckled Villa fans on board. We had a whip round for the fine for the beer. When the Vice Squad got involved over the video however, we all decided it would be best to keep a low profile.

The Fat Squad

You know when you've met the Villa Fat Squad, you can't miss them. The Fat Squad has five main members, Big Paul, who is really Mr Aston Villa and never misses a match. You then have Fat Stan, Duncan Disorderly, the Postman and Rolls. People drift in and out depending on weight gain. Jez has recently become a fully paid-up member, well once we established he wasn't actually pregnant. The Fat Squad don't run. The Fat Squad never run. They can't run. Don't get me wrong, these men are athletes. You don't get that kind of frame over-night. It takes a lot of time, endeavour, blood, sweat and tears to obtain. Not to mention an absolute fortune. They have now reached the pinnacle of their field in my opinion.

Fowler: We were locked up in Japan. We had tried to get into the World Cup there. Bruno and Jez were fast asleep in a cell. Pete said to me, 'I can't believe those two are asleep, it's still early.' It was only about 1pm. We'd been travelling all night so we were trying to keep awake so we wouldn't be up all night. I said, 'Are you mad Pete? Jez will wake up, have some food and go straight back to sleep again!' We got hold of a guard and told him we wanted some food. We wanted a McDonalds or something. He came back with a sheet. It had pictures of animals on it and burgers. The idea was you picked a chicken and a burger for a chicken-burger and so on. I went into Bruno and Jez's cell. They were still snoring their heads off. I said to the guard, 'I've asked these two mate and they don't want anything!' You should have seen them both move. Jez was up like a shot, shouting 'Cheese-burger! Cheese-burger! I want a cheese-burger! I want large fries and a large Coke!' We were all in bits. I turned to Pete and said, 'I told you!' Jez moves like a cheetah when food is involved. They brought us the McDonald's and we ate it. Good as my word, Jez went and lay down. Within minutes he was snoring again.

Pete Mc: We had a fight outside the Jester, a pub on the Queensway in Birmingham city-centre. The Jester was a gay pub. We somehow got into a fight with the regulars just as it was emptying one night. We had it toe to toe with them for quite a while. Then some punks or something like that poked their noses in. One of them, who was about 6'10 and four foot wide, grabbed Roly. He tried to pick Rolls up and throw him over the Queensway under-pass. It was about a 50ft drop. On seeing the drop, Roly filled his shreddies. We had only eaten a curry half an hour before. It saved Roly. This punk

decided Roly was too heavy and smelly. He dropped him on the pavement. It was funny as fuck from a distance.

Dandy: We were at Dom's girlfriend's birthday party. There was a buffet with a big birthday cake in the middle. It was dark, and to be fair it didn't look like a birthday cake as such. I said to Jez I bet you can't eat that big cake there. He went over and grabbed a massive chunk of it and ate it. He did this a few times. Suddenly they turned the lights on and announced they were going to present the birthday girl with the cake. We thought it might be wise to leave at that point.

Fowler: We were in Tenerife for Tuckers 40th birthday. There was one of those snide KFC places, Tennessee Fried Chicken or something. They had a sign up saying 26 pieces of chicken for 10 euros. When we got there Pete told us Jez had already been over and ordered one just for him. After he had been to that place a couple of times I don't think we saw another chicken on the whole island for the rest of the holiday. I also saw him heading back to his room with 7 Cornetto's the one night. I remember thinking to myself that there'd be a nice Cornetto waiting for me when I got back to our digs. When I got back he'd eaten the lot. I shouted, 'Jez, you greedy bastard, couldn't you save me one?' 'I had to eat them all Fowl, they were melting!' he replied.

Big Paul: We attended a UEFA cup match against a team called Varteks Varazdin in Croatia. It was very nearly a full Fat Squad turn-out. Nostrils, Dandy, Duncan, the Postman, Stan and I travelled over. Nostrils bird at the time worked in a travel agent. She had got us a cheap flight but also access to a business class area in the airport which had a free bar. We were all slaughtered by the time we got on the plane and we were really loud. We ended up getting the whole plane singing, 'everybody on the right do the wap bam boogie, everybody on the left do the boogaloo!' We had the whole plane rocking. We landed in Trieste and caught the train onto Croatia. We travelled through Italy and Slovenia and finally got to the city, Varazdin, in Croatia. We were still bladdered as we'd been drinking all day. In the taxi I was in the front passenger seat. Duncan, behind the driver put his hands over his eyes and held them there. The driver struggled and I steered. How we haven't died on some of these away trips I just do not know.

Jez: I stopped at Nostrils house the one night after we'd been out on the lash. I woke up in the middle of the night starving. I went to the fridge and there was all this chocolate in there. I steamed into it and before I realised I had eaten the lot. What I didn't know was Nostrils girlfriend was a diabetic. She had a turn the next morning and needed the sugar, she ran to the fridge for her chocolate......

Pete Mc: I remember getting chased by the bouncers from Snobs. It was a night club. We all used to frequent the place and always ended up getting slung out for one reason or another. We used to give them grief when we'd been thrown out and they'd try and grab us. Seeing as we were fit in those days, well some of us were anyway, we'd get away. One night we'd pushed the bouncers too far and they came after us. Most of us were young and fleet of foot. They gave up on us and focused their attention on Fat Stan. He wasn't quite as fast as the rest of us shall we say. They were gaining on him. They had almost caught him as he ran up the road by the Copthorne Hotel. To their disbelief, and ours, Fat Stan decided to jump the barrier and over into the building next to the Copthorne. Fat Stan had amazingly and quite athletically, somehow managed to vault the barrier. All we heard was 'AAAAHHHHHH!' He had subsequently dropped 30ft into a subway and some bushes below. He reappeared hobbling with a broken ankle about half an hour later, happy days.

Big Paul: We went to Romania, to see Villa play Steaua Bucharest. We landed at the airport and four of us piled into the first taxi we could find. The Postman, Dandy, Duncan and I got into this taxi. It was similar to a Trabant type car. It had, frankly, seen better days. We sped into the city-centre from the airport. Duncan was sitting in the front, he said, 'I could murder a KFC.' I said to him 'Fucking hell Dunc, you doughnut. Where do you think we're going to find a KFC in this dump?' At this point the car turned a corner and Duncan gave out a yell, 'There's a KFC!' We all went wild singing 'KFC! KFC!' We were bouncing up and down in the taxi. Suddenly there was a loud bang, and the taxi came to shuddering halt. The taxi driver jumped out and we jumped out. Well we extracted ourselves more like, as quickly as we could. We'd completely snapped the suspension. The axle had snapped in half. The taxi driver was rubbing his head. He couldn't believe his livelihood was in ruins because the Villa Fat Squad had spotted a KFC. We simply unloaded our bags and hailed down another passing taxi. 'Where you going?' asked the driver, 'KFC kidder!' I said, pointing across the road. We found our digs and before the match we were all drinking in this bar called the Sydney Bar. It was a sort of Australian theme pub. The barmaids in there were a bit tasty and we were asking them if we could have our photographs taken with them. They agreed and we'd walk round to their side of the bar and have our photo taken by one of our lot the other side. What they didn't realise was that every time we went behind the bar we were swiping bottles of alcohol. We did this for ages. Each member of the Fat Squad was taking it in turns to pose (and steal beer!) with the individual barmaids. We were slaughtered by the time we left to go to the match. We got in a taxi, and we refused to pay when we got to the ground. We literally barged through these numerous army checkpoints, (Steaua is an army team, connected to the Romanian armed forces) eight or so inebriated members of the Fat Squad barging through these armed soldiers. We should've been shot really, looking back. We'd have deserved to be.

Birmingham City Vs Aston Villa League Cup 2nd Round
21st September 1993

We drew Birmingham City in the Cup. We had been pottering around in low numbers but following the draw for the cup it was all people were talking about. A lot of lads were coming out for it. Everyone you saw the question was, 'You going to Blues?' We'd turned them over in 1987. We were then promoted and the whole football violence scene had died a death. Those of us who were still bothered and not off our faces on ecstasy every weekend, felt robbed by it. As soon as we heard the draw for the 2nd Round of the League cup we knew something was bound to happen. It was Villa-Blues, it always did. The hatred between the two sets of fans is so substantial that confrontation always occurs. Even between the normal 'scarfer' types. One shout or challenge soon escalates and both sides have never been backwards at coming forwards in that respect.

I had met Jonesy on the day of the game. We travelled to the Bagot Arms. We had arranged to go with Steve Norton and some lads from the Bagot. Around 20 of us met just after dinnertime and things were already looking good. I remember feeling confident as I looked round and saw what lads had met up there. This was only a small portion of what we would be taking. We travelled towards the game stopping off in a few pubs along the way. I think we were in the King Edward on Lichfield Road Aston when someone came in and said it was kicking off close to Aston University. There are a few pubs scattered about by the university. We heard that some older lads had received a good hiding. We decided to make our way up there. Obviously if Blues were about in large numbers it was a risk but we decided we would head up there regardless. We made our way towards Aston. We met another Villa fan, Ross. He told us everyone was meeting at a pub called the Ben Johnson just on the outskirts of the University. We made our way up there.

Tucker: Mark, Dom, Fowler, Dave Rammel and I met at the Sack of Potatoes by Aston University. We heard that Blues had landed at the Pot of Beer which was close by. Brains, Smudger, Gary Williams and a load of Chelmsley Blues lads had landed. They had battered the Villa in there. We had heard all the Villa lads were meeting at

the Ben Johnson. We headed there.

As we arrived at the Ben Johnson it appeared closed. We knocked the side door out of view from main road and it opened slightly. 'You Villa, lads?' a voice said from the gap which had opened. 'Yeah we're Villa mate,' I replied. The door swung open and we went in, or at least we tried to make our way inside. The place was packed. It's not a small place but there must've been hundreds in there. As we made our way through the pub I recognised nearly everyone in there. There were a few new faces but mainly old faces I knew. We found a space and got the drinks in while we waited to head to St Andrews. All of a sudden it was time to go. Someone gave the shout, 'Come on! Let's fucking go!' Everyone roared in unison and filed out of the boozer. The landlady looked bemused. She turned to a barmaid and said 'I thought this lot were going to a football match, not to a war?' We swarmed over the road and walked through the University campus. Everyone was up for it. Anyone who did have second doubts had the opportunity to make their own way to the game. There would be no excuses tonight.

Tucker: We must've had 200 lads plus as we left the Ben Johnson. We headed through Digbeth and landed at the Cauliflower Ear pub in Digbeth. We trashed that and moved on. We carried on and got to the Forge Tavern, a few Blues came out and they got slapped straight away. We carried on. We didn't feel like we could be stopped that night.

We emerged from our back streets route to the game and we landed at a pub just off Digbeth, the Cauliflower Ear. They saw us approach as we swarmed towards the pub. Unnoticed by police we had arrived within a stones throw of their ground. We overwhelmed them. They ran back inside and the doors of the pub were quickly bolted. Mayhem ensued. The windows were all smashed. The doors were almost kicked off their hinges. Missiles were flying in and out of the broken windows. 'Villa! Villa! There was no response and the pub was totalled. As this was going on a police van screeched to a halt on the road opposite. He was obviously radioing through warning the police control we were there and on our way to the game. Within seconds the sounds of sirens could be heard. We moved on. It was pointless hanging around when we had done enough already to that pub. We were determined to cause as much damage as we could. We headed towards the ground and other well known Birmingham City pubs. Before long the police appeared and got hold of us to a fashion. They tried to stop us at the front. 'Who are you lads? Are you Birmingham fans or Villa?' We noticed they didn't have West Midlands accents. They managed to get us into some sort of order. They sealed either end of the road. More and more police were arriving. A conversation broke out with one of them. We found out they were from Derby. They'd been lent to the West Midlands force to boost the numbers for the nights potentially explosive derby match. They seemed satisfied that we were in a sort of order. They decided to march us to the ground via the back streets of Digbeth. They didn't seem to know where they were taking us. I was walking with Victor, close to the front. They were marching us straight towards the Spotted Dog, which was a notorious Birmingham City pub. We couldn't believe it. The Old Bill were oblivious to what they were leading us into. We were rubbing our hands but keeping quiet about it. As we approached the pub faces appeared at the windows. They weren't at the windows for long. We threw everything at them and swarmed towards it. The Police didn't know was going on. The spontaneity and ferocity of our assault took them by surprise. The doors of the Spotted Dog were already locked when we arrived. Some people decided if they couldn't get in through the doors they'd go in through the windows. 'Villa! Villa!' rang out once more. Victor was half hanging out of one of the windows trying to drag one of them out. Missiles flew in and out as the Police struggled to get a hold of the situation and drive us away from the pub. We were on the move again then, towards who knew where next. The way the Derbyshire Constabulary were handling things, we would probably be marched straight into the home end. We carried on towards the ground. We were still on the back streets of Digbeth. Our escort was more strung out now as they battled to restore some order to proceedings. We turned onto another street. Some Birmingham fans turned the corner, a small mob of them. We ignored the police and ran at them. They were almost walked over as our horde streamed towards the island at the end of the road.

Stan: As we came to the island I remember some black geezer jumping out in the middle of the road shouting. 'You're fuck all Villa! We ain't scared of you!' He was virtually walked over. We carried onto towards the park. We could see them now. They were in front of us over the road.

Tucker: We got to the island. We could see Blues across the road. We ran towards them. A few old bill tried to stop us. One of the police, who seemed to be in charge shouted, 'Let them go! Let them go!' Blues came down to meet us. They saw our

numbers and ran back up the road.

Suddenly a roar went up, 'Zulu!' There they were. It was their firm. This is what we had been expecting. They were standing over the road beckoning us. We were still spread out so they seemed to outnumber us at the front. As one we surged across the road towards them. They just ran. We were then hit with a hail of bottles and bricks. It temporarily checked our advance. There was a much bigger mob of them standing at the end of the road next to the park. I saw many of the faces I'd travelled with earlier in the day flood forward.

Tucker: I remember seeing Bruno running towards Blues. A big police horse came out of no-where and knocked him flat over. The mad cunt just did a gambol and kept on running towards Blues. If any of them saw that, it's no wonder they didn't hang around!

Birmingham tried to make a stand on the side of the park, on Garrison Lane. They were raining missiles on us but we had the momentum. Half or more of the Zulu's didn't like the look of things and were already running away across the park. Some of them stood their ground. Hand-to-hand clashes ensued. They were being backed off and suddenly they were in full flight across the park. We had never had it this easy at Birmingham City. We poured through the park sweeping everything before us. The police were running around not knowing what to do. They didn't know who was who (we certainly did) and they were constantly surprised as fighting seemed to be flaring up everywhere. They were now trying to scatter the two groups, except they didn't know which side was which and were invariably forcing us upon each other.

Birmingham rallied at the top of the hill. They were trying to boost their numbers and intimidate us at the same time with their tried and tested 'Zulu' war cry. It didn't appear to be having its usual effect. It didn't slow our surge toward them. They tried to stand their ground. Some of their familiar faces were there that night. I remember thinking, 'these aren't going to run.' They did. As we approached they had a good look at us and turned tail. We swarmed after them - the police now were just a slight annoyance as you randomly bumped into one and felt the force of their truncheons. We were singing now. The joy was obvious, 1987 wasn't an accident. It had now been qualified by us repeating the feat. We headed up Garrison Lane, in pursuit of the now running Zulus. We saw more Police running down from the ground. This time they were West Midlands Police. They were in no mood to mess about. 'Fucking wait there, what the fuck do you think your doing?' Some of us attempted to walk past. They made it obvious they weren't going to allow that. We were not taking the piss anymore. They generally need no excuse to go over the top. We were finally halted. The Derby force was bringing up the rear. They still didn't know what had hit them. An easy walk to the ground for them had turned into a running battle. We were elated. We were marched towards the ground, noisy and euphoric at our achievement once again at St Andrews. We were then penned in by the away end and forced into the ground. Villa won a highly contentious game 1-0 and we were ecstatic as we left the ground. We were marching back down Garrison Lane away from St Andrews with the park to our left. The Police presence was massive and we noticed that our Zulu friends had appeared and were also heading down the same way inside the park. They were shadowing us as we headed down towards the island at the bottom of the road. It didn't take an expert to realise that something was afoot. They'd usually started throwing things at us by this point. They'd been embarrassed and they wanted to hit us head on it seemed. At the bottom of the road they had a large mob waiting for us. The group waiting for us at the bottom let fly with a hail of stones and bottles. The group to our left exited the park and surged into us. Fighting broke out in the road.

It was dark. Things were confused. People were spread out and the shower of missiles was still raining down on us. There were normal fans with us as well. We were forced to come down the road together with the normal supporters. The police baton charged the group annoying us with the missiles and the fighting was broken up to our left. We were forced right at the island by the police and back towards Aston. We walked up the road, the police using their batons to hurry us along. We went up Lawley Middleway and past an estate on the right. Now we were away from the ground our police escort became more relaxed. Out of nowhere there were lads walking down and just punching members of our group at the front. They'd been that embarrassed some of them had decided to do a suicide mission. It was pointless. They managed to surprise the people they hit but they were soon overwhelmed by either us or the old Bill. We carried on up the road towards Aston. All of a sudden in front of us about twenty black lads emerged from a bus stop. They'd been hiding in there and had remained undetected. They flew into us at the front. Their familiar chant of 'Zulu!' could be heard but we were far from impressed by that. Big Tony launched the first one who approached us. They hadn't got the numbers and the shock value of their surprise tactics soon dissipated. We overwhelmed them and the ones who could, turned and ran. We left the ones who were foolish enough to stand in our wake where they had fallen. We finally arrived at Pump Island by the Aston Expressway and the police decided they had really had enough. They employed the horses and we were split up and forced in all directions. We decided then to call it a night and headed home. It was another job well done at Birmingham City. They were good once, very good but they'd had their day. Reputations only last so long.

Sunderland Vs Aston Villa League Cup 3rd Round 26th October 1993

Fowler: We'd gone up in a coach, it was a Tuesday night, and I was with Dom, Seth, Barmy H, Sedge and his brother Dave. There were about 20 of us on the coach. It was a pathetic turn out. We'd loaded up from an off-licence on the way up there and were drinking all the way to Sunderland. We were stinking drunk when we got there. The coach dropped us off near the ground and we went into a pub close by. When we get in there was some cunt in a Blues shirt. I don't know if he was working up there or simply taking the piss. H just walked over and smashed a glass into the geezers face. The pub was in uproar. There were glasses flying everywhere. It was fucking madness. Four or five of us were fighting the rest of the pub. Someone walked past with a tray of drinks I just grabbed it and fucked at these Sunderland. It was bad really, looking back. People were screaming and scrambling to get under tables. We were going mental, totally pissed. The old bill landed. H and Dom got nicked. I tried to do one out of the door. As I was going out someone piped up 'that's him, he's one of them!' I got nicked as well. We were in the cells, they asked me if I've ever been in trouble before, and I replied no. I always do that. Fuck 'em. Let them find out for themselves. I was let out to be interviewed and the female sergeant said 'So you've never been in trouble?' and I said 'No of course not!' 'What about this, and this and this then?' she said. She had got a list.

We were held in the cells there. Three days later we were in court. The prosecution wanted us remanded in custody. The magistrate agreed and we were remanded to Durham Prison. It was in all the local rags and news, 'Football fans that caused mayhem are remanded.' We expected a hard time. We said to each other 'We'll have to stick together here.' When we got there they were all fucking Newcastle, the whole fucking place. They hate Sunderland, so we were fine.

All the evidence was pointing to H. He had long hair and it was obvious from the statements it was him. All the depositions went in and we went for bail. If you're knocked back you can go to Judge in Chambers, to have it reviewed. We got knocked back in November. I went to Judge in Chambers. I got knocked back. In December, H went to me, 'I'm not going for JC. If you got knocked back there's no way they'll give it me!' He didn't think he'd get it because of the evidence. We were up for bail on the 16th of December. If we didn't get it Dom and I were going to go for JC. H wasn't. It was about the 14th of December and H said to me, 'My solicitors going for JC. I don't want him to. If I get knocked back for JC I automatically won't be considered in court!' Just before we were to appear in court we were all in association. H came off the phone. He had been talking to his mom. 'Our mom's mad,' he said. She's just gone to me, 'where are ya?' 'Where do you think I am?' he said, 'I'm in prison!' She had replied, 'No, no, you've got bail today!' We laughed. 'Your Mom is mad H!' I said.

We thought nothing more of it. Dom and I were sharing a cell. H was next-door. We heard a screw come up. He lowered H's hatch. We could hear it clear as anything. He said 'get your shit together you're going out in the morning!' Dom and I were open mouthed. We said, 'What?' He's only gone and got JC the jammy git!' Dom and I watched H leave. Fair play to him, he turned round and said, 'Sorry lads, what can I do?' We could see the yard from our cell. We watched him walk across the yard out of the place. We watched him go, we couldn't believe it. I contacted my brief 'You'd better go for JC!' We knew we'd get it then but we had to wait another week to apply for it.

My solicitor met me in prison. 'Listen Steve,' he said. 'They have nothing on you. They shouldn't really have held you this long. If I were you I'd sue them. You can't really do it through us because of the distance. If I were you I'd find a local solicitor and sue them.' They eventually dropped the charges against me and Dom. I went and saw a solicitor in Brum and started suing them. I was in my house one day and there was a knock on the door. It was the old bill, 'Smudger' from Castle Vale police station. He knew me from over the years. He said, 'Alright Steve! Have you been fighting up north?' I thought it was something to do with the compensation. I replied 'Oh yeah.' 'We're going to have to charge you again I'm afraid,' he said. They'd dropped the charges when we were released from Durham. Now, because I was suing them they re-charged me so it didn't look like they had held me for nothing.

We were up and down to and from Durham court. I was on trial in Durham Crown Court a few months later. Villa and Blues were playing that night. I went to the doctors and got a note for court so I could go to the match. I faxed it up to the court and went to the Villa. The Judge went mad apparently. He wanted me in court the following Monday. So I had to take a day off on the Monday. I was on my own as Dom and H had turned up the previous Wednesday. I walked in and gave the usher my name. She said, 'Oh you're Steven Fowler are you? You can go now. The Judge said you're bailed.' They'd made me go up there just for the sake of it. We were eventually transferred to Newcastle Crown Court. We appeared there and they gave us a, 'If you plead guilty to a lesser charge you can go as you've served enough time in prison for that charge,' so we did and we walked.

Tottenham Hotspur Vs Aston Villa League Cup Quarter Final
12th January 1994

We were buoyed by our successes on and off the pitch against Birmingham City. We had drawn Tottenham at White Hart Lane in the League Cup quarter-finals. We travelled down on a coach. It dropped us off at Kings Cross. We planned to catch the tube to the ground. We had around 50 lads. It was a mixture of old and newer faces. We all knew each other or via other people. We stopped off at a few pubs en-route to the ground as we made our way across London. We ended up in the Northumberland pub just down from the ground. One of our older lads Joycey had been glassed in this pub a few years previously. We were all talking about getting revenge for that, when Spurs turned up. Some bloke with ginger hair walked into the pub. He asked how many of us there was. There were enough of us. It was our firm at the time and a few more Villa. He said they would be coming down the road shortly. We spilled out of the pub and onto the road. I don't think Spurs were expecting as many of us as there were. We saw them and we just ran at them.

Roly: We knew Spurs were coming down the road. We piled out and marched down Park Lane. It kicked off half way down the road towards the ground. It kicked off in the middle of road and we backed them into a housing estate. I remember the old bill saying, 'You can't come here and do this!' We had and we were.

We ran into the road and into them. They tried to stand at first but pretty soon were backing off and then running. There was an estate to the right and a load of them ran on there. I saw Jonesy chasing a group of them. He was waving a plank above his head. 'Jonesy, don't go on there!' I shouted. He took no notice and disappeared into the darkness. It was still going off into the road. Spurs were being backed up the road. They were only saved when police on horseback came ploughing into us to beat us back. Everyone started to chant, 'The Brummies are here!' We were taking liberties. The momentum had started. We were starting to become a firm. It was still going off on the estate where Jonesy had run onto with another load of Villa. The police took horses on there to try and quell the trouble. A stream of lads came off the estate, all Villa. Spurs had vanished. We really took this piss that night. We marched up to the ground just seemed like there was Villa everywhere. Scuffles broke out in front as we neared the ground. Small groups of Spurs tried to have a pop. We were just walking through them like they weren't there.

Villa won the match. Big Fat Ron Atkinson was making a massive impact. We weren't just winning. We were playing some fantastic football. On the pitch and off the pitch we were on a high. We were one step away from Wembley, somewhere we hadn't been for 12 years. The draw was made and we avoided Manchester United and Sheffield Wednesday. We got the seemingly easier draw of Tranmere Rovers. A two legged semi-final, with the first leg away at Prenton Park the home of Tranmere Rovers. They're the lesser known of Merseyside's three football clubs. They'd always been a lower division club but recently had witnessed an upsurge in their fortunes. They were playing attractive attacking football and challenging for promotion to the Premier League. There was a massive demand for tickets for the match. I queued with Jonesy and Paul D. We missed out on tickets. We were about 10 from the counter when they announced they'd sold out. We got into my car and drove up to Merseyside the same morning. We found Prenton Park and entered the ticket office which from memory was a portakabin. We weren't sure if we'd get the tickets but we did with no problems. We purchased a few tickets for the home section to pass onto the lads.

Grimsby Vs Aston Villa FA Cup 4th round 25th January 1994

Tucker: I did a coach to Grimsby. It was a 21 seat executive coach from Claribels Coaches. We used them a bit in those days. There was Jeensey, my mate Mark, Little Ginge, Reidy and a few others. We landed in Cleethorpes where the ground is situated. We found this big old pub in a big long road. A couple of vans had turned up. There must have been about 60 of us there. The gaffer of the pub was standing at the door with two big Rottweilers. Grimsby came round and they made an entrance into the pub

singing 'Shit on the Villa!' I threw a drink over the one geezer and Fowler hit another one.

Reidy: Tucker had organised a coach. 'Tuckers Tours' as it was known to the lads. Half an hour before the game, Grimsby came steaming through the doors carrying weapons and hurling bottles at us. I picked up a table as a shield. Jeensey, who was standing by me, caught a bottle full in the head. I started kicking him and saying to him 'Get up you wimp!' I was still holding the table. We recovered from the shock, rallied and ran at them. Grimsby were chased back outside and were on their toes. We spilled out of the pub just as the police were landing. Jeensey was carted off to hospital to have stitches in his head.

Fowler: We met the lads up there. We'd travelled independently by minibus. Grimsby came into the pub. Tucker threw a drink over the one and I stepped forward and chinned him. The whole pub went up. They were all outside. I ran out of an emergency exit with a pool cue and ran into them. We heard the sirens. I panicked a bit. I had only just come out of prison for Sunderland. Skinhead Neil's brother who is a football intelligence officer came walking down the road. 'Alright Mr Fowler?' he said. I wondered how he knew my name. 'How do you know me?' I said. 'It's my job to know about people like you,' he said in reply. He had heard about the whole Sunderland thing obviously.

Screwdriver: We'd been on the ale all day. I was sick with drink. I hard a roar outside the pub and Grimsby were there. They were surrounding the pub and I remember the one Grimsby lad head-butting the windows of the pub through.

Tucker: At the end of the match Grimsby came on the pitch. A few of us got on as well, around ten of us. We were standing there and there were hundreds of them tearing towards us. We stood and the police managed to get the horses on. They kept them away from us, pushing us into a corner of the pitch. We'd have been murdered otherwise.

Fowler: Grimsby came onto the pitch at the end. Some of us scaled the fences and ran onto the pitch to meet them. There must've been 200 or so of them running towards us. As they ran towards us I turned round and shouted, 'Come on Villa!' Most of the Villa had stopped on top of the fence. There were only a handful of us who had gone onto the pitch. We enjoyed that trip so much we were all saying, 'When is the next one?' We couldn't wait to go to another with our little mob.

Tranmere Rovers Vs Aston Villa League Cup Semi-Final
16th February 1994

A group of us travelled up to Chester on the way to the match. Reidy, Stan, Carl S, Carl and Russell, Ginge and Clive, Skinhead Neil, myself and a few others. Small groups of us were still travelling independently with a view to meeting up later in the day. We all knew each other by this point but were still disjointed as a group. We met Phil, who lives there and had a drink in Chester. As the afternoon wore on we became louder and were asked to leave a few pubs. We were all spannered by time it came to make our way to the match. We travelled on the train and made our way to the ground. We got in one pub and everyone seemed to be bladdered. We had a bit of a scuffle with some Villa fans in the first pub. It was just the drink. There were no Tranmere about it seemed.

Tucker: I did a coach to Tranmere. We met in the morning at the Bar St Martin. We were all drinking Thunderbird wine and a drink called 20/20. We ended up in a Wetherspoons pub in the middle of Birkenhead town centre. A load of Bagot lads joined us and we had a really good drink. Jeensey was the first person to be nicked. He was bladdered as usual. After a few scuffles on the way to the ground, he started swinging his belt round his head. He got lifted by the police. There was a queue to get in. We surged into the crowd for a laugh. Stan and me, we got nicked. We never saw the game!

We went into the home end. We found a place next to the section for the Villa fans. We weren't bothered, we spotted a few people we knew in the Villa end and acknowledged them. Just before the match started we were spotted by our police. Police came into the home end and escorted us out to the Villa end. Villa weren't doing too well on the pitch. We were losing 3-0. A number of us became restless. Someone suggested we went round to the home end and have it with them. A large group of us left the ground. The police must've presumed we were heading home dejected. We walked straight round to the other end of the ground.

Big Tony: Villa were losing. A load of us, about 60 strong, went round to their end of the ground. We steamed in. Just as we did Villa scored a goal and we went ballistic. They sussed out who we were and a few of them started to come towards us. We just ran at them and they scattered.

Kas: The police surrounded the sixty of us in the home end. They escorted us out. They had dogs and one of the dogs bit Tucker.

Mark B: We were kicked out of the game. We headed towards the pub nearby. We followed a small group of about 8 lads inside. There were a handful of Villa in there. One of the group we were following turned to us and said, 'Come ed, here's Villa in here, let's give it them!' We just steamed them straight away. The Villa inside also steamed them. We went right through them, cheeky Scouse cunts.

Ginge: I'd left at half time with Skinhead Neil and gone into this pub. Some Scousers came in and the atmosphere was tense. More came in and one of them said 'There's fucking Villa in here!' I told him I knew there was and I hit him with a stool. Some more Villa came in through the doors at the same time and steamed them. It went off proper. I was hit on the nose and I was grabbed by the old bill and arrested. There was blood everywhere. They took me to an ambulance. They left me in there on my own. When they'd gone I just jumped out and ran for it. Funnily enough the same Tranmere lads would back us up when Everton landed on us at the Big House years later. It's funny how things turn out.

Somehow we ended up in the Town centre after the match. There was a few Villa knocking about, in small groups. I found Ginge and a few others in a pub. There was about 8-10 of us. All of a sudden these lads filled the pub. There were about 30 of them. We were sitting over the one side by a pool table. As soon as they came in we knew they weren't Villa. We stood up and fronted them. We had to. We were outnumbered. If we hadn't they'd have killed us, we'd have been sitting ducks. We threw everything at them and managed to hold them back long enough to get out of a side door. I was last one out and by the time I'd backed out of the pub holding a stool some of them had come round from the other door. One of them went for me. I clattered him with the stool and lost it in the process. I couldn't run anywhere because there were metal railings dividing the pavement from the road. They were around me, five or six of them. One of them pulled out a blade. I froze, this is it I thought. No Villa in sight, they'd all disappeared. He was going to do it. I could see it by the look on his face. He made a lunge for me and I jumped back. He caught me on the arm. I was proper bricking it. Out of nowhere Skinhead Neil vaulted the railings. He was straight into them. 'Come on! We're Villa!' he shouted. I shocked them. Their mates were coming out of the pub and it looked like my reprieve had only been temporary. Suddenly, a few Villa came running over

'Come on let's fucking have it now!' I shouted. More and more Villa appeared out of the dark Merseyside night. We fired into them. They didn't fancy the more even numbers. A few of them stood but we clattered them. They legged it. I've never forgotten what Neil did for me that night. You don't. He didn't have to. He saw the blade, but he was straight into them, no messing. That's the thing with the football. Things happen and you form bonds that you never forget.

Tucker: I was taken to this police station. I was released with another Villa fan, a bloke from the Black Country. When we got out his mates were waiting for him. They had to go to another police station to pick up another of their mates. When we got there, there was our coach waiting. They thought I was in that station and were waiting for me! That sums our lot up. Jesus it was rough when I went to court in Birkenhead. It was full of smack-heads. I received a £200 fine and was bound over. I wasn't too upset about that.

Aston Villa Vs Manchester United League Cup Final
27th March 1994

The cup run brought us all together. We were different factions all travelling together. We didn't think about a name for our group. I think we realised it could all end as soon as it had started. Everyone wanted to be attending matches. The football under Big Ron was exciting and we were expecting Villa to win more often than lose. The final was due to be played on the Sunday. We travelled down to London on the Saturday morning.

Big Tony: We were drinking around London and we got talking to this cockney. He was friendly and he told us to go to this pub called Deans Bar. It was somewhere in North London. There were six of us. We found the pub. It was a massive and on three floors. We went into the basement bar. We weren't in there long when a load of Cockneys came in. They were all United fans. There must've been about 50 of them. They were Cockney Reds. We thought it was going to go off but they were alright, at first.

Kas: They were alright at first. Then the atmosphere changed a bit. One of the Cockney's told Vic it was his round. Vic said it wasn't and they started arguing. Vic said he'd toss a coin and whoever lost would buy the drinks. The cockney agreed and

he lost. He went and bought the round. About 20 minutes later the same thing happened again. The guy came over and they ended up tossing a coin again. Vic lost this time and went to the bar. They wouldn't serve him or any of us. They'd still serve the Cockney's but they wanted us out. Vic explained this to the United fan. He said he wanted Vic's drink. Vic said he wasn't having it and they started arguing again. Vic simply poured his pint on the floor. We decided it might be best we left.

Big Tony: We walked out and turned right. We had walked about 100 yards down the road when we saw that Deans Bar had emptied. They were coming straight for us. We ran. Kas and I ran into some sort of community centre. There was a dance going on. We ran straight through it and out the other side. We had lost them. We didn't know were the others were. We were shouting them. We somehow met up with them and we travelled back to Kings Cross were we were staying. Victor was saying he wasn't going back until he'd hit a Manc that night. We scoured the streets looking for some. We started singing that 'Championies' song they were singing at the time. All of a sudden most of the windows in the hotels on that street opened. They were all full of Mancs and they joined in the singing. We told them to come down and we'd have it with them. None of them seemed keen. The only people who did come down were some of the Scott Arms lads, Dog and Big Dave. They had thought it was going off and that we needed help. Dave had his trousers falling round his ankles; he'd got dressed to quickly. The police came and we made ourselves scarce.

There was a tight little firm of us, around 40 in number. We were drinking round the West End on the Saturday. We expected to but didn't see any United around whatsoever. We heard they were drinking in Kilburn. Then apparently they were drinking in Finchley. We made a move up to Finchley and plotted up in a pub up there called O'Henry's. There was no sign of them so we made a night of it. We were outrageous in there to be honest. We were swinging off the light fittings, we were roaring drunk. More Villa joined us and we had around loads of lads in there. We ended up making our way back into London and found a pub just off Piccadilly. There was already loads of Villa in there. A lot of the Youth were staying at a hotel nearby. We were in there having a laugh when suddenly someone shouted United were outside. We flooded out of the pub. It took ages to get out because that many people were struggling to get out of the doors. By the time I got out United were nowhere to be seen. Some of our lads had been battling with them but when they saw the pub empty they had run.

Reidy: While I was fighting, one of the Mancs had come behind and tried to stab me. The police arrived within seconds as they always do in London. Carl pulled me to the side and said 'Where did he get ya kidder?" I still had no idea what he was going on about. They were saying to me 'You've been stabbed!" Further inspection showed they were right, I had been stabbed. A thick leather belt that I had been wearing at that time had taken the blade and stopped it going in any further. I've always looked back and thought someone was looking after me that night.

Ginge: The next morning Neil and I had gone over to Euston. I was meeting my brother and Neil was meeting his wife. We hooked up with a few Villa lads from Brownhills. They had got off the same train. They joined us as we travelled back towards Wembley. There were about 20 of us. We boarded the tube to cross London. The train stopped for longer than normal at Dollis Hill. We thought nothing of it. It was there for ages with the doors open. A few lads walked down the steps and onto the platform towards the train. They were United lads, about 10 of them. Words were exchanged. A few of the Brownhills lot got off the train and steamed into them. The United ran back up the stairs. We didn't bother to chase them. They were shouting as they ran. We walked back to the train. Then we heard it, a roar. No exaggeration but what must've been hundreds of them flooded down the stairs and onto the platform. They steamed straight into us. A lot were Cockney Reds, we found out later. They forced us back onto the train and followed us on there. They kicked fuck out of us. They were coming through the doors in front of us. They were using the doors on the other carriages and coming through into ours. We had no chance. People were screaming. Normal members of the public caught up in it were diving out of the way in terror. I had my nose broken, again. We literally got knocked over by their weight of numbers. We were so squashed you were restricted to head-butting, or biting in one of their cases. One of them bit half of Skinhead Neil's ear off. I eventually fell over. Luckily I landed on top of Carl. They were still going for it and continued to batter us. One of them, an obvious Londoner said, 'Right lads, leave it, they've had enough!' Fair play to him and they left it. They just stopped. Funny thing was they stayed on the train. We all ended up travelling to the match together. It was very odd. We were even talking to some of them. That's when we found out that quite a few Cockney Reds were with them. The geezer who stopped them, he obviously had a lot of sway over the Northerners who were with them. When we got off the train at Wembley we all went our separate ways. Neil went off to hospital to have his ear, or what was left of his ear, seen to.

Kas: We were in the Green Man close to Wembley stadium before the game. The pub was split into two sections. Villa were on the one side of the pub and United at the other. There was a lot of singing, it was a laugh. A Villa fan ran over to the United side of the pub and threw a bottle at them. It went off as soon as he'd done that. Bottles, tables and chairs were flying across the pub. I got a bottle straight in my face. I ended up going to hospital and having to have seven stitches in my face. I got to the ground just as Atkinson scored the first Villa goal.

United were on for the treble. The League Cup was the first trophy of three they hoped to win that season. Villa annihilated them on the pitch and cruised to a 3-1 victory. After the match their end emptied. We obviously stayed in the ground to watch the trophy being presented. When we got out it was just Villa everywhere. United had long gone. We made the trip back to Euston expecting a Dollis Hill type ambush but it never came. There were a few in Euston when we got there but the police had the place well under control.

Leicester City Vs Aston Villa FA Premier League 3rd December 1994

Villa's start to the season had been disastrous. By November we were at the wrong end of the table. Ron Atkinson paid for Villa's poor start with his job. Villa sought a new manager. We have always had a thing with Leicester since I can remember down the Villa. We had gone there in April 1984 with the Villa Youth and had running battles before and after the game. It was a day which we'd all enjoyed and spoke about for ages. After that day we just naturally assumed whenever we played Leicester City that it would go off. It did 9 times out of 10. We played them for the next four years every season with trouble occurring at virtually every fixture home and away. This match was the first time we had played them for seven or so years so we had been looking forward to it. Leicester's Baby Squad hadn't yet had the pleasure of meeting Villa's Hardcore. We aimed to give them a nice surprise by turning up in large numbers. Added to all this on the 25th November, a week or so before this game, on his 41st birthday Aston Villa had named former Villa legend Brian Little as new manager. Little who was then in charge of Leicester City had been linked to the Villa job when Atkinson was sacked. He was asked in the press if he was interested to which he confirmed he wasn't. Villa then made an approach to Leicester for permission to talk to him regarding the post. Villa were refused permission to talk to Little. Little then resigned as Leicester manager but was adamant he wasn't interested in the Villa job. He was unveiled as Aston Villa's new manager the next day.

This inflamed Leicester's support who had stuck by Little as he had repeatedly attempted to get Leicester into the top flight. We didn't go to the game. We stayed in Leicester city-centre drinking.

Fowler: As the game was ending we left the pub we were in and made our way towards the ground. We walked towards the home end. We were going to be there waiting for them when they came out. We must've had 100 lads with us easily. We didn't get to the ground. As we walked down this one road we could see them coming up toward us. I wasn't at the front but I ran forward barging people out of the way to get into them. I started rowing with this geezer in the road. The old bill were there straight away and I was arrested. Jonesy was arrested shortly afterwards. We were sitting in the van together. It was still going off everywhere.

Jonesy: Filbert Street was situated amongst terraced housing. We got 800 yards from the ground. There was no sign of any police. They must still have been inside the ground. A few people were leaving by this point. We noticed a small firm of lads, about 20-25 of them. They were pointing towards us. We advanced toward each other. They didn't realise our numbers because we were just turning into the street. About ten of us charged straight toward them. They backed off. Only five or so of them stood their ground. The adrenalin was rushing. We steamed straight into them. I picked one of them out, as you do. I aimed a kick at him and put him down. As he went down I started punching him. Unbeknown to me there were two mounted police over the other side of the road. They were about 25 yards away. They charged into us as we were fighting. We all scattered. I ran straight forward. One picked me out and shouted, 'Come here!' I ran off towards the direction of the crowd which was now leaving the stadium. I ran into Walnut Street. I didn't realise but there was loads of police down there. I literally ran into them. The mounted police were in pursuit still. He shouted to them to stop me and I was wrestled to the ground.

Fowler: I kept on being bailed and had to keep going backwards and forwards to Leicester Magistrates Court. Suddenly it was my trial. I didn't have a solicitor. In those days it was just football. I thought they would put it back again because I wasn't ready. I went to court and told the magistrates that my witnesses were unable to make it that day. They said to me that they were still going to deal with it that day. I told them I hadn't got a solicitor. They informed me I would have to conduct my own defence. The trial started and I had to cross examine three police officers. To be fair the prosecution said they would help me out as much as they could. They would tell me when to speak. This copper stood up and gave his evidence. When he had finished they asked me if I would like to ask any questions. I stood up and said to him, 'There were hundreds of people fighting in the street. In your statement you state that you witnessed me, run from the back of one gang, to the front and start fighting?' He replied, 'Yes I did.' I continued, 'You actually pinpointed me in all those people throughout the disturbance till I was arrested?' 'I don't understand the question,' he replied. 'I just cannot believe that you are being truthful when you say that you picked me out of what must've been 100 people,' I replied. He was adamant he had. In the end I was summing up, giving them all the spiel, they had to stop me from going on. They went and made their decision. While they were out the prosecution approached me. They informed me that if I was found guilty they would not be applying for a banning order. I had told them I usually took my son to the matches. Because of the ill feeling I told them I had decided not to take him to the Leicester match. I had no record for football then. I had been arrested at Sunderland but it hadn't been dealt with then. To all intent and purposes I was a normally law-abiding citizen who had been in the wrong place at the wrong time. The prosecution said that they could see I was not a football hooligan. The magistrates came back in. They said that on the balance of the evidence from the police they were finding me guilty. They continued that they could see it was out of character for me. They bound me over to keep the peace and gave me a couple of hundred pound fine. I was buzzing afterwards as I left court. That was a proper result.

Jonesy: I travelled to court with Fowler. I went not guilty. I had to appear at Leicester Magistrates Court three times. One of the policemen was an atheist and wouldn't swear on the Bible so they wouldn't let him give any evidence. There was only the word of the one mounted officer against mine. I tried to humour the magistrates by explaining that a man of my stature could not employ a flying kick as the prosecution had suggested. That didn't go down very well. I thought he was going to put a black cap on. I was found guilty. I received a £500 fine and a one year banning order. That was my second ban from football.

This is taken from a police statement by a police officer who arrested Jonesy. My attention was drawn to the defendant who I now know to be Jones. Jones beckoned to four friends and they charged towards the Leicester City fans waving their fists in the air. Jones appeared to be the ringleader. I followed and saw Jones run at a Leicester City fan who was facing them in the middle of the road. Jones let out a flying kick as he got to this youth, an unknown man, knocking him to the ground on impact. Jones then dragged the male person up and punched him several times in the face and body. The other male fell over and I managed to grab Jones who was swearing and shouting. He was shouting and swearing towards nearby Leicester City fans. Jones broke from my grip and ran off in the direction of the traffic lights. The persons with Jones returned to the group of Aston Villa fans following other confrontations. Myself and another officer continued after Jones who ran onto Walnut Street where he was detained by uniformed officers as I shouted to them.

We were getting it together now. We were becoming a recognised group. We were socialising with each other and now, in the main, travelling together. We had made new acquaintances. We had resumed old friendships. New people were coming to prominence in our group Steve Fowler being one of them. The younger lads, mostly the ones who came from the EJH Coaches were also appearing. We were becoming one group now the old smaller groups were disappearing as we intermingled with each other.

Barnsley Vs Aston Villa FA Cup 3rd Round 7th January 1995

Tucker: We all went up to Barnsley. There must've been about 40 of us on this coach I'd hired. We were roaring drunk by the time we got there. We walked round the town, nothing, no Barnsley about. We then walked up to the ground, still no Barnsley about. We were up for it. Some of the lads went into the match and others including myself decided to go to another pub while the match was on.

There are about eight of us who didn't go in, Skinhead Neil, Dom, Mark H, Rammel, Fowler and a couple of others. We went in the social club by the ground. It was a bit moody in there. Not long after we get in there someone said, 'It's going to go off here,' they meant with the locals. The landlord then refused to serve us. He could see what was going to happen if we stayed in there any longer. All of a sudden it went off. They launched everything at us and we were forced back towards the door. Skinhead Neil grabbed a big wheelie bin from just outside and hurled it at them. We disappeared before the old bill got there. We'd been told that their lads drank in a pub near the ground called the Bear or something. We'd arranged with the rest of our lads to meet us there when the game finished as we were going to go in to this pub and kick it off after the match. Eight of us were standing outside this pub as the match finished or it was about to finish. A few Barnsley came up the other side of the road. It was clear they were lads and also clear they wanted it. A bit of bouncing went on and a few punches were thrown. The old bill arrived. We were running away from the old bill up the road. A dog handler let his dog go. The dog ran after us. We were all pissed. It caught my mate Mark. It dragged him to the ground. The dog was biting him. I ran back and just jumped on it. I bit it. I started biting the dog. It let go of Mark and had a go at me. The copper caught up with us. He started hitting me with his baton. The dog saw this, jumped up and bit him as well.

Fowler: Our coach was getting a police escort out of Barnsley. I was angry because we were leaving one of our lads behind. I went up to the coach driver and said, 'Oi!

Mate, pull over, we're not leaving our fucking mate behind!' He ignored me. So I said, 'Mate, pull over or I'll smash your fucking head in!' He pulled over. 'Right, everyone off the coach, they can't nick all of us! I shouted. I jumped off the coach. The old bill jumped out of the one car and came towards me. 'We're not leaving our fucking mate behind. Until we've got him, we're going no-where!' I shouted. The copper walked up to me and chinned me! I tried to tussle with him. The lads seeing this and more coppers arriving were thinking, 'Fuck this,' and shut the doors to the coach! They arrested me for assaulting the copper! They didn't go through with it. It was just a holding charge. I was locked up and released the next morning with Tucker, his mate Mark and some kid from the Black Country. We had to catch a taxi back home. I had to attend court in Barnsley and ended up with a bound-over, result really.

Chapter Three: Villa Hardcore. Landing on Them

We fancied our chances against anyone now really. We were now an organised group. Not just a loose collection that turned up now and then. It was exciting to have once more. We had a firm to be reckoned with. Wherever we went the arrogance of our group made it odds on that trouble would occur. We knew no fear. I was once again viewing forthcoming matches with respect to the potential for trouble rather then events on the pitch. To the older ones amongst us, myself included, after the way football violence had suddenly ended in 1990 it was like having a second bite at the cherry. We wanted some recognition. We saw the West Ham game coming up. We decided that we'd land on them. It would enable us to find out how good we actually were. We would take it to West Ham in East London. Tucker had been working with one of their lads so he had inside information where to go. We needed to do a small amount of planning. Getting there undetected was the main problem. We decided to hire a coach and get it to drop us off in London. That way we avoided the police at Birmingham New Street. The Transport Police there have taken a real dislike to us and were always on the lookout for us in New Street station.

Tucker: I'd been working at the National Exhibition Centre near Birmingham. I had started talking to a painter from London who reckoned he was old West Ham Inter City Firm. I had been telling him we'd got a tidy little mob together at Villa and fancied taking it to West Ham next time we played them. The game was coming up in the next few weeks. He had laughed but had drawn me a map of where their lads could be found before or after a game. I'd told him that we wanted to have a pop at them. I don't think he believed me. He told me that Liberty's Bar or the Boleyn pub were the best places to pay a surprise visit.

West Ham Vs Aston Villa Premier League 4th November 1995

The look of surprise on the faces of the police on horseback, outside the station, said it all. Seventy of us flooded out of Upton Park tube station onto the main road. It was a dreary wet November day. East London looked as dirty and as miserable as ever. One of the mounted police shouted into his radio, ahead to whoever, 'Aston Villa's hardcore have arrived, in numbers!' This wasn't the Aston Villa they were expecting. As these words were uttered,

Fowler, who was leading us, turned and announced, 'That's what we'll call ourselves, Villa Hardcore! That's the name!' It was original anyway. The name was decided. We had our identity. Not just 'Villa fans,' not just Aston Villa's hooligan element. We had our own identifiable name and one we would follow and build upon for the next decade and beyond. It suited us down to the ground. Everything about us during the last couple of years had been 'hardcore.'

Screwdriver: We bowled out of the station and onto the road, there was an old guy standing near the station. He looked like he'd been about a bit. I think he may have been selling programmes. 'Fucking hell!' he said, 'Villa have only gone and brought a fucking firm!'

The fixture in question was usually a very low key affair with the visitors who did travel posing no real threat. Admittedly West Ham weren't what they had been in the 80s. Obviously once we had flooded on to the main road from the station it must've been apparent that possibly things might be different on this occasion. To say we were up for it would be an understatement.

The last time I can remember any trouble being caused by Villa fans at this fixture was in the 1989 quarter finals of the League Cup. Unexpected numbers of Villa fans had travelled from Birmingham, (when you could still pay on the gate) and over crowding in the away end just before kick-off had forced us onto the pitch. It soon developed into scuffles at pitch side as some of the home fans took exception and welcomed us in that typical East End way they have down there of entertaining visitors. They're fucking horrible there. Some of us were forced into the West Ham seats to the left of the away end. Not the most pleasant experience I have ever spent and ended up having to spend a considerable part of the game in there.

Back in November 1995 however, things were going to be very different. We wanted to put ourselves on the football map. We knew what we had. We knew what we were capable of. Our police certainly knew what we were capable of. The reverses some teams had experienced after coming up against us in recent years were hardly going to be publicised by the people who had been on the receiving end. We were coming up against people, teams with reputations and turning them over more and more frequently. We were surprising them, just like we planned to surprise what was left of West Hams ICF that day. Yes we'd had our bad days and we are the first to admit that. We were doing it for the sake of it, win or lose. Kicking off for kicking offs sake. Getting turned over has never mattered to us apart from where Blues were concerned. Making a show was what we were about. If we lost then so be it but we have been there and they will remember us. Even if we didn't have the numbers we'd land and let whoever know where we were. We had something that was a bit special. We had new faces with us, people that were going to make an impact, not just locally in the West Midlands, but nationally.

In the underground world of football violence West Ham has always been a bit of a catalyst. They led the way in the early to mid 80s. Hooligans ruled the terraces and if you wanted to make a statement there was no better place to do it than West Ham or Millwall. We'd taken a large firm of 300+ to Millwall during the 90s. We'd surprised them and the police by getting off the tube at Surrey Quays. We walked the back way to the ground. You could see the curtains twitching of locked up pubs but no-one challenged us. Nothing of note happened but the police escort we had afterwards was huge. We'd never quite managed to make an impact at West Ham however.

Tucker had been organising our travel requirements for some time. Tucker's Tours we called it, motto 'Bound to end in tears.' He had hired a top of the range double-decker bus and it had taken 70 of us to Euston station. Every one of our group was known by each other, people we had grown to know and trust over the last few years. We had made our way towards the east-end via our usual stopping off point in King's Cross.

Following our exit from the tube, we made our way down from the tube station towards Upton Park. It was obvious that our arrival had been noted. Small groups of Cockney's were making their way up the road towards us. Our general demeanour and numbers initially put them off. They thought it was little old Villa turning up. They were wrong, it was Villa's Hardcore. We were roaring. Everything was getting trashed in our wake, bins, street furniture and pedestrians were being scattered. Any West Ham about made sure there was a certain distance between us and them. We were on a roll. We were still moving as a group but stretching out now as the more eager of us vied to be first into anyone that stood in our way.

There was a general air of 'who the fuck are these cheeky Villa bastards, coming down here trying to take liberties?' We didn't care what they thought. We didn't worry about other people. We did what we liked and if they wanted to try and stop us, let them. Whoever they were, opposition or police they would have a fight on their hands. We carried on down towards the ground. Police were running from the stadium towards us and trying to contain us. The police from the tube station, still in a state of shock or disbelief, were trying and failing to get some kind of control over us. As one of the police officers ran toward us he shouted 'who the fucking hell are you lot?' The surprise which ensued following our arrival was obvious. We had surprised both the police and West Ham. 'We're Villa mate,' I said, 'we've landed.'

We made our way down towards the Queens pub on the way to the ground. We decided we were going to try our luck and try and get inside, with or without the approval of the locals. That is what we had come for. We hadn't come for the game, fuck the game. We'd been travelling to games recently with little intention of seeing a game of football. We'd come to antagonise and if possible have it with the home support. By the looks of it wc weren't doing too bad a job up to then. It must've been pretty apparent by this time to the police and West Ham what our intention was. The people behind the doors of the pub weren't having any of it and they locked the doors. We tried to beckon them out with the usual abuse and an announcement of who we were. Missiles flew from our group in the direction of the pub. Windows started to shatter but they didn't come out, they wouldn't come out. The police started to make their weight felt and employed their batons, dogs and horses to force us away from the pub and towards the ground. A running engagement broke out between ourselves, the police and small numbers of West Ham. As soon as we saw any West Ham we made our way towards them. They were taking exception to us showing up on their patch and taking liberties. They weren't however that keen on exchanging pleasantries. We were still heading towards the ground virtually unopposed.

Close to the ground the police finally managed to stop us and round us up. They soon found out we hadn't got tickets. They were met with our usual excuse if we wanted to rid ourselves of unwanted police attention on match days. 'We're not going to the game mate. We've just come down for a drink.' They were having none of it. We were surrounded. They informed us in no uncertain terms that we were going to pay into the ground otherwise we would be arrested and spending the rest of the day in the cells. It wasn't much of a decision, we paid into the ground. We ended up in the seats behind the goal, possibly one of the worst views you can get anywhere in football. Villa did surprisingly well on the pitch, they won 4-1. It certainly was turning out to be a day full of surprises. We now had to match that achievement.

Tucker: This map gave directions from the ground so there was only one thing to go wrong, getting tied up by the police afterwards when the match finished. Luckily after the game, we managed to stay under the tunnel behind the away end and get through a car park gate and file silently away from the police, who were intent on escorting the

visiting supporters away from the stadium. We filed passed the West Ham Social Club without comment. We weren't here to bully normal supporters we were here for their firm or what was left of the ICF. I pulled the map out to try and see which way to go. Someone said 'You want to get rid of that Tuck, for fucks sake! They'll throw the book at you if you're caught with that!' I had one last look at the map and tore it up; we carried on making our way towards the place from memory.

Suddenly, someone shouted 'There it is! That's the fucking place!' We saw Liberty's sitting there, across the road in front of us. As soon as everyone clocked it they just ran toward it. No-one needed any encouragement. Some were giving it the 'Youth! Youth!' chant that we used to give in the 80s. It happened quickly but I can still see the look of surprise on the faces of the West Ham standing by the windows and outside the place as we piled round that corner and flooded towards it.

Big Tony: West Ham wouldn't come out at first. We swarmed round the entrance. It was only when we started trashing the place a few of them decided they'd have to have a go.

The West Ham outside scattered. Screwdriver picked up a litter bin. He launched it towards the window. It arced in what seemed slow motion towards the main window and towards the open mouthed faces of the West Ham punters inside. Amazingly it bounced off.

Screwdriver: I picked up this bin and hurled it at the windows. It bounced off so I picked it up again. This time it went straight through. Then suddenly it was thrown back out again. So I thought I'll have a bit of that. I picked it back up and through it back through the windows.

Fowler: They were all in the pub. We saw them turn round as we approached it. The look of surprise on their faces was a picture. We went straight in through the doors. The whole pub went up, the windows the lot. Bruno ran over with a tin of CS Gas. He sprayed it at some geezer but had forgotten to take the safety catch off. You know what it's like. Football violence, it's basically hit and run. Only a couple of us managed to get through the doors as the whole pub launched everything at us. You could only get 2 or 3 through the doors, and anyone who says, 'Oh yeah I walked in the pub and did this that or the other,' is bullshitting, the whole pub came at us. We were backed out through the doors.

Some of them had managed to try and get out at us. They had either been put on the deck or forced back inside the pub. The bin had been picked up by now and had finally made an entrance into the pub via the windows. The bin came back out again into us as we tried to gain entry to the pub. A hail of missiles were being exchanged through the now extinct pub windows. Bottles, bricks and street furniture were being traded vigorously between the two groups. They made another concerted effort to come out and slightly forced us back. We had the numbers required in the limited space of the doorway and we knew none of us were even slightly thinking of backing off. There was no need, we appeared to be winning. The bin made another couple of trips back and forth through the now empty window frames. This was going even better than we could've hoped for. Just then we noticed they must have gotten out of a rear entrance and they came at us from the side of the pub. As soon as this happened, we noticed that the Boleyn pub up the road was emptying and more West Ham were now heading down towards us from there. Fowler was standing his ground shouting 'Stand your fucking ground, we're fucking Villa! We're Villa, no-one fucking run!' The shouts went up and we defended ourselves against the ensuing assault. They flew into us. They just didn't seem to hold back. They knew we'd taken the piss before the match and now we were doing it again. They wanted the chance to try and get even. We'd had the element of surprise earlier. Now the numbers were in their favour and we'd walked straight into it.

Kas: A pub up the road emptied and so did Liberty's. We stood our ground and met them head on. The police were arriving and they surrounded us. West Ham seemed to come from everywhere.

Fowler: We had them coming at us. The old bill, West Ham and we were in the road. It was going off everywhere. It was mayhem. We'd landed, and we'd done it. We were a football firm, we still are. We went everywhere we did. No-one can say we didn't. Every single town or city we went to we had a row.

We split in both directions to meet them head on and to deal with the punters in Liberty's. Bins were being hurled; road signs and bottles filled the air. We were dividing our numbers by facing both sides. Their higher numbers were becoming more and more apparent. Suddenly the whole thing didn't seem like such a good idea after all. Most of us present had known each other for years through following the Villa. Some were newer faces but were still known by and introduced by people who we had known for years. It was amazing that day, looking back how quickly the tables turned. We were eager and had scored points for shock value. When it came to it, we lacked numbers. However they didn't get it all their own way and we managed to stand our ground and back them off a couple of times. We weren't going anywhere. We had to stick together now though. Some people were now getting concerned and shouting for people to group up and 'Get it together Villa!' P.C Flynn, or Flynnie as he was known by us, was on the scene. He was our football intelligence officer. Aggie was on the floor being kicked to pieces. Flynnie and some other old bill waded into the group surrounding Aggie and pulled him up off the floor. There were 70 of us, standing our ground. Mind you by this time we had them either end of the road so it was a case of fighting them on each side so our numbers were virtually halved. We were slowly being backed off, with the police desperately trying to stop flashpoints which were cropping up everywhere as opposing members of each group were discovered amongst the other side. The old bill were smacking us and the West Ham in a desperate attempt to separate the two groups.

Screwdriver: The police managed to get some of us in a group and surround us. West Ham were coming into the group and just kicking it off with us. We weren't bothered but the old bill didn't have a fucking clue.

Suddenly the gaps between the two mobs disappeared and everyone was mixed up together. That's when we knew it was over and it became damage limitation. Numbers outweighed us and people had to look after themselves and do the best they could. We split up into two different groups and the fighting continued with our group being backed off. Some of ours who couldn't leave the scene ended up hiding in front gardens of local houses rather than be caught by the West Ham. The cockneys were by now eager to avenge the victory we had gained by attacking one of their main watering holes. It seemed a hollow victory at the time, when you're in fear for your life, but we'd be talking about this for months.

Big Tony: The police surrounded us. They tried to escort us up the road. West Ham were still trying to have a go at us. We'd done what we came to do. The police escorted us back to the tube station and on to Kings Cross.

Dandy: A few of us tried to make our way from the scene and back to the tube. We jumped on a bus headed for Plaistow. You could sense as you looked out of the windows

and passed pubs in the area that something was afoot. Pubs were emptying and people were making their way to the area we had just come from. Anyone who says they can experience something like this and not be scared is simply lying in my opinion. It's more than apprehension, it is proper fear. West Ham were out and looking for us. We were unsure which way we were going. We were all split up. We were simply making our way the best we could back to Kings Cross as arranged, to re-group. East London is grim at the best of times and our journey now was not a pleasant experience anymore. We made our way in the general direction we knew we had to head in. We suddenly came upon Plaistow Underground Station. Standing on the platform of the station waiting for the tube we suddenly saw what seemed like hundreds of feet appear above us on the stairs. It looked as if West Ham had landed at the station and our luck was going to run out. On the platform we prepared ourselves as best one can when they're about to have their head caved in on a London tube station. As they came down the stairs we realised it was the rest of our lot. Fowler, Tucker and Loz were the first faces that appeared, they'd also managed to get back to Plaistow.

There was a bit of back slapping and relieved laughter as we headed back across London. We met with the rest of our lot back at the Flying Scotsman and were standing around. We were in and outside the pub drinking and reliving the day's occurrences. West Ham away! We'd got away with it! Fucking brilliant! That was the general theme. 'Did you see such and such do that? I thought so and so was going to get killed' and so on. Suddenly the Old Bill came screaming round the corner in riot vans and pulled up with a screech outside the pub. Flynnie jumped out and he started ranting at us. He delivered the sort of lecture I hadn't had since primary school. 'I suppose you lot are proud of yourselves! Look what you've done down there! Something to be proud of is it? We looked at him in stunned silence, and then one of us said 'Well, yeah, we are proud of it actually. We've just took it to West Ham on their manor.' Flynnie was having none of it, 'You're an absolute disgrace you lot!' He stormed around checking who had actually made it back and who was missing and possibly still a potential source of trouble. The police just couldn't understand that being a disgrace was the last thing from any of our minds. We had made an announcement. We'd been doing it for a few years now with regularity. We were the first major hooligan 'firm' at Aston Villa since the late 80s. We were going to be the best, not just the best Aston Villa had witnessed but good enough to take it to anyone in the football world. We made our way back across to Euston and then on to Birmingham on the coach. We knew we had done something special. We would all be reliving this for weeks. After doing this we couldn't see ourselves being turned over by anyone, whoever they were. In our world it doesn't get much better than West Ham away.

Months later, the following year, the corresponding fixture at Villa Park spurred many rumours that West Ham were coming up to give us some pay back.

We were excited at this prospect and gathered in numbers at the Britannia pub on the Lichfield Road opposite Aston station. The pub is about a mile from Villa Park. We expected them to get off the train at Aston. If they didn't we had spotters placed upon the station platform to annoy the fuck out of them and get them off the train. The night turned out to be a damp squib. West Ham didn't show, whatever the reason. Our presence, in numbers suggested to the police that something was going on. The pub couldn't contain the 200 plus of us who had turned up and many were standing outside drinking. All eyes were firmly fixed on Aston station.

Danny Hutton: We had a right firm outside the Britannia pub by Aston Station when we next played West Ham at Villa Park. They never turned up. We couldn't believe it, we had taken a diabolical liberty down there. They never gave us any comeback.

Eventually as the game approached the police decided to disperse us from the area. They employed dogs and horses to do so. Some of us were having none of it and missiles were aimed towards the police. They didn't back off of course, this was West Midlands police, 'backing off' doesn't appear to be in their manual. They charged us and most of us crammed inside the pub. We were hurling abuse and missiles at them from, what we thought, was relative safety from arrest and a truncheon round the head. One of the mounted police rode his horse into the foyer of the pub hitting us with his baton. The police made a cordon round the pub and we were eventually allowed to leave, but only in small groups. We re-grouped out of eyeshot and made our way down Village Road towards Witton Station were we were convinced West Ham would be. We were of the opinion that the police had forced us away from the station when a train full of West Ham had come through. It wasn't the case, as we arrived at Witton, which is the other end of Villa Park we could see the only West Ham that night in attendance were the scarfer variety. There were 'lads' walking about in one's or two's but we wanted a firm.

Things changed after the West Ham away fixture. Fowler really came into prominence. Not at first because he was one of the lads. When you saw him in action it wasn't long before people were saying, 'Who the fuck is that?' You had to respect him. He put himself in there. A few of the older lot I knocked about with didn't like it at first. Once you'd talked to him you realised he wasn't after personal glory he was totally for the Villa. It rang a bell with me and I could see he was something out of the ordinary. People like that you just have to encourage. If you don't you should look at your reasons for doing so and I'll wager they're solely selfish reasons. Me, I was just eager to see how far we could go.

Chapter Four: Villa Hardcore. Having It

Aston Villa Vs Gravesend and Northfleet FA Cup 3rd Round
6th January 1996, The Black Horse

Fowler: We were playing some non-league team. We didn't bother with the game. We all went to the boozer instead. Blues were playing Wolves. I said 'Right, let's go and have it with Blues.' We decided to go and land at one of their pubs. We got as far as the Black Horse in Nechells. The only reason we stopped there was because it was pissing down. We hit the first pub we could see and thought that we'd ring them from there to find out where they were. We had walked and we were soaking. There were a few Blues in there drinking after their game. We wanted their lads so we left them. Liam Daish was in there, he played for Blues at the time. He was in there with some other geezers. Something was said and Daish got a bit lairy. I said to him, 'Shut your mouth, I don't care who the fuck you are. Just because you're a footballer doesn't mean I won't smash your fucking face in!' We weren't there for him or normal people. We weren't out to smash just anyone. We wanted Blues. Daish disappeared then round the corner. We were all in there totting and getting dry and warm. To be honest by then we'd forgotten about the violence.

Youngy: We stayed in The Vine on Lichfield Road during the game as we did most weeks at that time. It was a case of the usual heavy drinking and drug abuse, ripping the piss out of each other, you know the score. Fowler then piped up that we should try and have a pop at Blues and look for them in Nechells. There was no complaint's from anyone who was left but then again. Everybody to the man was either steaming drunk, on amphetamines or both.

We walked into Nechells and got as far as the Black Horse. It was raining and it seemed to take ages to get there. We entered the pub and saw Liam Daish and a few Blues drinking in there. As we entered a few words were exchanged. Daish disappeared round the corner. In hindsight he went to make a phone call. About five to ten minutes later the front doors of the pub went in and we heard the Zulu chant. There seemed to be loads of them. They were mostly black. Most of us did one out the other door of the pub.

Danny O: Most of us disappeared. A few of us tried standing but there was just too many of them. I remember Daish standing in the road fronting us with them. He was shouting 'Get the one with the ear-rings!' Fowler had obviously upset him.

Fowler: All of a sudden Blues come in the one door. Daish had obviously rung them. I saw them and said 'Here you are lads Blues are here!' Again this book is about honesty and a lot of our lot shit it. They ran out of the other door. I was rowing with Blues. Reidy was grabbing me and trying to pull me out of the pub. Reidy was saying 'It's too on top Fowl, let's get out!' We left out of the other door at the side. We ran down the road. There was what seemed like hundreds of Blues. I had an earring in each ear in those days and I could hear Daish shouting 'Get the cunt with the earrings!' We reformed, got tooled up and went back. By this time Blues had vanished and the old bill were just landing. Looking back we were silly to go there really with only twenty or so lads. We went looking for it and we certainly found it.

Youngy: All I remember after that is being dragged onto the grass verge outside by several of these Blues and kicked and bricked to shit. Later I found I had developed the skin condition impetigo due to one of the dirty unwashed fuckers having his finger in my mouth. He was trying to rip my cheek off. One of them kept on shouting 'Kill him' during the beating. I remember that more than anything to this day. I remember thinking that a knife was going to go in at any moment. They also stole everything from me. They took my wallet, my earrings and my watch. The next thing I remember is our lot coming back tooled to the hilt. Blues were nowhere to be seen. I had internal bleeding and was in hospital for a couple of days.

It was a learning curve for us. No-one looked upon the Black Horse as a defeat. We had simply been outnumbered. We had gone with low numbers. It was something which we did as Hardcore regularly. We went looking for it with too few numbers on many occasions. Blues wouldn't and have never done that. Blues would only land somewhere if they knew they had the numbers. They would be sly about it. They would make sure that they outnumbered whoever they were landing on. They would put spotters into pubs and wait for significant numbers to disappear before they landed. We never did that. We just landed whatever the numbers. We have always done that. It works for us. We don't take ourselves as seriously as them. It must've worked, they hate the Hardcore. Just like a lot of other teams up and down the country hate the Hardcore. We've landed, sometimes with smaller numbers and taken it to them.

Aston Villa Vs Wolves League Cup Quarter Final 10th January 1996

We'd drawn Wolves in the League Cup quarter finals. We'd got our name now. We were Villa's Hardcore. People always flock to a banner. They become proud of the name just like we had when we were Villa Youth. It becomes important to you. It becomes your identity. We needed some more big results to establish ourselves nation wide. At that time, Wolves had decent numbers and were pretty active, especially on the England scene. We knew a few of their lads from England games. We presumed that they would show up for this one. We met at a pub close to Snow Hill train station. We expected them to come off at there. Someone brought us news that Wolves had got off a train at New Street instead.

Tucker: Someone came in and said, 'Wolves are here!' I said 'Nah, Wolves are going to ring us when they get here.' He shook his head, 'Nah they're here. I've just seen them go into the Prince Hotel at the back of New Street station.' We left the pub like a shot and made our way down there. There couldn't have been more than 50 of us.

We headed down there straight away. We split up and around 50 of us walked undetected in the rush hour crowds. It was busy with city-centre workers heading home and a few late afternoon shoppers. We walked through the Pallasades shopping centre onto the station concourse in case any Wolves were there. Then out onto the front parking area which overlooked the Prince Hotel. We could see a couple of lads waiting outside. They were obviously spotters posted to look out for either us or more Wolves. They didn't notice us as we hurried down the stairs. The stairwell was covered. The first thing they knew about us was when we burst out of the doors at the bottom. We were about 30 feet away from them. They were open mouthed, they couldn't believe it. We flooded down the steps towards the pub. As we hit the street a roar went up, and the spotters disappeared inside the pub. We swarmed round the pub. A few of us, led by Fowler, tried to get inside. It was mayhem. A battle ensued for control of the door area, the vanguard of Villa fought with the Wolves inside. The usual street furniture put paid to the windows. Missiles rained in and out and a table even flew out at one point.

Tucker: We trashed the place. Gilly, one of Wolves main lads has said to me since, 'You had ammonia and were spraying it into the pub. You had this you had that!' We didn't. It went off for ages, until the old bill finally arrived and scattered us.

The road the Prince Hotel was on Stephenson Street was normally busy at this time of day. The traffic was stopped dead. Above the roar being emitted by the combatants the sound of sirens filled the early evening air but no police arrived. The police were stuck in their riot vans up the road. They were prevented from getting any nearer by the traffic being at a standstill. We couldn't have had it better if we had planned it. Some police started arriving on foot but not enough to stop the battle. We ended up getting a foothold in the pub as the Wolves lads inside battled to try and stop us getting in any further. They were appearing at the smashed windows hurling stuff out. A few were grabbed and had to fight furiously to free themselves from people who were just as furiously trying to drag them out of the windows.

Botch: I was outside. We were trying to get into the pub. Wolves wouldn't come out - they were shitting it in there. There was this small hole in the window and this bottle came flying though it. I remember watching it as it flew through the window and hit me. There was blood everywhere. I had to get out quick when the police finally landed.

Someone ran up to the windows. They emptied a can of CS Gas into the pub through the broken windows. They still wouldn't come out. They had nowhere to run. We were now trying to get into another door at the other side of the pub and if we had we would have outflanked them. Wolves were fighting for their lives and desperately trying to keep us out. The Police started arriving in more and more numbers. They were running down the street towards the hotel. They still couldn't get their vans down there. We were forced back by the police to where we had come from. We ran back up the steps back onto the train station concourse. We stopped upstairs and viewed the carnage below we had caused. People were being led out of the pub. Some were limping; some were covered in blood, all with various cuts and bruises. The article in the next days Birmingham Evening Mail showed an outraged car owner and the wreckage of what was left of his car standing outside the pub.

Tucker: We scattered when the police finally came. There were around ten of us hanging round the entrance to New Street. Wolves came up with an old bill escort to get onto the train. There were loads of them. We were gobbing off at them as they came past. I had some glass doors behind me. New Street has a line of glass doors leading into the station. I was thinking if they came for me I could just back through the doors. They surrounded us. Most of them had clocked who we were but the old bill were the other side of them. This big black guy drop kicked me. As he did, I tried to back through the door. I picked the only door that was locked to stand in front of. I didn't go anywhere. They all steamed us and the old bill had to come flying in.

Villa won the match 1-0. We were embarking on yet another cup run. Fowler led us that day. When it came to it he was first inside the hotel. It didn't go unnoticed. From that moment on really he started to call the shots. I was quite happy to let him as was Reidy and others like us. Yes, a few of us had been around for a lot longer than him. A few of us had reputations. We lacked ideas though. We accepted a lot of things and on reflection it needed a newer fresher outlook. If one of the older hands had started leading us we'd have fallen in with our previous views and some teams would've walked over us simply because we presumed they would. Fowler's new outlook tore that theory up. We would now treat people as we found them. We were new. As far as we were concerned it was year zero. Other firms would have to earn our respect from scratch. As we showed at West Ham we respected no-one.

Tucker: A few months later we travelled to Wolverhampton for a friendly fixture. We had a mob of around 80 lads. They were told of our arrival and they headed towards us. We prepared for them to enter a pub we were plotted up in. We were waiting inside, poised at the door. We had a couple of spotters posted outside. As soon as they were spotted we prepared ourselves. Pint pots, chairs and tables were all utilised as we were told they numbered at least 200. They were obviously fired up by what had happened at the Prince Hotel a few months previously. They came well prepared numbers wise. Unfortunately they were swiftly followed by West Midlands police who made sure that they only got to the doors of the pub. They were soon driven off as a few of ours tried to make our way out to them. We were herded up and sent straight back to Birmingham after the match.

I got to know Gilly, one of their main lads, quite well afterwards. Skinhead Neil and I went to meet Clinchy, Simmo and Baker in Brussels during Euro 2000. Fowler had already been turned back. We were in Brussels looking for the rest of our lads. It went off with some Arabs in Brussels. Neil and I were standing outside a bar. Some lads approached us. One of them went, 'Are you Tucker?' 'Yeah I am mate, who are you?' I replied. 'We're fucking Blues, you Villa bastard!' he said. He had a handful with him, enough to turn me and Neil over. He was obviously going to go for it the way he was talking. There were a few lads milling round. Someone turned to me and said, 'Alright Tucker?' I didn't know the bloke and I replied, 'Yeah mate, sound.' I was thinking 'Who's this?' It was Gilly with a small mob of Wolves. He went to the Blues, 'We're fucking Wolves. We're with Villa!' With that, the Wolves, followed by me and Neil fired into them. It wasn't long after Wolves had landed and had it with Blues on the Moseley Road. I think that is was that which prompted them to back us up. Following that incident Gilly and I have always stayed in touch. I know the Albion and a few teams don't like him but he's never done me any wrong.

Birmingham Evening Mail Thursday 11th January 1996:

CUP FANS RAMPAGE IN CITY HOTEL BAR

FOOTBALL thugs transformed a peaceful Birmingham city-centre bar into a battleground.

Windows in the Prince Hotel bar were smashed and ammonia was sprayed as supporters gathered before last nights Coca-Cola Cup match between Aston Villa and Wolves. Hooligans burst into the hotel in Station Street, outside New Street station, after Wolves fans gathered for a drink. They smashed furniture and fittings and fought. Bar licensee and hotel deputy manager Anthony Shelvington, aged 27, became sandwiched between rival gangs as he unsuccessfully tried to bolt the doors.

The thugs threw a fire extinguisher through the window of a car and damaged a police van then ran off as officers arrived at the scene. Three men were arrested at the scene. Mr Shelvington said: 'One minute these people were peacefully enjoying a couple of drinks and the next they were animals. There were about 30 Wolves fans here. They weren't drunk. Most were on about their second pint when the windows were smashed and ammonia was sprayed. Then it just turned into a battleground. They picked up chairs and smashed them around. It was a miracle no-one was hurt. I made sure regulars and staff were safe and the police response was very good. The bar would be open as usual tonight,' he said.

Supt Tony Garbett of Steelhouse Lane police station said that officers were investigating whether the attack could've been planned. Nineteen people were arrested outside Villa Park for public order offences.

Aston Villa Vs Leeds United League Cup Final Wembley
24th March 1996

For the second time in two years we reached the League Cup Final. Our opponents were Leeds United. We all headed down to Wembley the day before. Nothing of note happened at all we couldn't find a Leeds firm in London anywhere. We heard it had gone off during the Saturday but who with was a mystery to us.

Big Tony: The game was on a Sunday. We travelled down to London the day before. We stayed in Kings Cross again. We had arranged to all meet up in Trafalgar Square

that day. We met up at 12 o'clock. We heard it had gone off up the West End. We went up to the West End looking for Leeds. They weren't about in numbers. We bumped into a few of them but they were too few to bother with. We travelled back over towards Kings Cross. We found a few of them in Kings Cross. There were about 10 of us and about 15 of them. We ran at them and they legged it.

Kas: On the day of the match we were at the Green Man by Wembley. Half of the pub was Villa and half of the pub was Leeds. This was also the case on the car-park. It was divided down the middle. Trouble started and bottles were thrown. To be honest Leeds had the better of things. They had a grass bank behind them where most of our bottles were landing so they weren't smashing. It enabled the Leeds fans to pick them up and throw them back at us. It went on for ages and the police didn't come for quite a while. It only ended because both sides ran out of ammunition and couldn't find anything else to throw at each other.

Late Kick-offs leading to too much drinking

POLICE WARN AS DRUNKEN FANS CLASH
(From the Express and Star 25th March 1996)

A police chief called for a crackdown on matches kicking-off late after hundreds of fans clashed before the Coca-Cola cup final.

The 5pm start at Wembley meant that fans had more time to spend drinking said Commander John Parnell of the Metropolitan Police.

Mr Purnell, head of operations for the game, called for an end to late kick-off's for important games.

Supporters clashed in pubs and outside the ground before yesterday's game, marring Aston Villa's victory over Leeds United.

Around 200 people were involved in a battle at one Wembley pub. Police made 50 arrests, raising fresh fears about hooliganism in the run up to the European Championships.

Mr Purnell said today, 'An evening kick-off enables a large quantity of fans to spend the time drinking and arriving at the stadium ready for trouble.' He said there had been a major disturbance at a pub in Wembley before the match involving about 200 fans.

Around 30,000 Villa fans travelled from the Midlands to watch the game.

Scotland Yard said a total of 50 fans were arrested - half Leeds and half Villa.

Most have been charged with drink-related public order offences and a few with possession of drugs. They have been bailed to appear at Brent Magistrates Court on April 24th and 30th.

More than 77,000 fans watched Villa's victory, which has booked the team a place in next seasons UEFA Cup.

Villa won the Coca-Cola cup two years ago and have now equalled the record for five wins in the competition.

Aston Villa Vs Manchester City 27th April 1996, Bar St Martin

The Adventurers close to Villa Park, was our base after games. The landlord was one of the few who would tolerate us drinking regularly in his pub. We had a reputation, most of it deserved. We played Manchester City and lost 1-0 at home. We had clocked Man City's firm before the game. They had Blues with them for some reason. That pissed us off. We had left the ground early to look for them and a few of us had a bit of a battle with a few Man City at Witton station. We all met up after the game at the Adventurers. We had the usual after match sing song. People were not satisfied with just that though. Most were pissed off at Blues turning up at Villa Park with Man City. 'Let's go up the Bar St Martin. Blues haven't travelled today. I know they're drinking up there,' said Tucker. There was widespread agreement. We'd gone up to the same pub a few months previous. We hadn't had it all our own way but put up a reasonable show. It was at the time probably their most prominent pub in Birmingham city-centre.

Tucker: I got nicked before the game for hitting a copper. We were by the away end at Villa Park. Man City had made an appearance. There was a few Birmingham fans with them, one in particular called Fletch. We went for them when we saw Blues. We took no notice of the police who were everywhere around us. I hit a copper accidentally and got nicked. I was taken to Bromford Lane police station. I was released about 7 o'clock. Fowler sent a taxi for me. I headed back to Aston to meet the lads. We eventually headed into the city-centre on the train.

We'd had a pop at a lot of pubs which Blues had used over the years. We were now slowly edging them out of Birmingham's city-centre pubs. We had a pop at them at every opportunity. One of their lads, Cockney Al was known to do the door at the Bar St Martin. They all used the pub and they took the piss in there a bit. He'd stood his ground on the door last time we tried to storm it. They'd put on a show and come out with the police breaking it up and chasing us away. We had unfinished business there, especially with Blues having the cheek to make an appearance at Villa with Man City.

We left the Adventurers. There were 40 or so of us. We caught the train up to New Street. The Bar St Martin was only a stones throw away from the station. We left through the front doors and walked through the car park of the station. We turned the corner out of the station and onto the road. We approached the pub. It was now less then 100 yards away. The excitement was building as our mob cut a path through the Saturday shoppers.

Mark B: I was inside the Bar St Martin. I'd gone up for a drink with some of my mates. I'm from a pretty staunch Blues area of Birmingham, Kings Heath. I know a lot of lads on the Blues side. All told, there must've been about 30 of them in there. All of a sudden a shout went up, 'Villa are coming!' They rushed to the front doors and shut them. Everything went through, the windows, the lot. You could hear people kicking the doors trying to get in. None of them made too much of an effort to go outside. You could then start to hear sirens. A few of them went out of the side-doors as soon as they realised Villa had left and were running from the police. One of them turned round to me and said, 'You're fucking Villa aren't you?' 'Yeah I am mate,' I replied. One of my mates intervened, 'He's with us,' and no more was said. More of them started to leave the pub to go and try and salvage something from the incident.

We saw a few faces at the door. I don't think they could believe it at first. They must've been thinking, 'Who the fuck are this lot?' they probably thought we were Blues. We should've played it cooler. We would in future years. It's hard to keep calm when there's such excitement and with Blues such feeling involved. We saw them and virtually all charged at the same time. There was a good few of them at the door. They saw us start to run towards them shouting. A couple of them stood at first. They scrambled back inside the pub and bolted the doors. The windows of the pub started to go through. People were taking it in turns to try and kick the doors down. You could hear screams, shouts and breaking glass, the sound of the mob. They wouldn't come out. I remember thinking there must've been only a few of them inside. After the police had baton charged us away they came out. I realised they had quite a mob in there.

Fowler: Carl walked up to them and one of them chinned him. We all then ran up and Blues ran into the pub. They shut the doors. All the windows went through. We

were swarming round outside. I went up and put my head through the broken windows. I shouted inside the pub, 'What the fuck you doing hiding in there? What the fuck you doing you divs? What you hiding for? We're here, Villa are here!' They were shouting back, 'Fuck off Fowler you prick!' Tucker put his head through the window and he was shouting, 'What you doing, we're Villa, come on we're here!' The old bill started to arrive. We made a sharp exit round the corner. They caught up with us in their vans. A policewoman came over to me and Tucker. She said, 'Can I have a word with you two please?' 'Yeah, what do you want?' we replied. She grabbed us both by the arm, 'You're both under arrest for criminal damage!' 'Is that right?' I said and shoved her out of the way. I ran. I was running up New Street with police dogs behind me. There were shoppers everywhere. I managed to get away.

Tucker: We were at the back. We followed after it had all happened. We'd clocked the old bill. Fowler went up to the smashed windows. As he popped his head through he said, 'Hmm, got done by Villa have you?' All of a sudden these coppers jumped out on us and said you're nicked. Fowler ran and I was about to do one, I looked round and the only place to run was into the Blues, who now the old bill were around, had decided to come out of the pub.

Fowler: A couple of weeks later my door went in. I was at work but my Mrs was at home. Twenty coppers piled into the house. 'Where is he?' She phoned me to tell me. I handed myself in and I went no comment all the way. They handed me the depositions. Cockney Al's name was on there. It said 'Steven Fowler and Gary Tucker put the windows through' etc. He was grassing us up. I didn't put any of the windows through. I don't do that. He'd made out to the old bill that it was me and Tucker. We went to court and he was there with Gary Williams one of Blues main lads. I walked up to them both. I was face to face with Cockney Al. 'You grassed me up you cunt!' I said to him. 'No! No Fowler! I wouldn't do that! I'm here to get you off.' 'Bollocks!' I said to him, 'I've seen your fucking statement!' He was shitting himself. He then went in the dock and said 'No it wasn't them.' My argument has always been why did he do it in the first place? If he hadn't grassed my door wouldn't have been kicked in. Why do it? I heard there was a big thing down the Blues about him grassing, I did hear that some of their main lads didn't like it and that's why he retracted his statement.

Tucker: Cockney Al and about six doormen turned up at my house on a Sunday night. They'd got my address from somewhere. They were in two cars. My wife and kids were in the house. They were just trying to bully me. It didn't go on for long but they did it a few times. They would drive past my house slowly in cars, thinking they were gangsters. It was football but they wanted to take it that little bit further. I heard someone at Blues had a word with him and stopped it all. I don't know how true that is.

Some of our lads were targeted by Blues following this incident. We would make sure it wouldn't happen again. We had more about us than that. They weren't going to treat us like we were mugs. We started finding things out about them. We found out where some of them lived. We didn't use the information but a few of us decided if they ever tried the out of hour's intimidation again we would return the compliment with interest. Luckily we didn't have to lower ourselves to their level but we would've if they'd have kept it up.

Coventry City Vs Aston Villa Premier League 23rd November 1996

Pete Mc: We had a good 40 plus out that day. I can't remember how we got there but we ended up in the Penny Black. It's a pub near Coventry city-centre. We hadn't gone to the game, as usual. We all just stayed on the lash. I think Cov had rung the landline of the boozer and asked to speak to one of the Villa. They knew we were in there. One of our lot acknowledged that we were there. We knew their arrival was imminent. A few of us had started to mill around outside. There was a shopping mall behind the pub. A small number of them had come through the shopping mall to the rear of the pub. A handful of us saw them and ran into them. It was roughly equal numbers and there was a big few lumps with them. They didn't look like hooligans. A few of them were wearing Coventry rugby shirts but they were calling us on so they got the same treatment as everyone got in those days. They had it on their toes as the rest of our lot came out the pub. As Villa flooded out of the pub Coventry's main firm landed out the front. There was a little token resistance from Cov but they soon scattered. As Cov were in full flight, West Midlands finest started arriving. They had dogs and horses. They set the dogs on us and everyone piled back into the pub. What we didn't know was that PC Flynn our police spotter had been watching us from the shopping centre all the time. Two of our lads Rob and Danny O got sent down for the incident; I had a stroke of luck that day and didn't get my collar felt.

Dandy: We came back into Birmingham on the train and passed through New Street station. We had quite a firm out that day. We always turned out decent numbers for Coventry, home or away. We headed towards the Square Peg and had a tot. We were in there quite a while. People started to drift off to go wherever. It was Saturday night and some of the lads had made arrangements. There were about fifteen of us left in there. Danny Hutton was sitting by the door scanning the road for any lads who might be knocking about. He suddenly shouted, 'They're here! Blues are here!' I ran over to the windows. I'm not kidding you, they filled the road. There seemed like hundreds of them. As Danny Hutton shouted the warning two or three lads who were already inside the pub jumped up and one of them ran over and punched him. These lads had obviously been in there some time. They had waited till the majority of our firm had gone. Then given Blues the nod to come and storm the place. Blues swarmed round the entrance to the pub. The pub employed bouncers at a weekend. To be fair to them, they battled to stop them coming in while we got ourselves together.

Stan: The Square Peg has massive windows. Some of the Blues were fighting with the doormen. The ones who couldn't get near the door were starting to put the windows through. They must be 20 foot sheets of glass in those windows. Normal people just out for a drink were scattering as the windows started to smash. Women were screaming as missiles were being thrown through the holes in the windows. They were throwing bins through these windows and smashing them in the middle. The rest of the glass, still intact above the hole, was starting to fall down and shatter. It was adding to the panic inside the pub. We knew what we had to do. Deal with the Blues in there and defend the doors.

Fordy: We were getting chairs, stools and tables thrown at us as we desperately fought to either force them out or force our own way out onto the street. I remember ducking as a bottle narrowly missed me and thumped into Bayo's head. He was standing behind me. There really did seem like hundreds of them.

Stan: They were shouting inside the pub to us. One of them this geezer from Kings Norton called Faye was shouting 'Stan! Where's your fucking boys now then?' and 'Stan you're fucking dead, we're gonna kill you!' They'd got in past the bouncers and into the pub. Fighting was breaking out as we hit them. One of them ran in came forward and shouted 'Which ones Fowler?' Fowler bounced over to him and said 'I am,' and put him on his arse.

Dandy: It must've been going off for five minutes or more. We were getting forced into an ever decreasing circle. Then we heard the sirens. Blue lights appeared outside. They stopped and started to leave. We followed them out and fighting continued on the road. I looked at the devastation as I left the pub. It had been packed and normal people had been caught up in it all. They were all huddled in a corner of the pub. I saw grown men crying. What with the massive sheets of glass going through almost all at the same time people must've thought it was a bomb going off. That image stayed with me. We carried on after a small group of them as they ran from the scene to avoid the police. We followed them down into Dale End. There must've been ten or twelve of us.

We spread across the road and shouted to them. 'Come on! We're fucking Villa! Lets fucking have it!' They stopped and thought about having a go. It was roughly the same numbers. A copper on a motorcycle came screaming round the corner and got in between the two groups. He was followed by a riot van. The van full of police mounted the kerb and came straight for us. They were trying to run us over. Blues were on their toes now. We scattered to avoid being hit by the van. As the van emptied we all just split up and melted into the night. Two or three of us hailed a taxi and got out of town.

Chapter Five: Villa Hardcore. All Abroad

European Championships Sweden June 1992

Fowler: I went with Dominic Byrne, Dave Rammel and our friend Kevin. We didn't have a clue. We were only young. We caught the train down to Harwich. We got a ferry then to the Hook of Holland. We then travelled overland to Sweden.

We met up with Pete and Bruno. It was expensive over there. It was £5 a pint which was a lot in the 80s. We'd got tickets for the game and we were buzzing. Our first England game and it was England against France in the European Championships. They'd erected these big tents for the England fans. They'd got security on there and they were serving beer. They had decided that they wouldn't serve the England fans normal strength beer. They were serving their equivalent of low-alcohol beer. It was still stronger then the stuff we were used to in the UK. Everyone was steaming drunk. They'd got a band on in there everyone was going wild. I was drinking this can of lager. You had a lot of Swedish coming into the tent. They had heard about the English and wanted to come in and party like the English did. Well we're great aren't we? Until we have too much beer that is. I don't think they appreciated that fact. I had this can of lager and there was some sort of melee involving the security guards. There was a scuffle and I ran over and bounced the can of lager on a security guards head. It exploded. It went off everywhere. It was a riot, literally. We were being charged by police on horseback and the England fans were getting big sticks and chasing the mounted police back up the road hitting them.

It was so expensive over there we were running out of money. We'd only been there two days but everything cost a bomb. England fans were rioting and doing smash and grab raids on shops. I remember we were running down the one road. There was a jewellers shop. Dom grabbed a big stick and ran towards the window. He smashed the stick against the glass. It must've been reinforced glass and the stick bounced back and hit Dom in the face. Dave Rammell was arrested shortly after all this and he was taken off in a police van. It was going off everywhere throughout the night. When we'd had enough we had nowhere to stay. We returned to the tents where we'd initially been. We slept in there, it was freezing cold. Most of the England fans had gone on to Stockholm for the next match so there weren't many left. We virtually had these big tents to ourselves. We were cold, hung-over and hungry. The next morning we found the police station. Dave was just coming out. 'Alright lads!' he said cheerfully. 'I've had a bang on night,' he said. 'The cells are brilliant here; I had a comfy bed and a cracking breakfast!' We couldn't believe it. We were undecided what our next move would be

We wanted to carry on to Stockholm but we had virtually no money left. A mate of ours paid for a flight from Copenhagen to Amsterdam. We had an open return on the ferry from Amsterdam to Harwich. We made our way back to Copenhagen and found the airport. We were late for our flight. We ran down the departures lounge and got on the plane. They'd been waiting for us. It was a business flight from Copenhagen to Amsterdam. The passengers looked at us as if we were off another planet. We had beer down us - we were in a right state. We flew back to Amsterdam and returned to England. After we went to the game I attended every England game. Up until France 1998 where I was deported and they stopped me following England. Up until then I went to every single game England played.

Holland Vs England World Cup Qualifier Rotterdam 1994

Fowler: We got to Amsterdam on the morning of the match. There was Dave Rammell, Brick, Pete, Barmy H, TB, me and a few others. Trouble started later on that day. There was fighting everywhere. We were walking down the one road. Our group was mainly Villa but we had a few other teams mixing in with us. All of a sudden a mob of lads came bouncing up the road. We ran towards them. They looked game. We thought they were Dutch. We were going to have a battle. They were Cockneys. We all joined up and then landed at another boozer. The pub was packed and had some Dutch in there. It went off of course. The police landed and nicked virtually everyone. They didn't nick me and Dave. We made our way to the square in central Rotterdam. We found a pub there and were drinking with a load of English. Someone said, 'The Dutch are over there!' We emptied the pub. We went over to this bar and it was full of Dutch. They were firing flares out at us. All of a sudden this big black rubber thing landed by us. 'What the fucking hells that?' shouted Brick. I didn't know. Pete shouted, 'It's a fucking bomb!' We all dived for cover as it exploded. We all had cuts and wounds from it. I was in one of the English newspapers the next day pictured in mid-flight as I tried to jump out of the way. They had thrown a bomb at us. The English went mad. We stormed the pub and smashed the living daylights out of the Dutch and the pub. They tried to run in and lock the doors but it was useless. We trashed the place. That must've been one of the biggest England firms I have ever seen. There must've been a thousand of us in all. We were walking by the train station and another firm came out. Again we thought they were Dutch but they were English as well. The police eventually managed to get us into this big square. They penned us in there and riot police were brought in. It was like trooping the colour the way they were manoeuvring ready to confront us. What they said as they were going to put us on buses and take us to the stadium for the game. We all got on and they took us straight to some military base. They kept us on these buses surrounded by police for what must have been four or five hours. In the end they got all the people who had tickets off the buses and they were allowed to go to the game. We were left there with a few police while they and the majority of the old bill went to the match. After a while we got restless and took advantage of the few police who were there guarding us. We smashed down a fence and started walking up the road. There must've been 300 of us. As we walked further up the road we could see the police in full riot gear at the top. As we approached them my mate TB said, 'I'm not having this Fowl.' He grabbed the truncheon of one of the police. They leathered him and starting wading into us. We all scattered. We were hiding in bushes and allsorts but we managed to get back into the town. After the match at Rotterdam train station a few of us encountered a few Dutch. One of the Dutch had a flare gun. He was aiming it at us. A few of us were trying to get near them but no-one really fancied a flare in their face at such close range. Fuck that. Eventually Bruno had enough and he waded into him and we scattered them.

England Vs Scotland European Championships Wembley June 1996

Fowler: We hired a big coach for this one. I think it was a 70 seater. We met on Corporation Street in Birmingham. We had a proper firm on there. While we were travelling down the motorway towards London someone noticed we were being followed. It was our football intelligence officers. I said to the coach driver that we wanted to stop at the next services. He pulled in and we went into the coach park. The police following us pulled in and they went into the bit which was reserved for cars. 'No carry on!' I shouted to the driver and we tried to lose the police. They were still following us but when we got into London we suddenly stopped outside a tube station and all jumped off. They couldn't find anywhere to park and we disappeared into the tube system. There was a meet arranged with the Jocks at Cockfosters in London. We decided we'd all jump off the coach at a tube station. We planned to go a couple of stops then jump out and get taxis just in case the old bill were still on our tail. When we got to Cockfosters there was police everywhere. They knew all about it. The old bill swooped on us. One of the coppers was speaking to someone on his radio. 'Its Villa, its Villa!' he was going, 'We've got them!' We were searched and allowed to leave. They assigned two coppers to us for the day to follow us everywhere. We went into London. We landed at Trafalgar Square. There was an easy 100 of us by this time - people who hadn't come on the coach had met up with us. The Jocks were in Trafalgar Square and it went off. There was this one Jock, fair play to him he was having it with anyone. He had a kilt on with a Celtic football shirt. Ginger ran into him. He clumped Ginge, sent him flying. I ran into him and just missed him with a swing. The old bill were quickly onto it and broke it up making a couple of arrests. We went to this pub, it was full of Carlisle. We went in and started talking to them. Some of the lads went to watch the game. Some of us stayed on the piss. After the match we all met up again. We were walking through London. I can't quite remember where. We saw a load of Jocks sitting outside this bar/restaurant thing. We walked past and something was said. We steamed them. Screwdriver picked up a stool to throw and as he swung it backwards it hit me straight on the chin. It was a deep cut and there was blood everywhere. I had a white Lacoste jumper on and it was covered in blood. We smashed the place to smithereens and wasted the Jocks. We disappeared into the night as we heard the police sirens. What a good day out that was.

Poland Vs England World Cup Qualifier Katowice 23rd May 1997

Some of us who had been away with England in the 1980s and very early 90s knew the score. We accepted there was a clear hierarchy. The new boys didn't however. On the England scene, you found that the smaller or less well known firms linked up to the established ones. They played the subservient role, frankly to firms who no longer deserved the reverence and who were washed up. Teams like West Ham, who hadn't done anything of note for years. We were supposed to hold them in awe. What for? For where they were born or for what club they happened to choose to support? Certainly it wasn't for what some of them had been doing over the last ten years or so. We didn't keep to the script.

Fowler: Villa had taken a few to England games in the mid to late 80s then it had died a death. It was decided that Aston Villa would remerge on the international scene and with no place better to start than Poland away in Katowice. We'd been going everywhere in England. We wanted to take a decent sized firm away with England. It was really the only thing we hadn't done as the Hardcore yet. Our plan was to fly to Berlin in Germany from Birmingham and travel overland to Poland on the train to Katowice.

The Poland game is one of the better and more attractive fixtures violence wise. The Poles are as game as anyone. It's one of the few places in my experience that England have nearly come unstuck over the years. We flew out of Birmingham two days before the fixture headed for Berlin. We were going this way to avoid any unwanted police attention. As we entered departures the police were there interviewing all departing fans. We were going to Berlin, days before the match, they couldn't stop us. The free drinks on the plane went down well, rather two well in fact. They didn't know what had hit them. Between 40 of us the bar was drunk dry halfway across the channel. We landed in Berlin. Everyone seemingly hammered by the alcohol. We made our way to the Zoo area of the city. We arrived there and plotted up in a bar. There were a few red-light attractions locally. A few of the lads went for a mooch. I stayed in the bar with a few of the lads and we continued to drink.

Reidy: Once we were on the plane, it was one of those duty free planes and there was Graham Norton look-a-like pushing the trolley giving out the drinks. After struggling to get down even a quarter of the aisle he gave up. Eddie took over. Instead of having a couple of miniatures each, we ended up with a box each! By the time we got to Berlin everybody was leathered. We were told once we get to Berlin to get in taxis and ask for a pub called the Soccer Bar which was by a train station. My taxi and two other taxis ended up in East Berlin going to three different pubs by train stations. The drivers hadn't got a clue what we were talking about. Eventually, after getting into our third taxi, we found it. When we got there the lads had already had an off with Leicester where Luddy and two other lads had been arrested. We'd only been gone an hour and half and they'd been in two fights. This was the start of what was to come.

Pete: Luddy didn't know we were spiking his drinks. He was kickboxing at the time so he was usually drinking orange juice. Every time I went to the bar I ordered him an orange juice and slung double vodka in there. Brian was doing the same. You could see him getting more and more hammered.

After about an hour or so we heard a rumour Leicester Baby Squad were about in the area. This obviously interested us because of our recent history with Leicester. We decided to go out and have a look. Leicester's lads were there. A small group of us approached a group of them not far from the bar. I thought I'd only had a couple of drinks. I didn't realise how bladdered I was. I went over and said 'Are you Leicester or what? You Babies are you eh?' One of their group replied they were Leicester. I half staggered into him and we exchanged a few slaps. Oldie was with them. Oldie is a staunch Villa lad from the Leicestershire area. It was a surprise to see him there and he was trying to calm it down. He was stepping in and suddenly Oldie and I were rolling about on the floor. It's easily done when the alcohol has been flowing. As we were rolling about I felt something hit me and hit me hard from behind. I felt a sharp pain on my head. Whoever they were, they were laying into me and Oldie. My

Villa Hardcore in Madrid.

The calm before the storm in Madrid.

Hardcore in Thailand trying to sneek into Japan for the World Cup.

A drink for Dave Moore R.I.P. on the Thailand trip.

Villa Hardcore in Lille.

Nostrils and Paul consider a hire car upgrade.

Big Paul, Dandy and a none too impressed looking Reidy now showing his age.

Pete bonding with the locals.

Shame . . . cuffed fan hides face under cap

Kicked out . . fan in handcuffs at Heathrow after return yesterday

Yobs are facing 5yr travel ban

By MARTIN BENTHAM and JOHN SCOTT

FOOTBALL hooligans face automatic five-year bans on travelling to matches abroad under a new crackdown by Home Secretary Jack Straw.

Courts will be ordered to "ground" any yob convicted of a soccer-related offence unless there are exceptional reasons.

If JPs fail to act Mr Straw is set to bring in laws to make the travel bans compulsory.

He told MPs yesterday: "We are determined to ensure that the disgraceful scenes in Marseille are not repeated."

Four fans branded Category C yobs — the worst — were kicked out of France in plastic handcuffs yesterday and banned from the country for life.

Aston Villa thugs STEPHEN FOWLER, STEPHEN BAKER and TERENCE COUGHLAN were frogmarched to a van after British police spotters saw them in a Toulouse bar.

Arrest

Coventry City yob RAYMOND RAFFERTY was arrested at a pub. All four were on a plane to Heathrow within hours. They arrived with French police and were then allowed to go.

Fowler, 29, Baker, 25, and Coughlan, 36, all of Birmingham, were involved in trouble at England's World Cup qualifier in Poland last year. Painter and decorator Coughlan protested last night: "I spent over £1,000 organising the trip to France and had no intention of causing trouble."

Jobless Rafferty, 36, said: "The only thing I'm dreading is meeting my mum. But I am no hooligan — I am a Jack the lad."

Police were seeking six more Category C yobs in Toulouse last night.

HOME IN SHAME

DEFIANT: Upset Rafferty yesterday

COVER-UP: C-rated troublemaker

LIFE BAN: No return to France

SHACKLED: One fan in handcuffs

Yobs France kicked out

By JEREMY ARMSTRONG

FOUR English football hooligans troop home in shame – the first to feel the weight of France's emergency action against World Cup thugs.

One tried to hide by pulling his T-shirt over his face as they were flown in to Heathrow yesterday. Another was handcuffed.

Two strongly protested innocence. But all four — Terence Coughlin, 36, Stephen Baker, 25, Steven Fowler, 29, and Raymond Rafferty. 36 — are ranked as Category C "extremely dangerous" offenders.

They were picked out by British hooligan-spotters in Toulouse. The four were kicked out of France and banned from the country for life.

Hours earlier, authorities there were granted emergency powers to either refuse entry to potential troublemakers or expel them even if no offence had been committed.

An official in Toulouse, said the four had been drunk and had no match tickets. He asked France's Interior Minister for an expulsion order "bearing in mind their previous convictions and their police records, particularly in connection with football matches".

The four were held overnight in cells, then flown to London guard-

ed by nine French officers. Warehouseman Rafferty, from Coventry, said: "I was drinking in a bar when I was grabbed, put in a police van, then deported. I have not been charged, done nothing wrong and been told nothing."

But he has been barred from Coventry City ground for beating up a Derby fan and is also said to have other convictions for soccer-related incidents.

Rafferty added: "The only thing I am worried about is seeing my mum. I am dreading it".

Coughlin, Baker and Fowler are all Aston Villa fans from Birmingham. Coughlin, a self-employed painter, said: "At the police station, the chief said we were known as hooligans and had to be deported.

"We'd had two drinks, minding our own business, and then we got kicked out. It's outrageous."

"I was arrested when 17 at a Villa match and got a conviction," he said. "But since then I have not been in any trouble at football at all." He admitted "some other convictions" for non football-related offences.

A fifth English fan was held in Toulouse after being "spotted" from the riots in Marseille.

● Voice of the Mirror – Page 6

VILLA FANS ARRESTED AFTER MADRID BRAWL

SIX Aston Villa fans have been arrested in Madrid after wrecking a bar and injuring two people, Spanish police said today.

The fans who were in the Spanish capital for the match against Atletico Madrid in the UEFA Cup tonight caused havoc when they smashed up a bar in the city centre and injured a waiter and a 21-year-old man last night.

On Sunday night, four other fans were arrested for a breach of the peace near the same bar.

Doug Ellis, chairman of Villa, said he was deeply disappointed by reports that a small number of fans had caused trouble.

"It is deeply regrettable, but it is a great surprise to me. Our stadium holds 40,000 people and they never cause problems."

Supporters were involved in two incidents last night which led to six arrests, police said.

The first was at 11pm at the Fontana de Oro bar, near the central Plaza del Sol — the same bar in which trouble broke out the night before.

■ **ELLIS: Disappointed**

Trashed

A group of fans trashed the bar and attacked a waiter, police said. The waiter needed medical treatment but the injury was not serious.

Five fans were arrested and the owner of the bar and the waiter have made a complaint against the men, aged 21 to 34.

In the early hours of this morning, police said a sixth Villa fan, aged 25, was arrested after attacking a 21-year-old man.

A spokeswoman for the Spanish police said all six were being held at the central police station. They were given a lawyer and an interpreter was appointed.

Spanish police have obtained a special security order from the chief of police to put into place additional safety measures, ready for tonight's game.

These will include a police escort for fans from the airport to the stadium, extra medical services and dog and horse patrols.

It is understood that 2,000 policemen — one for every Villa fan — have been put on duty for the quarter final match, which kicks off at 8.30pm British time.

The police spokeswoman added this was the normal procedure to prevent any violence at a football match. It is adopted for national as well as international games and is the same as the measures used in Britain, she said.

● **Big match preview — back page**

Villa fans are held in Spain

FOUR Aston Villa fans were arrested early today after allegedly going on the rampage in the centre of Madrid.

The supporters, in Spain for tomorrow's UEFA Cup match against Atletico Madrid, wreaked havoc in the Spanish capital after a night on the town turned violent, police said.

Five fans were involved in fighting inside the La Fontana de Oro bar near the central square of Sol, injuring several people who were drinking there and damaging the bar.

After being thrown out of the bar, they allegedly smashed four shop windows in the main street and overturned a parked Renault car and a motorbike before four of them were arrested by police early today.

The fans, aged 21 to 27, spent the night in the cells at the central Madrid police station.

A spokeswoman for Madrid police said it was not yet known whether the fans would go before a local judge charged with damaging property or whether they would be released in time to watch the game.

A dozen Villa supporters caused damage to the hotel where they were staying in Madrid on Saturday night, the spokeswoman also revealed.

● **Big-match latest - Back**

Queries? Just ring the boss

BOSSES at Wolverhampton-based Birmingham Midshires are claiming a first — by including their home telephone numbers in the building society's annual report.

The eight-strong executive team plus chairman John Leighfield are making their home numbers available to the society's one million customers.

BOOTED OUT FAN: I DID NO WRONG

A BIRMINGHAM football fan deported from France today declared: "I've done nothing wrong."

Terry Coughlin, aged 36, was one of four West Midlands men booted out of France ahead of last night's World Cup clash in Toulouse between England and Romania.

Coughlin, an Aston Villa season ticket holder, was today banned for life from attending games at Villa Park.

The club's chief security officer John Hood said: "These are not true football supporters. They have caused trouble and we do not want them at our ground."

By MARTIN BANKS

Life bans have also been imposed on two other deported Villa supporters - Stephen Baker, aged 25, of Sheldon and Steven Fowler, aged 29, from Castle Vale. Ray Rafferty, 36, of Coventry, was also deported.

They were the first fans to be ejected under new emergency powers which allow Category C hooligans - all with football-related convictions - to be expelled even if they have committed no offence.

Back home in Blackrod Road, Wyrley Birch, Mr Coughlin, a self-employed painter and decorator who lives with his mother, insisted he had done nothing wrong.

"We all took a week off work to watch the World Cup in France. We were not there to cause trouble. The only reason I was deported was because I've got a police record and I didn't have my passport with me. The whole thing is a nightmare, he said."

He admitted he had a criminal record but said the offences were minor and not related to football.

Offensive

"The last time I was arrested at a football match was at Villa Park against Man United in 1981 for offensive behaviour. I've not been in trouble since. I've been to the World Cup before and Euro 96 without any problems," he added.

Mr Coughlin was one of six supporters who left Birmingham ticketless last Saturday morning in a hired van. He said they planned to stay in France for one week and hoped to buy match tickets shortly before the games in Toulouse and in Lens on Friday.

"We booked into a hotel after about an hour, ten French policemen burst into the cafe.They asked to see our passports but when I said they were in the hotel they didn't want to know and arrested us."He said they were handcuffed, bundled into a van and taken to a local police station where they were questioned and held for about 16 hours in a cell. "The only thing the police seemed interested in was whether we'd been causing trouble in Marseille. I told them we were still in England then but they didn't want to know."

The four landed at Heathrow airport yesterday morning accompanied by nine French police officers

■ TERRY COUGHLIN: Banned from Villa Park for life

■ STEPHEN BAKER

■ STEVEN FOWLER

UEFA droht:
England fliegt raus

...wenn Krawalle bei der EM nicht sofort aufhören

Bruno, I ain't dun nothin wrong (again).

attacker was in full riot gear complete with truncheon and shield. He wasn't alone either and a group of German Polizei surrounded me. I kicked and punched out at them. The drink had taken over. I wasn't going anywhere. Not for them that day I wasn't. I managed to fight the first couple off. I was kickboxing in those days and fancied my chances with anyone. More and more of them appeared. They managed to gas me and get me on the floor. The lads were trying to free me from their grasp. They were forced away by the police who used gas and batons to disperse them. At least three of them pinned me to the ground trying to handcuff me. Their weight on me was crushing. They were holding me to the ground. Their knees were pressing my face into the concrete. I feigned an epileptic fit. They weren't expecting that. I was pretending to gag and swallow my tongue. They were shocked. They removed their weight in concern. They released me. At which point I jumped up and steamed into them. I sent at least two of them flying. It was England against Germany now, in my mind anyway. They'd now seriously had enough. They gassed me square in the face and jumped on me mob handed. I must've had five or six pinning me to the ground as they tie-wrapped my hands behind my back and my legs together. Three of them dragged me to the waiting van. I used my feet against the step to the door to push against them head-butting the one with the back of my head. I couldn't get free thanks to the tie wraps. They beat me again. They beat me continually until I collapsed in a heap in the floor. I was scooped up and put in the back of the van. I still wasn't finished, not by a long way. At this moment the van doors opened and Oldie entered the van. 'Fucking hell Luddy what are you doing? You're fucking nuts!' he shouted. The Polizei took us both to a local police station. They cut the ties from my legs so I could walk, I wouldn't leave the van. They pulled and pulled but I would not leave the van. I was leathered I wasn't listening to any sense or reason. In the end they filled the van with CS gas and I was dragged out and beaten again. They put me half unconscious into a cell and I gradually came round. I eventually sobered up and realised what I had done and dwelled how long I would now be spending in Germany. I couldn't understand it. I'd only had a few drinks. The cell was 3 brick walls with a completely glass/Perspex barrier at the front, enabling them to fully view the whole of the room. Oldie was next door. I shouted to him. He reassured me by telling me he thought I was in deep shit. During the evening they took me out and took my DNA. Nothing was being said to me about what would happen. The way I'd behaved yesterday and the number of Polizei I'd clattered, it was not looking good.

Reidy: It was now about 3 o'clock on the Friday afternoon. We'd taken over this pub in West Berlin. The one good thing about Germans is they make great beer. All afternoon we had the German police sitting in the vans outside. All the lads were in good spirits having a good sing-song. Eddie the plastic Blues fan is a mate of mine. He came to a few games with us in those days. He decided to start hurling abuse at the German police. He was saying things like, 'Your grandad bombed our Chippy,' or 'You bombed my grandad's shithouse with me grandad still on it.' After five minutes the coppers had had enough and they came over and dragged him away to one of their vans. After five minutes, a couple of the lads went over to the police. They explained that being a Birmingham City fan, it was his first time abroad to watch football. After another fifteen minutes of trying to explain what Birmingham City was I think they just got pissed off with us. They decided to let him go. It was about seven o'clock on the evening. The old bill had had enough of us. They escorted us to the train station where we were catching the overnight train to Katowice. The train was huge, about 20 carriages long, like one of our pre-1970s trains. There were about 5 compartments in each carriage and a gangway wide enough for just one bloke to walk down.

Fowler: There was a bit of a scuffle with Huddersfield on the train. I didn't see it. We had some Wolves with us who had latched onto us. The Poles are nuts, absolutely nuts, I was trying to get my head down. They were waiting to attack the train at 5am in the morning. For fucks sake! I remember I was asleep in the carriage. A Wolves fan opened the door and shouted, 'Fowler, Fowler! It's going off, come on!' As I came out the compartment, all the Poles are standing down the end of the carriage. I thought I'll have a bit of this. I ran down towards them. They were throwing things at us. Brick's said, 'What the fuck you doing you nutter?' I love that sort of thing me. I have to get in there. I ran towards them. The Poles ran. A couple of them barricaded themselves in the toilet. I was trying to kick open the toilet door. Others had joined me now but I was having these cunts. I kicked the door open and punched the life out of the one Pole. There was blood everywhere. I just laid into the two of them. It was fucking madness. I just kept hitting them. One of the Wolves lads was shouting, 'They've had enough! He's had enough Fowler!' I turned to him and said, 'He's had enough when I decide he's had enough!' This Polish geezer was battered to fuck. I stopped and he and his mate ran past us out of the train. They jumped off the train. Then they turned round and started again. They were shouting 'Come on!' and attacking the train again! He was pouring with blood. It was everywhere! I remember thinking to myself, 'These aren't real these aren't! They're fucking nutters!' He'd been clattered to fuck and they still wanted to have another pop! I remember thinking God knows what we were letting ourselves in for when we got to Katowice.

Reidy: There were lots of other firms on the train. The arguing began more or less straight away. I nearly got involved with Huddersfield. It ended up with me and a black lad facing each other, in the gangway, with our lads behind me and his lads behind him. He was going on about 'Where's your gobshite Combat 18 lads?' Our firm has no association to the BNP or Combat 18. However I would be lying if I didn't say a small number of the lads are right-wing within the firm. With me as well as many of the firm however, if we're going to have a row, it will be about football, not racism. I said to this lad "If you want to kick off, me and you are going to be wedged between both firms where the pair of us would probably take a kicking. I said to him, 'This isn't the place. We're not Combat 18 but if you still want to row when we get to Poland we'll sort it there.' I recently read in one book that Huddersfield reckoned they had given us a few slaps once we got to Poland. That is utter bullshit because we never saw them again until we got back to Berlin. At that time, I don't think they realised just how many there was of us but once they found out they kept away. The train was attacked a few times by Poles at different stations. A couple of the lads including Pete were actually thrown off the train in the middle of the night by the police, in the middle of Poland. The only incident after that to talk about which was funny was the plastic blue-nose Eddie again. He decided he wanted to get in on the fun of the night. He gave a Pole a slap round the face on the train. The Pole went and got the police. Once again Eddie was arrested. He was made to stand in between the carriages with his hands on his head facing the window. We went and had a word with the Police. They said they were going to let him go once they got to the next station which was about half an hour down the road. We were winding Eddie up saying, 'They told us they're going to take you to one of those prisons like in Midnight Express!' You could see the tears running down his cheeks. We arrived in Katowice about seven o'clock in the morning.

Back in Berlin I hardly slept during the night and was woken up by a German prodding me the next morning, 'Come! Come now!' he gestured in broken English. This is it I thought, I was off to court, with a bit of luck I would be deported back to England. At worst I was looking at a bit of an extended stay in Germany. I had no idea what had happened to Oldie. He was no-where to be seen or heard. They took me into a room; there was a form on the desk, 'Sign! You sign!' said the one who had been waiting outside while the other woke me. 'I'm not fucking signing anything' I replied, 'I'm not signing anything without a fucking solicitor!' He looked at me bemused,' You sign you go', he said. What? I couldn't believe my ears, 'You sign, and you go! Leave Berlin, leave Germany! We do not want you English hooligans here!' I could not believe my luck; I didn't fancy staying myself after all this. I signed the form and they escorted me out of the station. Oldie was waiting outside. 'You're fucking mad' he laughed. 'You're fucking lucky I've waited for you, you mad bastard. You were out of order starting on those Leicester yesterday. They were with me!' I gave Oldie a half hearted apology, 'I didn't know they were with you did I eh? How do we get to the train station to get to Poland?' He shook his head and we headed off together into Berlin. We managed to hail a taxi and he took us to the train station. When we got out of the taxi, there were some lads hanging about. They were Leicester. Luckily they knew Oldie and they weren't bearing a grudge about yesterday's episode. We jumped on the train which was heading for Poland and eventually Katowice.

Fowler: We got to Katowice. We were playing up, a bit too much really. We were confident because we had the biggest firm out there. It got to us a bit. We were swaggering round, some of our lads had taken slaps on the train from other firms and it had pissed us off. Due to the length of the train a lot of us didn't know what had gone on until we got to Katowice the next morning. If I'm honest we took the piss. We were probably a bit naughty with other England fans. We were young and naïve to the England scene then. It's something which I think we all regret about that trip.

We got to Katowice and scoured the place looking for our lads. We met them coming from the city-centre. It had gone off down there and there were large groups of Poles. They were tooled up, looking for the English. We joined them and headed for the Hotel Katowice which had been pinpointed as a place where the English lads would gather. The city-centre was proving to be too hot with the Polish police liberally dishing out severe beatings to any English they found involved in trouble. We entered the hotel. There were loads of English there. No real firms but small groups all mixing and having a drink. We found a place in the lounge. We plotted up and discussed the events of the day and the night before.

Reidy: The first confrontation I can recall was with Newcastle. We had a phone call from a lad in a bar about 200 yards from us saying Newcastle's firm were giving it large. We got the rest of the lads together. We walked in and showed our faces. Newcastle walked out. They didn't say a word. By mid-day there had been quite a few skirmishes with Poles and the police. One of the first ones I remember was by a Hotel. It went off with some Poles. Then I heard a sound that I would continue to hear all day long, whack, fucking whack. We were getting battered by the Polish police. The police hated us more than their fans I think. They just seemed to hate the English. The bats

they had were about four foot long and quite flexible and they fucking hurt once they hit you. There must have been some kind of competition amongst the Polish police force of who could hit the most English. Whoever won would win a Skoda at the end of it. There were some nasty looking lads about. There had to be, this was Poland. We saw Bruno. Three coppers had set about him with these bats. At first all we heard Bruno say was 'Is that all you've got?' I'll try and give a little bit of advice here. First thing, if you're totally outnumbered and you think you're going to get a kicking. Mingle in with the home fans and try and adopt the accent of the day. It might work? Secondly, do a Linford Christie. The third one a couple of Blues fans have told me about. They said 'stand there and cry.' It's worked for them on a couple of occasions. Well, back to Bruno, he decided to stay and show them they couldn't hurt him. What a mistake that was. 'Whack fucking whack.' He did the best thing he could do in that situation and that was to collapse and start screaming. After about five more whacks the coppers got bored and left him alone. It seemed all the fun of it had gone once he'd stopped screaming and moving.

We decided we'd have a walk back down towards the town and see what was going on. We left the hotel, about 40 of us walking down towards the city centre. We'd got about half a mile when three or four riot vans pulled up. The vans emptied and the police ran over the road towards us. We thought they were just going to herd us back towards the hotel. They didn't want to herd us anywhere. They simply wanted to batter us senseless. We were forced back towards the hotel by the riot police. The police decided to follow us into the hotel. It was their first mistake of the day. As the first couple came through the door, they were hit hard by a table being propelled by two large Englishmen. It knocked them clean over and the England lads surged out into the doorway forcing the old bill back, dragging their half unconscious colleagues with them. 'Eng-er-land! Eng-er-land! En-ger-land!' The chant reverberated round the hotel as England lads tried to encourage the police to have another pop at getting access. We were taunting them. They didn't fancy coming in, you could see that. Bottles and glasses were being thrown at them. This is what we had come for but at the same time with the police completely surrounding the place it was hard to see how we were going to get out. They couldn't get in but at the same time we couldn't get out. Some of the lads were running out of the doors and hurling missiles and taunting the police.

Things quietened down and the police decided on a policy of containment. They surrounded the place with ever increasing numbers. While things were calming down Blues came in. They had smaller, much smaller numbers than us. One of them who knew Fowler from Castle Vale came over and had a chat. We decided to leave them. A few of ours were game to clatter them. They would've if the tables were reversed. They'll prove that later in the book. 'We're not fucking Blues, that's why we're not going to clatter them', said Fowler. It was obvious Blues were expecting it to go at any minute. It was good to see them squirm. That was enough for most of us. The place was still surrounded but someone found a side exit. Knowing the odds were not in our favour with regards to the Polish police everyone flooded out of this side exit.

Fowler: We'd all got split up. I was walking round looking for the lads, I went into a bar. There were a few lads in there. I spoke to some West Ham at the bar. I said to them 'Do you remember when we landed on you?' The one geezer replied, 'No I don't remember that?' I said 'Of course you do, Liberty's! We trashed the place and you don't remember it?' He was giving me some attitude. I said 'Who the fucking hell are you lot eh, you think you can mouth off at me like that? I'm not a fucking liar!'

Reidy: We were in a bar. It was like a marquee and had no sides. The bar was in the middle. Fowler came in with a couple of lads. He came up to me. He was really pissed off. He was slagging West Ham off. West Ham were saying they hadn't heard of us doing a couple of their pubs a couple of years earlier. Fowler was getting more agitated. I was looking him in the face pointing at my chest. I knew directly behind me was the streak of piss Dodd and his Carlisle firm. They were sitting with West Ham. Fowler went to the side of me. He said 'Are you West Ham?' With that Doddy and his firm stood up and said 'Yeah we're West Ham!' Cue a mass brawl.

Fowler: I then had a walk round still looking for the lads and I eventually found them in another bar. I walked in and up to Reidy and the lads who were sitting outside and said 'Fucking hell I've just spoke to some fucking Wes Ham in some bar and they were giving it loads,' Reidy said 'Sshh! There's a load of West Ham behind us. I looked at these lads sitting behind him. I said 'Are you fucking West Ham or what? They stood up. One of them, who I found out later was Carlisle said, 'Yeah we are, what you going to fucking do about it?' I banged him. We went into them. We had a pitched battle outside the bar. Chairs, tables and glasses were flying everywhere. I'd put the Carlisle geezer on his arse. The riot police landed, in numbers. They laid into the lot of us with these long batons they had.

Reidy: There were punches, chairs and tables being thrown on both sides. Some other English shouted "Stop! Stop, look what's coming!" There was only about a third of our firm in this bar along with other English, there was probably was about 50 of us in total. We were in a square and we looked over and there must have been about 300 Poles running at us with sticks and bats and everything. If the coppers hadn't have got there in that split second we would have taken a good kicking. Whack, fucking whack, the coppers were back on us again telling us to get out the pub. They got us outside and started marching us down the road. We didn't know where we were going.

Fowler: We all got split up and I was left with Brick. He isn't really a football fan but comes with us as he is a very good friend of mine. He spotted the Carlisle bloke over the road with a couple of other lads from the fight, 'There's that mouthy cunt, fucking do him Fowl!' 'I'm going to, but there's old bill around,' I replied. There was some old bill milling about but I didn't want to lose the opportunity. I walked over. I put my arm round his neck, as if we were friends. I later found out his name was Dodd and he fancied himself as a bit of a lad. He was going to me, 'What? What you doing?' I said to him 'Shut your mouth you fucking div! Let's have a walk round the corner. We'll have a fucking straightener!' He was going 'I don't want a straightener! I don't want a straightener Fowler!' 'Let's just go round the corner and have a straightener,' I said, 'No, no! I don't want to Fowler!' he whined. It was pathetic. He looked a right twat in front of his pals. I actually started to feel sorry for him. I couldn't bang him. Yet you read some fucking book they've written. It says me and Fowler, exchanged bats. Did we fuck! He shit himself!

Reidy: Fowler fronted Dodd. Dodd wouldn't agree to fight even to save face in front of his mates. All he did was walk back in circles. He was full of shit, he'd got no bottle. He said he was England's number 1! He didn't have the bottle to have a straightener. Obviously, he needs a firm behind him. We would see Carlisle later however. It was about 5pm now. Our entire firm had got together with about 300 English. We were standing outside a pub drinking and singing. The police had surrounded the pub with their batons and shields on full show. They were just looking for one reason to be able to get stuck into us. Then they found it. Some English were battling at the top of the road about 800 yards away. Some more English decided that was the time to start throwing bottles at the Coppers, big mistake. A whistle went. From all sides the coppers attacked us. Big Dean, who is probably the hardest lad I know, and me were standing about five yards away from the main group. The police laid into us. We stood there, put our arms up and started crying! Guess what? It worked! Blues did have something in that idea after all! By the time everybody had got into the pub there were at least a dozen English lads lying on the ground. They all had bad cuts to their arms and heads including, guess who? Yes that's right, Eddie the plastic blue-nose. Blood was pissing from his fingers. 'What happened?' I asked him. 'Well,' he said, 'I heard the whistle. I thought we were all to line up in an orderly fashion to be escorted to the ground. I didn't know it was their cue to attack us. I'm never coming with you lot again. You said this would be like going to Blackpool!'

I was walking up the road with one mob of about 20. All of a sudden Polish riot vans pulled up and police in riot gear jumped out and steamed into us. Everyone scattered. I ran across the road narrowly avoiding traffic. It was a bit of a walk, you knew something was going to happen. We had a loose police escort. I had the impression that the Poles were about and would hit us at any time. We walked across the park near the stadium. A mob of Poles appeared. They were obviously up for it and their police had a go at forcing them back. England started to move towards them and we were also beaten back by the Police. Sporadic fights broke out between those of them who have made it through or any English who did vice-versa. The police steamed in and forced us towards the ground. When we go there they tried to force us to go into the ground. Most England fans were intent on having a look around the stadium first. The Poles were around us but no real lads. A small group came up the road chanting. They were confronted by us. We ran into them. They scattered. The police had had enough and started herding everyone into the ground. The ground was a relic from the cold war. It was completely fashioned out of concrete, including the benches which you were supposed to sit on. There was quite a few English who have travelled. The Polish parts of the ground were soon filling up. Their support was getting lairy behind a fence to our right. Fighting broke out in there. They were ripping each other to bits. The Polish police entered and dragged out around 10 blokes who had seemingly taken on the whole end. We were cheering. We thought they were England fans. As they were taken out we can see they're not English. They were Poles fighting Poles. Just goes to show the Poles are up for it. They used their match against Europe's hooligan elite to settle domestic affairs. The match was a comfortable 2-0 win for England. It was absolutely freezing there.

Reidy: There were two trains back to Berlin. One left abut two hours after the game, it went via Posnan and took longer. One left during the second half, direct to Berlin. We decided to get the earlier train. Guess who was just paying into the ground as we were leaving? It was Eddie the blue-nose. He had stitches in his fingers and his hand bandaged. 'Fucking hell!' he said. 'I've been arrested twice. I've been whacked, punched and taken to hospital. Now I won't even get to see the game! I'm never going anywhere with you lot again!'

Fowler: The game was shit and the weather was bitterly cold. 'It's fucking freezing! What time is that fucking train back to Berlin?' I asked Reidy. I said to everyone 'Come on let's fuck off!' We made our way to the train station.

Stan: As we walked into the train station Danny Hutton called me. I turned round and he was having it with three or four Poles. I ran over and punched one of them. As I've hit him someone has hit me from the side. I turned round and the kid who had hit me must've been about fourteen or fifteen. They're mad those Poles.

There were a few Poles milling about the station. Poland was a dirty, depressing place. It was all you imagined a typical Eastern-bloc country to be like. It was all grey concrete and it was freezing. There was a few other English waiting for the train. We ignored them as we headed for the warmth of the train. We eventually set off on our 13 hour trip back to Berlin. We settled down in a few carriages and tried to get our heads down.

Fowler: As we got to the station, I saw a few lads. I thought to myself they're Carlisle they are. As I passed them one said, 'Alright mate?' I replied casually, 'Yeah alright lads,' and carried on nonchalantly. They were testing the ground with us before they got on the train. My reaction had assured them we either didn't know who they were or we weren't bothered. I thought to myself I wasn't going to do anything there and then. I'd let them get on the train first. Then we would have the fuckers. We got on the train. We'd been battling all day. We'd been battling Poles and we'd been battling English. We'd been battling the Polish police. We were all knackered. We settled down on the train. We were leaving Katowice. I remember overhearing some of the lads saying, 'Don't tell Fowler, but some of those Carlisle are up there. 'Don't tell him cause you know what he's like,' I laughed to myself. After about 20 minutes I stood up and said, 'Right get your shit together!' They looked at me and said, 'What?' 'Don't bullshit me, I know those Carlisle are down there,' I said. We went down the train. We were ripping all the doors open looking for them. There was one compartment we couldn't get in. They'd barricaded themselves in there. We could see them through the cracks in the blinds. I said, 'Right Clinchy, get your fucking gas ready!' We levered the door and it opened. Clinchy sprayed the compartment. We shut the door. They had their heads hanging out the small window on the window side gasping for air. They were gassed to fuck. Those compartments are small. There were eight of them in there. The space was limited. The door opened and Big Dean and Reidy piled in there. All you could hear was smack, smack! Their lads were fighting back, but against Reidy and Big Dean even eight on to two is still not reasonable odds.

Reidy: Somehow the lads managed to prise the door just far enough open for two of us to get in. The door shut behind us. Big Dean had slipped over as he went into the compartment. Punches were thrown but no one was getting hurt because you just couldn't move. They started pleading for us not to do them. Everything calmed down then and the lads decided we weren't Blues. We left them alone.

Fowler: Reidy said to Clinchy 'Give it here, give it here!' Clinchy handed him the CS Gas. 'No not that! My ear, give it here!' Reidys false ear had been pulled out during the fight. He wanted Clinchy to pick it up for him. Him and his fucking ear!

Mark B: Wattsy and I missed the train that the other lads caught. We had to catch one which was going via Posnan. We were sussed straight away but luckily there were Polish police on board. 40 of them and they spent the whole journey protecting us from the Poles. At each station everyone seemed to be leaving the train. The Poles had a big scrap at every station. When the train was leaving they would then all get back on and continue on their journey. At the next station they'd all get off again and repeat the process. It was madness! The Poles were fighting each other and the police all the way to Posnan. It was freezing. Every window on the train had been put through. We spent eight hours on that fucking train I have never seen anything like it.

We were getting into Berlin. Carlisle still hadn't emerged from their self inflicted prison. The mind boggles how they coped with the obvious necessities of a long journey and a confined space. I suppose that's Northerners for you. They were probably sharing a bucket. The Polizei were waiting for us. They were waiting in numbers for us when we got off the train. No hanging about, we made our way to the nearest bar and plotted up there. We now had a permanent police presence as we made our way round Berlin drinking. They were following us everywhere and making their presence known by parking riot vans outside every bar we went into. Half our group were going back later that day the rest of us, around ten of us, were staying in Berlin for another night.

Italy Vs England World Cup Qualifier Rome 11th October 1997

Wattsy: We went to Rome to watch England play. It was a crucial World Cup qualifying match. England needed a result. Either a win or a draw would see England qualify for the World Cup Finals being held in France the following summer. Fowler, Bruno, Baker, Steff, Mark B, Danny Hutton, Clinchy, Liam and I all travelled over with some other Villa.

Fowler: We were on our way to the stadium before the game on the tube. We were on a platform waiting for the train to arrive. The train arrived and there were loads of Italian football fans giving it the big one. We steamed straight onto the train and we hammered them. We leathered them. The doors started to close and we jumped off. I suppose it was a case of no-one knew who was staying on the train so everyone jumped off. As soon as the doors closed the Italians started giving it loads again. Suddenly the doors opened again so we jumped back on and clattered them again. We leathered them everywhere and jumped back off again. I looked down the platform as the train pulled off. There was one solitary copper and he had Liam. Liam was flapping so I walked over. I smacked the copper plum on his chin. I put him on his arse. Liam ran off. The copper was on the floor. He pulled out his gun and pointed it at me. Bruno was standing next to me. Bruno was shouting, 'Shoot me then, fucking shoot me!' I looked at Bruno in amazement. I went to the copper, 'Yeah shoot him!' We just ran off. It was going mad outside. There were police everywhere. There was a helicopter hovering in the sky above us. It was a police 'man-down' situation. They had all rushed to where their colleague was down. Clinchy and I ran into a restaurant. We walked through it into the toilet at the rear. We were in this toilet at the back of the restaurant waiting for it to all die down. Suddenly the door opened. A hand appeared and pulled Clinchy out. Jesus we're in trouble I thought. I thought it was the police who had grabbed Clinchy and I was waiting for them to grab me next. I waited a while and nothing happened. It was quiet so I peeped out. Clinchy was standing there. 'Where have they gone? I asked him. He shook his head, 'It was some bird Fowl, all she said to me was one at a time.'

Wattsy: The match was a 0-0 draw. We had got the result we wanted. England were through to the World Cup Finals in France. Everybody was pleased but there was a tense mood as we left the stadium. It went off proper with the Italian old bill. There was a car park just outside the away fans section. They kept us in for an hour after the game. When they let us out scuffles broke out between the England fans and the police. The police weren't messing about. They were clobbering anyone they managed to get hold off. This inflamed the England fans and the police certainly weren't having it their own way. We finally got out of the car park. We were walking down the road. All of a sudden 20 or so lads came bouncing down the road. We thought they were Italians at first. They were all hooded up and had scarves round their faces. It was Oldham and Carlisle. I remember that a few of them had full cans of beer which they were using. It seemed a little odd but that's what they had. Some of us stood on. It only went on for a few minutes before the Italian police split it all up. We were scattered in different directions. We'd been there since the Friday night. A few of us had even been drinking with Oldham in one of the bars. They'd said nothing when it was even numbers. A few of them in hindsight had been reluctant to talk to us. They'd obviously planned that attack long before it had happened.

Fowler: It was going off all through the game. England fans were fighting with the Italian old bill all through the match. There was a big riot on the car park afterwards as the Italian old bill wouldn't let the England fans out. Eventually we got out. I was starving. I spotted this little stall which was selling hot pork sandwiches. I went over and bought one. It was a freezing night and it tasted lovely. It was just what I needed. All of a sudden I felt a blow to the side of my head. It was nothing major. I was more worried about my pork sandwich which was now on the floor. I tuned round and grabbed the geezer who had hit me. I said, 'Right mate, you're in fucking trouble!' I gave him a smack back. A load of them just jumped all over us going, 'Give it the Villa bastards!' There must've been about 20 of them. It ended up with about four of us fighting them in the road. I always say a lot of our lads got jobs behind the burger vans that night. A few went missing, it happens. They were all jumping over me. I'd just got the one geezer in my sights. I was concentrating on the one who made me drop my pork sandwich. The old bill landed and they broke it all up. I could still see him behind the old bill now. They dispersed us. This bloke, he was Carlisle's main lad at the time, not Dodd. Dodd is just a prick; this was their proper main lad. He walked up the same road as me. As soon as we were out of sight of the police I steamed straight into him and head-butted him. He went straight on the floor. I said to him, 'Come on you cunt! You want it now do you eh?' All of a sudden this big fella grabbed me from behind. It was these Newcastle fans that Reidy knew. 'Fucking hell Steve, what are you doing man?' they dragged me away telling me it was too on top with the police. Thing is we'd have had it with Carlisle and Oldham if they'd have wanted it. They outnumbered us but they still had to jump us to have it with us. Maybe that says more about us than it does them in a way.

Athletico Madrid Vs Aston Villa UEFA Cup Quarter Final
3rd March 1998

We had a little run in the UEFA Cup. We drew Atletico Madrid. The first leg of the tie was to be played in Madrid. We made our way there in groups. We were flying from different airports throughout the UK. We knew where we were going to meet. We knew where we were going to get our digs. We had it all arranged weeks before the fixture. Although it wasn't Real Madrid it was still an exciting and a relatively big fixture for us at that time. Our team were doing well on the pitch and we were doing well off it. We were feeling unstoppable. The times when we were plying our trade and being allowed to by lax policing we were coming out on top. We had the numbers now. We also had our fair share of lunatics who were willing to take things up a level. The police had become aware of that fact. We flew out on the Sunday. We met as planned and had a relatively quiet night around the Playa de Mayor area of Madrid. There was one Irish bar we took over. We also returned there the next day for breakfast.

Simmo: We were sitting in a bar in central Madrid, Nostrils, Fowler, Liam and me. There were a few others. Someone told us it was a Real Madrid supporter's bar, where their 'hooliganos' drank. They'd been playing someone and about twenty of them came into the pub. We just exploded. We totally trashed the place. The bar emptied and we spilled out onto the street. There was a skip outside. We emptied it and put all the windows through. The next day it was on the television. Along with all the other devastation we had caused. We watched them on prime-time news announcing that Villa fans had smashed up Real Madrid's bar. We certainly made an impression over there.

Birmingham Evening Mail Monday 2nd March 1998:

VILLA FANS ARE HELD IN SPAIN

FOUR Aston Villa fans were arrested early today after allegedly going on the rampage in the centre of Madrid. The supporters, in Spain for tomorrow's UEFA Cup match against Atletico Madrid wreaked havoc in the Spanish capital after a night on the town turned violent, police said.

Fans were involved in fighting inside the La Fontana de Oro bar near the central square of Sol, injuring several people who were drinking there and damaging the bar. After being thrown out of the bar, they allegedly smashed four shop windows in the main street and overturned a parked Renault car and a motorbike before four of them were arrested by police early today. The fans aged 21 to 27 spent the night in the cells at the central Madrid police station.

A spokeswoman for the Madrid police said it was not yet known whether the fans would go before a local judge charged with damaging property or whether they would be released in time to watch the game. A dozen Villa supporters caused damage to the hotel where they were staying in Madrid on Saturday night, the spokeswoman also revealed.

We obviously started early that day and by the early evening of the Monday we were starting to get out of control. There was no opposition to speak of in Madrid. None we could find anyway, only the police. We were having a laugh. We were being outrageous but nothing too bad. Then the atmosphere suddenly changed. At around midnight we exploded onto the street looking for some excitement or at worse another bar. I can't place what exactly started it. We moved down the street which the Irish bar was on. People in our group began trashing things at random, cars, motorcycles and windows. Alarms were going off. It wasn't too long before we were virtually rioting. A van load of Spanish police appeared at the end of the road. The sight of the Police who jumped out of the van did nothing to calm the situation down. We just saw them as an opponent. Finally, after a day of drinking and frustration at not encountering any opposition we exploded towards the Police at the end of the street. Scaffolding on the street was utilised. The police stalled as we ran towards them. We approached them with more enthusiasm than they perhaps anticipated. They stalled, we gained momentum and it wasn't long before our missiles were raining down on them and their van. They managed to scramble into the van and speed off as our faster members got to them. Scaffolding poles were hitting the roof and sides of the van as it sped off into the Madrid night. The destruction continued. The whole street, exclusive designer shops were being smashed to smithereens. Then sirens could be heard. Not just one, more than that. A car was overturned. The sirens competed with the noise from the destruction which was occurring. The police started to arrive in force. We kept the police at bay with a hail of missiles at first. They soon got their act together. They started made a concerted attacks to disperse us. Our momentum was failing. We were slowly being backed up the street from which we had come. Our backtracking turned into a full scale retreat as we ran from the police. The consequences of getting caught were severe as the Spanish police fought each other to lay into anyone who had been detained. We were now running back through the absolute carnage we had caused. Sirens, burglar alarms and shouting filled the Madrid night air. Madrid has a lot of small streets and alleyways. It wasn't hard to make yourself scarce. Some of us managed to reach a bar round the corner from the incident. We sat in there trying to look inconspicuous. The owner was pleased to see us. We settled down, we were laughing. The Police arrived outside the bar and stormed in, shouting. The owner immediately jumped to our defence. He started telling the police we had been in there all night. We were nothing to do with the trouble round the corner. The Police eyed us suspiciously as they left; half convinced we were the people they were looking for.

Birmingham Evening Mail Tuesday 3rd March 1998:

VILLA FANS ARRESTED AFTER MADRID BRAWL

SIX Aston Villa fans have been arrested in Madrid after wrecking a bar and injuring two people, Spanish police said today.

The fans who were in the Spanish capital for the match against Atletico Madrid in the UEFA Cup caused havoc when they smashed up a bar in the city-centre and injured a waiter and a 21 year old man last night. On Sunday night four other fans were arrested for a breach of the peace near the same bar.

Doug Ellis, chairman of Villa, said he was deeply disappointed by reports that a small number of fans had caused trouble.

Supporters were involved in two incidents last night which led to six arrests, police said. The first was at 11pm at the Fontana De Oro bar near the central Plaza del Sol - the same bar where trouble broke out the night before.

TRASHED

A group of fans trashed the bar and attacked a waiter police sad. Five fans were arrested and the owner of the bar and the waiter have made a complaint against the men, aged 21 to 34. In the early hours of this morning, police said a sixth Villa fan, aged 25, was arrested for attacking a 21 year old man. A spokeswoman for the Spanish police said all six were being held at the central police station. They were given a lawyer and an interpreter was appointed. Spanish police have obtained a special security order from the chief of police to put into place additional safety measures ready for tonight's game. These will include a police escort for all fans from the airport to the stadium, extra medical services and dog and horse patrols. It is understood that 2,000 policemen - one for every Villa fan - have been put on duty for the quarter-final match which kicks off at 8-30pm British time.

Fowler: We were all standing on a corner, in the middle of Madrid. It was the day after we had rioted. The main Villa Supporters Club was by now over in Madrid and they'd brought their own security with them. These security guys were walking round like they owned the place. We were standing on a corner. A car pulled up. These two blokes got out. The one is a big black feller. Someone said, 'Who do these two think they are eh?' This big black bloke strode over to us. 'What did you just fucking say?' He was pointing at one of our lads. He carried on, 'Do you know who I fucking am?

121

I'm fucking head of Villa's security!' I turned round and said, 'Oh yeah? Are you?' I swung at him. I hit him plum on the chin with a haymaker. He keeled over and hit the deck. Clinchy bent over him and said, 'Get your P45 you're sacked!' We were crying with laughter. His mate had shit it. The geezer was trying to get up. His legs were like Bambi's as he struggled to get back to his car. He was with the Spanish police the next day trying to point someone out for it, but he didn't manage to finger me.

The next morning, the day of the actual game we were all worse for wear. We brightened up towards the afternoon as the game approached. We noticed we were starting to attract media attention. Spanish prime-time television news came into the bar we were in. They started a live broadcast. We thought it was a recording until we started to see ourselves live on the televisions in the bar. They managed to obtain an interview with two of us, Loz and Ginge. It went something like this; Interviewer: Why have you come here? Ginge: To smash the place up. Interviewer: What do you do at home? Ginge: Smash things up. Interviewer: What will you do once you have smashed everything up? Ginge: Go somewhere else and smash that up. A very constructive analysis. I'm sure the people of Spain were a lot wiser after receiving those pearls of wisdom from him. Most of us were camera shy. We made it clear in no uncertain terms we didn't want our faces on the television. There was no telling what coverage would get back to the UK. We all had jobs to go back to. Then someone came in and said they'd just seen my mug on the 6 o'clock news.

As the match neared you could sense the tension which was gripping the city. They were expecting it to go off. They thought the previous night's damage was just a pre-cursor to more trouble. The police started emptying the bars to get us out of the city-centre and towards the ground. They were steaming into the pubs hitting anyone in sight and moving us towards the ground. We came across another bar nearer to the ground. We stood outside drinking and taking in the situation. We looked over the road and there was a small mob of Spaniards. They were chanting 'Hooligano! Hooligano!' Some of us ran over to have it with them. They were having none of it. The Spanish bolted pursued down the road by a number of us.

This spurred us on towards the ground convinced we were going to get some action there. The police were waiting for us. They herded us up and made us wait for other Villa fans and escorted us to the ground. As we neared the ground, with the glare of the floodlights in full view, it hit us. A barrage of missiles filled the night sky. They were raining down on us. We could see a large group of Spaniards over the road and some of us made an effort to get over the road towards them. We were beaten back by the police. The escort was stopped and we had to stand and endure this hail of missiles crashing into us and around us. Bottles were smashing on the floor. Bricks and bottles, of all shapes and sizes, were hitting people in our large escort, smashing to the floor around us. The police managed to force our tormentors away and we carried on towards the ground. We had purchased tickets over there and we were in the top tier of the stadium in a small section surrounded by Spanish. The supporters from Birmingham who had travelled officially with the club were at the opposite side of the stadium. We settled into the terracing and waited for the match to start. We were surrounded by police. Just before the start of the game, before the teams came on they unfurled a huge 'Gibraltar is Spanish' flag in the Spanish section of the ground. This obviously annoyed the travelling support and people started getting rather lairy towards our Spanish hosts. This in turn inflamed the riot police surrounding us and they were dragging people off the terracing, downstairs and giving them a good hiding. The atmosphere was electric and both sets of fans added to the atmosphere as flares and smoke filled the night sky from the Spanish zones of the ground. The match was a good battling performance from a Villa side obviously not in awe of their surroundings. We ended up holding Atletico to a goalless draw.

We were not happy at our treatment by the Spanish either before or during the match. Some scuffles broke out between Villa fans. Some of them had traded scarves with their hosts. People took exception to the scarf swapping after our treatment inside the stadium. We emerged from the stadium and began to walk back into the city. There was a bar over the road from the stadium with a large number of Spanish outside. We approached it with no particular urgency. We went unnoticed by its Spanish patrons. As soon as we were in spitting distance we gave a roar and the Spanish scattered. I steamed straight into the group of Spanish. Some sought refuge inside the bar some ran into the night. The tables and seating outside the bar were thrown through its windows. We roundly trashed the bar. A cigarette machine was ripped from the floor and thrown through the windows. They were cowering inside. Coaches containing Spanish supporters nearby were also trashed. It wasn't long before the Spanish riot police made their presence known. The Police made charge after charge into us and we were forced back up a hill towards the town centre.

Fowler: We're getting chased by the Spanish old bill up this big hill by the side of the ground. I was shouting to the lads, 'Walk! Fucking walk! If you run they'll steam

you. If you just walk they'll leave you alone,' A few of us walked, and then I heard a whack! The Spanish old bill had caught up with our group. I got a whack. I thought fuck this. I ran with the rest of them! I could hear people getting crunched behind me, it was a nightmare.

We were getting chased up this hill. If the Spanish police caught you, they were going to beat you senseless. The police were in no mood to take prisoners. Everyone who was caught was hammered by riot police. They were crowding round their victims and hitting them repeatedly. You could see our lads going back and hurling things like waste bins into groups of Spanish police who were grouping round fallen Villa fans. It was breaking them up and giving them a new target. We sought refuge in the bars of the winding streets of Madrid. We'd done a lot of damage over the last couple of days. We had made the papers back at home with the Birmingham Evening Mail labelling us as 'Scum!' Great! We drank into the night before returning to our various hotels, ready to fly out the following morning.

Birmingham Evening Mail Thursday 5th March 1998

VILLA FANS SPAIN AGONY

AN Aston Villa fan suffered a suspected fractured skull after he was hit over the head with a truncheon by Spanish police as he queued up to see his team's UEFA Cup quarter final match in Madrid. He was taken for first aid by officers, pickpockets stole his wallet containing credits cards and cash.

Aston Villa have made an official complaint to the British Consulate in Madrid about the police's 'heavy-handed' treatment of fans following a number of incidents at the match. John Hood, head of security and safety operations, said the behaviour of officers was the worst he had ever seen on his travels with the club abroad. Mr Hood who travelled with the fans, said: 'There was an over-reaction by police who seemed intent on causing trouble with our fans and ignored the bad behaviour of their own. They were shoving and pushing people and sending our fans around the stadium where they had to walk past Spanish fans who were throwing bottles and missiles. I have made my feelings known to the British Consulate in Madrid. When their fans come to England for the return game they will be made welcome.'

Six Villa supporters were arrested after a bar in the centre of Madrid was attacked. But Hood insisted: 'The fans who caused problems were among the

124

150 who had travelled independently and were nothing to do with the official party. The club has no time for these sort of people. Of the 2100 fans who travelled with the official party there were no incidents at all.'

The six Villa fans who allegedly went on the rampage were held in detention and missed the tie. They were all released after appearing before an examining magistrate in Madrid. They were accused of public disorder, aggression and causing damage. No bail was imposed and they were free to return to Britain.

The return fixture was just two weeks later. We were still boiling at the treatment we had received in and around the ground. We met at the Vine on the Lichfield Road and intended to walk straight into any Spanish that were in the vicinity of Villa Park. We wanted revenge. We had conveniently forgotten our mini-riot in Madrid. We now perceived ourselves as the victims from the previous fixture. We approached the Witton Arms. We could see from outside that it was full of Spanish. Instructions were passed round that we were simply going to walk into the pub. Once firmly installed in there we were going to kick off. It seemed as soon as we entered the place it erupted. The Spanish spilled out and some inside took a beating. Bottles were flying through the air, chairs being flung, tables being tipped over. The Spaniards were running behind the bar. They were diving for cover. They were jumping over the bar, and hiding behind the pool table. We surged through the pub hell-bent on revenge. It didn't take long for the police to arrive and they rounded up a few of us. Baker was arrested. Some Spaniards were complaining to the Police, but it was too late, it had happened to us over there and was now being paid back with interest.

The match finished as a 2-1 defeat for Villa and our European dream was over, but this had given us the taste for causing havoc on foreign shores and we would do once more given the chance.

The World Cup France June/July 1998
Marseille

Dandy: Ten of us hired a minibus. We travelled over two days before England were playing Tunisia in Marseille. We drove straight to Marseille from Birmingham. Marseille was full of Arabs. Not just the Tunisians who had travelled there for the game but Moroccans and Algerians who obviously lived here. We were debating whether to pitch the tent on the beach, luckily in hindsight we didn't. We found a campsite up a mountain about 15 minutes drive from the City. The next morning we drove into Marseille itself. We were all hung-over. We had a mooch round by the beach and up toward the ground. The ground was only 5-10 minutes walk from the beach. As we neared the ground we could see scuffles going off here and there. There were police 'snatch-squads' in plain clothes running in and nicking England fans. The police weren't fucking about. We headed down towards the beach again.

Jez: There was this Radio 1 road-show on the beach. There was a giant screen with disc-jockey's and celebrities appearing. You could tell what was going to happen. There was an atmosphere. The prats from Radio 1 were oblivious to it. The only surprise was that it didn't kick off earlier than it did.

Dandy: We walked down to the big screen. It wasn't long till kick-off. It was a mixed crowd which had gathered to watch it. It was just a big screen plonked on the beach. They'd put some terracing behind it which people could sit on. That was full of Arabs and we stood in front of the terracing between them and the screen. England scored. Bottles started raining down on the England fans standing in front of the terracing. Now you've got to understand, it wasn't just lads in the England crowd, it was a mixture of families as well. The bottle throwing inflamed the England fans. We stormed up the terracing after the Arabs who had thrown the bottles. We steamed up there and fighting broke out. Most of the Arabs didn't fancy it and some of them were jumping off the back of the stand. It must've been a good 30 feet drop and some were writhing in agony at the bottom where they'd fallen and injured themselves.

Jez: We stormed up the seats into the large group of Arabs at the top. It was toe to toe fighting at first then they just bolted. We chased them out of the arena and thought that was it. All of a sudden a big mob of them came steaming round the side back into the arena. We ran into them and they scattered. This time we followed them out and the fighting escalated to the beach. It was toe to toe for a bit then the police broke that up by firing tear gas into us. The police didn't seem to want to get involved at first and just stood there firing tear gas onto the beach.

Dandy: We thought that was the last of it but they steamed round the side of the stand in a bit of a mob. We steamed into them yet again and fighting broke out onto the beach proper. It was mainly missiles and no real fighting as such. Whenever we got near them they backed off or ran. They were flashing blades at us. There was one van-load of police watching all this. They did nothing. A few more police arrived. Even then they wouldn't come in between us. They fired tear-gas into us. It was quite windy and

it blew back in the faces of the police. This enabled the fighting to continue. There were more press there in the thick of the fighting, filming it all, than there was police. The fighting must've gone on for 20 minutes or more. It always seems longer when you're involved but this was no five minute thing. We got together and decided to leave the beach area as more and more old bill were landing. The air was full of sirens. We found a bar just off the beach and plotted up in there to watch the end of the game which was still going on. The match finished and we left. We had a mooch round the town. It was complete over-kill by the police now and English police were with them pointing out people. We decided it was too on top so we got in the minibus and drove back to the campsite. Now I think I mentioned it was up a mountain and on the way back the van was really struggling. A queue of traffic had built up behind us and some were sounding their horns. One of the lads took exception to this and sprayed a can of CS Gas out of the window behind the minibus. Suddenly there was no queue, the road behind us was clear. We got back to the campsite and walked into the bar. There were some Scousers in there and they said two of us, Steff and I had been on the news fighting on the beach. We decided we'd get an early night and fuck off to Spain the next morning.

We then travelled back up to Toulouse for England's next group game. We knew Fowler and a few others would be there and had arranged to meet them. When we got there we found that Fowler, Bruno and Steve Baker had been arrested. They had been deported apparently. The rest of the lads were there however. As the day wore on it kicked off outside this bar we were in. It was full of English and some Arabs had walked past. Something was said and it had proper gone off with a running battle outside. We spilled out of the bar and headed for the big square in the centre of Toulouse. It was well moody. Scuffles were breaking out. There was a Burberry shop and everyone was saying 'Let's do it, let's do the fucking shop!' The old bill clocked onto this though. They formed a wall in front of the shop. They charged the English who were contemplating doing it. As this happened a group of Arabs entered the square to have a pop. The English turned on them and they ran and didn't come back. As the night wore on we started heading back to our camp site. We were given a lift by some crazy French student types. When we got back we found that we'd pitched our tent on an ant hill so we all ended up sleeping on the road and in the van. We decided that we weren't going to watch the last group game in Lens where it was being held. It was too on top with the police so we decided to travel to Ostend to watch it on the telly. As we were driving into Ostend we passed a coach. It was full of lads, who were obviously English. We were told later they were Stoke. We were beeping our horn and waving at them. It was only when we were just passing them we realised they were all handcuffed and it was a police coach. They'd all been nicked the night before when it had gone off.

Fowler: Clinchy, Steve Baker, Bruno, me and another lad went over. We had been playing up bad at the time and we were getting recognised everywhere. Poland had given us the spotlight but it had its adverse effects. In Berlin on the way to Poland the year before, I saw two blokes. One of them was gesturing towards us and saying to the other, 'That's them.' I went over and said, 'What did you say mate? What did you fucking say?' He pulled out his warrant card and said 'We're Police!' Of course I left it. I thought nothing more of it. We headed towards Toulouse where England were playing their second fixture of the group stage. It was getting late so we stopped at a place where Scotland were playing their group match. We got there and all the Jocks were there. We found some digs and decided to stay the night. We were in a boozer on the evening. I said to the lads, 'No trouble here right? We're not following England here, it's their show.' We were in this bar it was full of Jocks. We started talking to some of them. It was all quite friendly. All of a sudden these Jock lads came in. They said to the ones we're talking to, 'Who the fuck are these? Are they the scum?' I had been adamant we wouldn't start any trouble. Now this lot were standing there calling us scum. Steve Baker jumped up and head-butted him. Baker said 'Who the fuck are you calling scum?' It went off. I got us out of there after a bit of a scuffle. The ones we had been talking to calmed them down a bit. We laid low for the rest of the night and next morning made our way into Toulouse. We got a bed and breakfast, one of the lads stayed in and the rest of us went into Toulouse to have a look.

We got round by the main square. It was raving round there. It was full of old bill and English police spotters. I said to the rest of the lads, 'Come on let's go somewhere offside, where there's no old bill.' We found a bar a mile or so away. It was a nice sunny day and we were sitting outside. There was an English bloke on the next table to me, I was chatting to him. He seemed like a nice bloke. He had come over for the football, fair play to him. No trouble or anything. The next minute, the next thing I know, I'm having a pair of handcuffs slapped on my right hand. 'What the fuck is going on? I asked. It was the French riot squad. There were loads of them. They had pulled up and jumped out without me realising. As I'm being nicked, I don't want any of the others to get nicked obviously. Human nature however makes you turn round and have a look to see if any of your mates have been lifted as well. As I turned round I saw these familiar faces. It was the police spotters from Berlin, the ones I'd challenged when I saw them pointing us out. I said 'I remember you two!' One of them said 'Yes Fowler, remember me from Berlin do you? Remember me do you Fowler?' I said 'You fucking wankers fuck off!' As the French police turned me round I saw that Baker and Bruno had also been lifted. The English police spotters were creaming themselves. 'We've got him! We've got him!' One of them was shouting into a radio. They were really excited about it all. They put us in the van. I think they'd left Clinchy because of his age. He hadn't been running with us that long either. They took us to the police station. They threw us in some holding cell. Bruno was trying to attract my attention. He was whispering, 'Fowl, Fowl come over here!' I went over and Bruno's telling me he's got something in the pocket of his jeans which he didn't want to have there when the police came and searched us. We had our hands cuffed behind our backs. There was a bin in the corner of the room, so he's had to stand there while I fished this object out of his pocket with my hands behind my back. I walked over to a bin in the room and hoped my aim was good. Luckily I dropped it straight in. The look of relief on Bruno's face was a picture. They then came in and took us upstairs to this room with a few desks in. We were each sat down at a desk to be interviewed. There was another lad sitting at one of the desks and he's said to Baker, 'Hey mate, who are you? What team?' Baker replied, 'We're Villa mate.' The kid nodded then said, 'You're not one of Fowlers lot are you?' 'Yeah as it happens we are. He's over there,' pointing me out. As I turned hearing my name mentioned, I see it was a lad called Raff from Coventry. They dealt with all four of us, Bruno, Baker, Raff and me. They deported us. This French copper then said to us, 'Take out your laces!', 'What?' I replied, he repeated it, 'Take out your laces!' so we took our laces out of our trainers. They took us down to these Perspex cells, where they made us leave our trainers outside before locking us up! French logic possibly? They put the four of us in one cell. We were starting to play up now, buzzing and banging the doors. We wanted something to eat and drink. They came to the cell and asked us what the problem is. I said 'You've had us for 7 hours and we've had nothing to eat or drink!' They let us have something to eat and drink but we had to pay for it ourselves. We had to give them permission to access our private property to get some money. Raff hadn't got any dough so I said 'No worries mate I'll buy you some food.' I bought him a roll.

They held us overnight and the next day took us to the airport. We were handcuffed to a plain-clothed French policeman. We had one at either side. They put us on the plane still handcuffed. It was a normal plane with other passengers. We hadn't done anything wrong but we'd got eight French old bill taking us back to England. During the flight I spoke to Baker, 'Hey Baker!' The one on my left said 'Sshh!' I said 'don't tell me to shut up you tool, who'd you think you are? Who did they think we are, the Mafia?' Anyway this stewardess came down and asked if we wanted a drink. 'Non!' the annoying copper on my left answers for us. 'Oi! Who do you think you're answering for you French twat? Yes I want a drink, remove the handcuffs!' I nodded down towards the handcuffs because I didn't think 'Clouseau' spoke very good English. 'Non!' he said again, 'Well what happens if the fucking plane crashes you clown?' I asked him, 'Well then I take them off,' he replied in perfect English. 'If you don't mate I'll wrap my arms round you and take you down with me if the plane crashes,' I told him. We landed at Heathrow. As soon as we got off the plane I started to play up. I was just cuffed now, not to them. They were trying to guide me and I was telling them to get their dirty hands off me. Our police were waiting. One of them said, 'Steve, calm down.' 'Tell these cunts to get their fucking hands off me!' I said, 'I'm on British soil now!' 'You're still under French jurisdiction until you get through customs,' one of them replied. 'I don't give a fuck I'm still in Britain!' The copper said 'Don't be stupid Fowler!' He motioned to the French to get their hands off me. We went through passport control and customs. We hadn't committed a crime in the UK. We certainly hadn't in France. We were free to go. 'I've got to warn you, there are a couple of press waiting for you outside,' said the one copper. 'Whatever!' I replied and walked off towards the arrivals exit. For fucks sake, a few press? It was blinding. There were flashes going off, film crews there, the works. I did start to think they must be waiting for someone else but then realised the lenses were following me. 'Have you got anything to say?' they were asking me. I didn't say anything. We got the tube from Heathrow to Euston and then a train from Euston to New Street. On the night I met my mate Brick. We had a drink in the Roebuck in Erdington. There was a television and the news was on. We were standing up the bar. I could see myself leaving arrivals at Heathrow. They were saying I was a 'Category C' hooligan and had been kicked out of France. This bloke behind me started going, 'Serves them right, fucking hooligans!' I turned round and said, 'What you saying mate?' he clocked my face. He looked at the telly again and said, 'No! No mate! I was only joking! Honest!' His face was a picture. I wasn't serious I just wanted to see his reaction, priceless. The next day Baker and I went and played golf. We were playing golf at a course up by the airport and my phone rang. It was Clinchy. 'Alright Fowl, what you doing?' 'We're just having a game of golf Clinch, we're in all the papers over here,' Clinchy said, 'We're travelling to Belgium. You're in every French newspaper over here as well!' 'Going where Clinch? Where are you going? Belgium?' I'm not banned from Belgium I thought. I turned to Steve and said, 'Baker d'you fancy Belgium?' We put the clubs away. We went straight to Birmingham airport. We booked two tickets for a flight to Ostend and nipped home to get some stuff. We hadn't been kicked out of Belgium. There was no World Cup in Belgium. We flew out, and we were in Belgium. We were sitting there having a beer before the lads got there. We then went onto Holland and Amsterdam and had a day or so there. Then we split up and we came home and the lads went to the next group game in Lens, back in France.

We were shocked when it made all the national press the next day. Seeing Fowler in a pair of shorts on the front page of the morning paper isn't the easiest aid to digesting your breakfast. The funniest moment has to be when Midlands Today tracked down Bruno at home. He answered the door with a tea-towel wrapped round his head and you could only hear muffled responses like 'Fuck off!' as the reporter was firing questions at him.

On the 23rd June 1998 The Mirror wrote:

HOME IN SHAME
Yobs France kicked out
By Jeremy Armstrong

Four English football hooligans troop home in shame - the first to feel Frances's emergency action against World Cup thugs.

One tried to hide by pulling his tee-shirt over his face as they were flown into Heathrow yesterday. Another was handcuffed. Two strongly protested their innocence. But all four ******* *******, 36, Stephen Baker, 25, Steven Fowler, 29, and Raymond Rafferty, 36 - are ranked as Category C 'extremely dangerous' offenders.

They were picked out by British hooligan-spotters in Toulouse. The four were kicked out of France and banned from the country for life.

Hours earlier the authorities there were granted emergency powers to either refuse entry to potential troublemakers or expel them even if no offence had been committed.

An official in Toulouse said the four hand been drunk and had no match tickets. He asked France's Interior Minister for an expulsion order 'bearing in mind their previous convictions and their police records particularly in connection with football matches.'

The four were held overnight in cells, then flown to London guarded by nine French officers. *******, Baker and Fowler are all Aston Villa fans from Birmingham.

The Daily Star 23rd June 1998:

THEY'RE SCUMMIN' HOME

FOUR shamed English soccer hooligans flown home in plastic handcuffs may be banned from France for life, write Gareth Morgan and Martin Stoned.

The category 'C' hardcore yobs arrived at Heathrow on a scheduled flight from Toulouse. They were arrested in bars, drunk and without England-Romania tickets by police spotters thwarting Marseille-type riots. Villa supporters Stephen Baker, 25, Steven Fowler, 29 and 36 year old **** ******* hid their faces with caps or T-shirts.

Regional prosecutor Alain Bidou said it was because of 'police records'. Sources confirmed that all four face a life ban from France.

Home secretary Jack Straw yesterday said: 'This sends a clear signal to hooligans going to France simply to cause trouble'.

The Sun 23rd June 1998:

YOBS ARE FACING 5YR TRAVEL BAN

FOOTBALL hooligans face automatic five-year bans on travelling to matches abroad under a new crackdown by Home Secretary Jack Straw. He told MP's yesterday: 'We are determined to ensure the disgraceful scenes in Marseille are not repeated.'

*Four fans branded Category C yobs - the worst - were kicked out of France in plastic handcuffs yesterday and banned from the country for life. Aston Villa thugs STEVEN FOWLER, STEPHEN BAKER and ******* ******* were frogmarched to a van after British police spotters saw them in a Toulouse bar. The men were all involved in trouble at England's World Cup qualifier in Poland last year. Police were seeking 6 more category C yobs in Toulouse last night.*

Scotland Vs England Euro 2000 Qualifier Hampden Park April 1999

England had struggled to qualify for the European Championships. They were to be held in Holland and Belgium in the summer of 2000. As one of the best runners-up we were drawn to play Scotland in a two-legged play-off. The first match was to be held at Hampden Park in Glasgow.

Dandy: A full coach of us travelled north for this fixture. A hotel had been booked in Dumbarton, which sits to the North-West of Glasgow. The intention was to stay overnight in Dumbarton and travel into Glasgow early the next morning. None of us had tickets. We wanted to put on a show, either with the Scottish or other English firms. We'd heard rumours Blues were going to make an appearance but we took that with a pinch of salt.

Jez: Fowler told us before we went into Dumbarton town centre that we shouldn't

bring attention to ourselves. By the next morning we'd made every major paper north of the border and a few more in the south.

Fowler: I said to everyone, 'No trouble tonight right lads? Tomorrow is the big one, England Scotland so let's keep out of trouble!' It was the first England match I'd attended since I was thrown out of France in 1998. I wanted us to keep as low a profile as we could before we landed in Glasgow. It could then be as high profile as anyone wanted. We got into this pub in Dumbarton. We were English weren't we? Straight away we knew it was on top. We had one of the biggest battles we've had as a firm. It was that naughty one of ours nearly died in hospital with a wound to the neck. They were throwing bottles at us. The bar staff were passing them full bottles out of the fridges to throw at us! An empty bottle is bad enough but the full ones were doing some right damage. Screw got cut badly, I'm standing at the door and the bouncer started getting shirty. I put him out the game with a head-butt. I dragged the kid who had the neck wound out of the place. Our lads were fighting them back to enable me to get him out.

Dandy: There was a confrontation at the front of the club with bouncers. Something had been said. The rest of the lads clocked what was going on. It erupted into a fight. The fight spilled out onto the street. 'You English bastards' was the general consensus amongst the local population as more and more Jocks joined the fray. We weren't having it all our own way. Many of the lads were injured. A volley of bottles came overhead. I shouted 'Duck!'

Up pops Bayo one of our lads from Aldridge and said 'you what?' and a bottle smashed straight into his head. The police were now arriving in numbers. Several of our lads were in a bad way. Quite a few were taken to the local hospital.

Tucker: We were in this one bar, it was fairly full. It was mostly locals. We were talking to some Dutch sailors. (Authors note: as you do) There was some sort of problem and the doormen said we had to leave. We were filing out of the place and it went off. The locals were launching bottles at us. Aggie went round the back and tried to have a pop at the back of them but couldn't get in. As the police arrived he got nicked. We flooded out of the pub. A pub over the road was emptying. They were coming out to have a pop at us, Simmo ran over to meet one of them. The bloke produced a rubber mallet and took a swipe at Simmo. Simmo ducked and then put the bloke on his arse. He was immediately surrounded by locals. We were all surrounded. It was total mayhem, shouts, sirens, screams, the lot. We eventually got back to our hotel. We were all fuming. A couple of our lads had been hospitalised. We decided to go back out. It was still mayhem and I flagged down a taxi. 'Forget it lads, we're just

133

going to get nicked,' I said. A couple of the lads joined me but the rest stayed out there. They all got nicked, except us who had jumped in the taxi.

Simmo: I got nicked. I was drunk and I remember swinging for this bloke. I swung at him, totally missed him and ended up on my arse. The old bill grabbed me and I was arrested. I was taken to Dumbarton police station. I was held for four days. I was transferred to Clydebank and Merry Hill while I was waiting to see if they were going to charge me. It was all skag-heads crying out for methadone, that type of thing, proper horrible places. The one copper asked why we went to Dumbarton. 'You must've been mad going there,' he said. Talk about stating the obvious.

Screwdriver: I was bottled and glassed in the club. I was taken to hospital. I could hear Bayo in the next cubicle getting his nose reset. He was screaming the place down. I peered out to have a look what they were doing to him. The police had come in. I could hear them, when Bayo wasn't screaming. They were asking about England fans that had been brought in. Once I'd heard that I didn't hang about. I slipped out of the hospital.

Dandy: The next morning the hotel was flooded with police. There were Scottish police and English police. With the English police were West Midlands old bill. PC Kelly was there, clueless as usual. They had been clueless since Flynnie was transferred from football intelligence. You'd think judging by the name, that one of the qualities of a prospective candidate would be intelligence. The local rag ran a story the same night. They were claiming that English skinheads had trashed the town. We laughed at that. We didn't laugh however when the paper then went onto say that we were English skinheads from Wolverhampton! The coach had had to be hired from Wolverhampton because we'd run out of Birmingham coach firms who were willing to take us. In usual press style they'd followed their noses and come up with anything but the truth. The police were busy taking all our details from the hotel management. As far as we were concerned we'd been attacked for being English. We were allowed to make our way into Glasgow.

Fowler: We were walking through Glasgow. We were all in a right state. We all had cuts and bruises. Walking through a park two under-cover police were gesturing towards us. One of them was going, 'Yeah that's them.' We found the first pub we came to and plotted up in there. We knew we'd been spotted so just got offside and hoped they'd go away.

Nostrils: We found a Wetherspoons type pub. It was called the Rat and Parrot. We plotted up in there. A few people popped out have a look round, to see what's happening. There was no sign of Blues. We wondered if they would show. They've never been really active on the England scene, not in numbers anyway. They have never had anything approaching the numbers we've pulled with England abroad. Liam provided the first of the morning's entertainment. He had a plaster of Paris on his arm. He decided to take it off. It wasn't the wisest move he's ever made after a night without sleep, loads of beer and copious amounts of narcotics. The shock of him removing the cast caused him to faint. There was an audible thud, he hit the floor. He whacked his head on a stool on the way down. People were creased up. We were trying to help him. He had spilt beer when taking the table down and it's covered him. Dandy was now shouting 'Look at Tinkle-pants' which made everyone crease up even more. Liam was sat up in a corner to recover, and to dry out.

Fowler: Blues were phoning me. They had been since the day before. They were coming to Glasgow. Whoopee! What do they want, a fucking medal? They never go to England games. Now one's just up the road they decided to land. There were two coaches of them apparently. It's no good turning up at one game they want to try doing it regularly like we'd been doing all over the world.

Stan: I could see this mob approaching the pub. Someone said to me, 'Who's this?' I remember saying 'Oh it's probably Reading coming back.' They had a mob up there and had left the pub not long before to have a look around. We'd been speaking to some of the Reading lads beforehand. One of them had said to me, 'Watch out, your rivals have got a right firm out today,' I remember saying, 'Yeah whatever,' we weren't really that bothered what Blues had out. We thought we'd be firmed up and have enough to deal with them. But by the point, when I thought it was Reading coming back, some of ours were outside, some of them were scattered around the pub and some had gone to get some food. This firm came in the door. They started shouting, 'Fowler! Fowler!' It was then I realised it was Blues. Fowler jumped up and shouted to them. 'Here I am! I'll have any one of you in a straightener now!' He was trying to take the heat off us, he knew we were outnumbered.

Tucker: We were all spread out in a packed pub and what seemed like hundreds of them came in. Williams came over and started talking to me. Fowler interrupted us, 'Did you just call me a doughnut Williams? Come on lets me and you have a straightener outside,' Williams wasn't interested in doing that at all. He had a chat with Fowler for a couple of minutes. Nostrils, Fowler, Screw and I were by the stairs, on a small stage area.

Fowler: Gary Williams was leading them. I stood up and said, 'Williams! What the fuck d'you think you're doing? Are you trying to mug me off?' 'What d'you mean

Fowler?' he replied. You've got it all wrong Fowler, it's not like that, sit down, let's talk about it.' We sat down and started to have a chat. 'What's going on Gaz? If you want it we'll have it. If you don't want it, take your firm and fuck off,' I told him straight.

Screwdriver: When I saw Blues come in I walked over to Fowler and said, 'What's going on Fowl?' He said it's gonna go Screw.' I had this pair of black leather gloves, I remember putting them on and saying, 'Right, I'm ready!'

Fowler: Half of them were Chelmsley Wood Blues and the other half were from Acocks Green, two Blues areas of Birmingham. Williams is a person I've got time for. He's the one who has led them against us the most during our era. He and the Chelmsley lot wanted to go. The Acocks Green lot were saying they wanted to stay and have it with Villa. They were mobbed up they want it. I stood up. For some reason I was chewing a golf tee. Don't think for a minute that Blues came in and it went whoosh! It didn't happen like that. They were in for a while before anything happened. Elvis, one of their lads was there and my mate is having a go at him. 'What you doing, this is fucking England! Not Villa-Blues!' One of them said to me, 'Tell your mate to shut his fucking mouth Fowler. Tell him to calm down!' I said 'Who the fuck you talking to?

Nostrils: It was their usual mixed race mob but it did seem to be majority black membership that day. Sitting to the left of the stage Pete had taken a seat. He moved slightly and nudged a bottle on the table. In what seemed like ages the bottle dropped to the floor. Pete made a grab for it, but it crashed to the floor. On hearing the bottle smash the whole pub thought the first bottle had been thrown. Blues steamed into me and the rest of us on the stage. As Blues did this they were subsequently attacked by the Villa behind them accompanied by the rest of the pub. England fans were joining in and pelting them with bottles. All they've seen is a mob of black geezers walk in the pub and start on some fellow England fans.

Tucker: All of a sudden a glass smashed and it all went off. I got a chair over my back. I hit someone with an ashtray. It was total mayhem.

Stan: To be fair, the other England fans in there just hurled everything at Blues. I think that's why we held our own for so long in there. We were badly outnumbered. Glasses were just flying everywhere, it was murder. When the old bill started to land everyone flooded outside.

Jez: When the Rat and Parrot emptied I'd lost everyone, I saw a group of lads up the road and just presumed it was our lot, and I ran towards them to catch them up

Suddenly my phone goes, it's Fowler. 'Jez you prat, someone's just seen you running up the road after a group of lads, I'd take your time if I were you cause it's a mob of Blues.'

Screwdriver: Blues surrounded me outside as I managed to get out of the pub. Williams was there and he told them to leave me as I was on my own.

Fowler: It was a free for all. Blues were going for it. We're getting backed up the stairs. We ended up on a balcony and are hurling tables and chairs down onto Blues. Some of their lads may tell you, those who are honest, that day even though we got backed off and had less numbers hardly any of our lads had injuries. Blues were cut to fuck and bruised. They were bleeding like fuck. None of ours had anything wrong with them. The old bill ran into the pub. We fucked off through a back door through a kitchen area. I'm thinking that if they spotted me at this I would be arrested. A result for Blues? Was it bollocks. We had it with them with less than half their numbers.

We came out a side entrance and I went to the game. I met up with three friends, we all had tickets. A lot of our lads didn't have tickets. We went to the match. I came out of the game, rang the lads, they told me they were at some club in Renfrew. We got to Glasgow Central train station. As we came out into the terminal, there were loads of Jock lads milling about looking for it. I saw this one Jock buy a paper and pull a blade out of his trousers and slide it into the paper. I said to my mates 'Did you clock that? They said that they had, the Jocks were milling around just looking for the chance. We got outside and a few jocks were following us. We spotted a black cab and hailed it down. We got to the club the lads were at. This big Scottish guy started talking to me at the bar. He was all over me, 'I've heard of you Fowler,' he was going, and 'I heard you had a wee bit of trouble in the town?' 'Yeah,' I said 'mate, it was something and nothing.' 'Well,' he said, pulling this fucking shooter out of his trousers, 'D'you want me to go down and shoot the bastards?' 'For fucks sake mate no!' I said to him, 'It's a bit of football violence, we don't want anyone fucking killed over it.' Madness, it was absolute madness. The place was fucking mad.

Bulgaria Vs England Euro 2000 Qualifier Sofia 9th June 1999

Dandy: We gathered at Birmingham International Airport to travel to Bulgaria for England's qualifying match in Sofia. We noticed some familiar faces in the terminal building. It was Blues. We soon realised there were around 20 of them. There were 35 of us, so the numbers were in our favour. The police had been tipped off and as we went through to departures they lectured all of us. 'There will be no trouble on the plane. If there is any trouble, the plane will land at the nearest airport and you will all be arrested. Plain clothes officers will be on the plane with you.' It was tense on the plane to say the least. Their group was led by Gary Williams. We filed into the plane and found our seats. Everyone was spread out everywhere. We were all sitting beside one another. As the plane took off the comments started to be made. 'Where's this prick Baker?' asked one blue-nose, 'I'm sitting next to you, you fucking doughnut,' said Baker. The nose shut up. He didn't say another word.

Screwdriver: Blues were mainly at the front of the plane. Steff was sitting up by them so he was hearing what they were saying. One of them, Fletch, was saying he was going to do this and that to the Villa. Some of our lads went up to have a word with them. There was a stand-off at 10,000 feet.

Dandy: Eventually the words from both sides became too much. One word too many was said and both sides stood up. We were 10,000 feet in the air and it was going to go off. The plain clothes police true to their word were on the flight. They stood up and stood in between the two groups. 'Come on lads, enjoy your holiday, it's not worth it' says one, adding 'not at 10,000 feet it's not anyway!' They were shitting it as much as everyone else.

Tucker: We had a couple of loose cannons on that flight, and so did they. We had Screwdriver and Sedge. Sedge was talking to Fletch. He was telling him what a twat Gary Williams was. Fletch said he would go and tell him. Sedge told him to carry on, he didn't mind. Then we had a mid air stand off which made everyone nervous. Even at the airport we were all on the same bus for hotel transfers.

When we got there Screwdriver said, 'Right, where the fuck are they? Let's go and look for them!' They avoided us all holiday. Only once did we see Williams, he came into the 'Mickey Mouse Bar' we were using on his own and had a drink, Screw went up to him and asked him what the crack was. He said they weren't interested. They didn't have the numbers. He didn't mention that they'd teamed up with Man City and had nearly double the numbers we had.

Screwdriver: A few of us went to the game. It was a 13 hour train ride to Sofia. We were playing cards on the way there. Mark B and I were playing with Liam. Liam is loaded and we were trying to hustle him. What we didn't know was that Liam was also trying to hustle us and he was quite good at it. He cleaned us both out.

When we got to Sofia we were plotted up outside this café with a load of other England fans. A mob of Bulgarians came round the corner. Everyone at the café was up for it and stood up to front them. But as this was happening a tram came down the street in between the two mobs. Everyone had to wait for what seemed an age for this tram to go past before they steamed into each other. It didn't take us long to have them running back to where they came from.

European Championship Holland and Belgium June 2000

Fowler: These were the first major championships since Bruno, Steve Baker and I were thrown out of the World Cup in France in 1998. We were thinking how we were going to get in to Belgium. We knew we'd be looked out for by the police. We had to get in somehow without being noticed. It was decided Jez would drive his car over. Baker, Jez and I would go in his car. Clinchy was going over as a foot passenger. I was in the passenger seat and Baker was in the back. As we were getting off the ferry on the Belgian side of the channel we noticed there was loads of old bill. They were checking all the cars. I said 'Fucking hell I bet that's for us!' I looked round and Baker was hiding behind one of the seats. He was going, 'What they doing now Fowl? What they doing now?' I had to laugh. I said, 'What do you think you're doing you daft cunt? If it is for us they're not going to miss you if you hide behind the seat are they?' It did make me laugh. The old bill swooped on us. They arrested us and took the three of us straight to a police station. Baker and I had been done before and Jez is obviously being nicked for association. We got to this police station and Baker was mouthing off at them. He was going 'Fuck off you Belgian pricks' and stuff like that. We knew we were not getting into Belgium. We were fucked now. They locked us in this police cell and the beds were at a fucking 45 degree angle. If you tried sleeping on them you were rolling straight off. Jez was naïve then. All of a sudden the hatch sprang open and they called Jez out. He was wondering what was happening and I started shouting after him. 'They'll never take you alive eh Jez! Don' let them take you alive!' He was shouting back, 'Where are they taking me Fowl?' 'You're fucked mate! They're all going to bum you!' I replied laughing.

Jez: They walked me down some corridor miles away and locked me on my own in some cell, why they did that is beyond me. When they took us out the next morning they put us on a coach. There was just the four of us on this coach. They'd shut the ferry port off to normal passengers when we got there. They kept it closed until our ferry had departed. It was all a bit over the top if you ask me.

Fowler: They put the three of us on this big bus. I'm not joking there were that many police around it you would not believe it. They had all the roads blocked off. There were police on motorbikes escorting us to take us back to the ferry port. All that fuss just for the three of us. It was unbelievable. They drove Jez's car onto the ferry. They escorted us onto the ferry to make sure we left. We were on the ferry going back when Tucker rang me. He was on his way over to Belgium with Bruno. 'Fowl where are you?' he asked. 'Well actually Tuck, I'm on the ferry on the way back to England.' I explained what had happened. 'We're on the ferry on the way over,' he said. I looked out of the window and I could see this ferry going in the opposite direction. 'You're not on the so and so ferry are you?' 'Yeah we are', said Tucker. I ran out to the deck and so did he. We were waving to each other as we passed in the middle of the English Channel.

Solo: When we went through the channel tunnel one week earlier, security had been tight to say the least. We'd all been checked out at the English border checkpoint in Ashford. NCIS (National Criminal Intelligence Service) had compiled a list of about 5000 known hooligans who would not be allowed to enter into Europe whilst Euro2000 was on. We were in two cars and two of our lads in the second car were pretty sure they were on the list. The police at the checkpoint paid them a lot of attention. Surprisingly they gave us all back our passports and waved us through. On the train we worked out that the banning orders couldn't come into force until we reached another country. They couldn't stop us leaving England but they would stop us entering France or Belgium or Holland. We decided to try our luck and the two lads who we thought were on the banning list transferred into the front car. The front car was about six cars ahead of the second one on the train. Another lad and I swapped over into the second car to replace them. We didn't believe it would work, but it was worth a try. The train pulled into France. The cars started to pull out one at a time. One by one the cars went through more police checkpoints without being stopped including the first car. Then as we approached the checkpoint a French Police and a British Police spotter stepped out in front of us. They waved us into a lay-by. There were more police there waiting for us. We all got out the car. Our passports were taken again. A senior officer with a smug look on his face was checking the list and comparing it with our names. He got to the bottom and started again. He checked them again. He called someone on his radio and waited. He came across to us and asked where the other two lads were. We said we'd never heard of them. He looked bemused at first. Then the penny dropped. He was fuming. He started to walk away, then turned and stomped back over to us and threw our passports back at us. 'Fuck off,' he said. We continued on our way.

We all met later that night in a bar on the outskirts of the Ostend. It was pretty warm so we were sat outside the bar at about four tables in a pedestrianised street. There were quite a few English spread around the town. Groups were milling about but the atmosphere was good. There was no sense of trouble. There were a few Belgian police walking the streets during the day, but it was low-key. It was noticeable that as the night wore on, their presence increased. They were suited up in body armour and helmets. Police trucks and vans were parking up in side streets around the town. A group of Norwegian supporters came walking up the street making a bit of noise. The police seemed to be paying them little attention. A police truck had parked on the corner since we'd arrived at the bar and they'd been eyeballing us from across the street. As the Norwegians passed by us, a skirmish broke out. It was the Norwegians fighting each other. It was two Norwegian teams who had met up earlier and after a few beers, differences had started to surface. The fight was absolutely pathetic with both sides posturing and slapping each other. They were rolling round on the floor like a bunch of mud wrestlers. We were all laughing and wolf-whistling them. The riot police came charging over. They ran straight past the Norwegians. They lined up facing us with riot shields. They moved forward pushing into us. They forced us backwards, knocking everyone off their seats. Tables and chairs were sent flying as they came forward. It seemed that the Belgian police were primed and ready for trouble from English fans. As soon as trouble broke out it was the English that were targeted. The reaction was so over the top it was a joke. We didn't even retaliate, yet they started using pepper spray on us. More riot vans screeched into the area with sirens blaring. We were all pinned up into a corner and searched. One by one we were dragged out of the bar area and thrown out onto the street. The town was effectively closed for the night, so we headed off to our digs.

Simmo: Sixteen of us travelled all in cars. I was with Tucker and Bruno in Tuckers car. We parked the car at Dover and went to board the ferry as foot passengers. We boarded the ferry with no problems. Halfway across the channel I had a phone call from Fowler. 'Where are you Fowl?' I asked. 'I'm on the ferry,' he said. 'You're on the ferry?' I replied, 'You can't be, I'm on the ferry and I can't see you.' 'Yeah I'm on the ferry, the fucking ferry heading back to England!' he informed me. We knew then we were going to have a hard time getting into Belgium. We had Bruno with us. Bruno had made the national papers being deported from the World Cup in France in 1998. We dressed Bruno up, gave him a hat, scarf and a big coat. We waited for the ferry to dock. True to form, Bruno sailed through passport control at Ostend. Tucker and I were topped and grilled on why we were visiting Belgium. When we eventually got through Skinhead Neil was waiting for us on the other side.

Solo: We arrived in Brussels in the afternoon. It was the day before the game. The sun was shining. The city was packed with England fans. The atmosphere was great.

There was not the slightest hint of any trouble. We sat at a bar just outside the top of the main square. There were more of us now. We'd been joined by a few Villa lads from the Vale, Erdington and Kingstanding. Most England fans would be gathering there because of the main square. Bruno and Clinchy joined us after a walk around the streets. They'd found a fair few English lads gathered in an Irish boozer called O'Reilly's. They said it was calm but was starting to get a bit lively. There was no sign of the Germans. British plain clothed police were checking out all the bars. They were trying to blend in but they might as well have had blue flashing lights strapped to their heads. Our football intelligence officer PC Kelly made an appearance and warned us all to keep our noses clean. First sign of trouble and he'd have us nicked.

Simmo: We struggled to get digs in Brussels so we all had to split up. I was with Tucker and Clinchy and we went out to have a drink. We found a bar with some England fans in. We were drinking outside, the weather was nice. All of a sudden a massive mob came round the corner; we didn't know who it was at first. It was a mob of English. They had just come back from the Moroccan quarter of Brussels. They had been having it with Moroccans.

Solo: The first riot van came screeching down the hill with its sirens blazing. It was followed by another and then another. Dozens of police cars and vans were tearing down the hill. The atmosphere had been totally calm and peaceful. Something was happening somewhere. We thought the chances were a German firm had landed somewhere and it had gone off. Or that it might have kicked off with the Turks. There were thousands of Turks living there. It was time to make a move. We all stood and started to make our way downtown. The lads in all the other bars had the same idea. There must've been a couple of hundred lads marching down the streets towards the sirens. The calm atmosphere had changed within seconds. It took fifteen minutes of walking through narrow streets to get to where all the commotion was taking place. O'Reilly's was on the main road. Across the road from it was a huge old town hall type building. It was surrounded by steps. Outside O'Reilly's there was a large group of about two hundred English lads. They were all standing outside the bar. Football, beer and sunshine, it doesn't get any better than that. Directly across the road from the pub were lines and lines of riot police with white helmets, riot shields and two-foot long batons. There wasn't any fighting or rioting taking place. It was just a major show of force by the Belgian police. As the crowd had grown, it had slowly drifted into the road. Without warning, snatch squads of plain clothed Belgian and British police picked off a couple of people. The treatment that was dealt out was extreme. Rapid baton blows to the legs as they were wrestled to the ground, arrested and dragged away to waiting vans. More and more English were pouring into the area. The sirens were like a magnet drawing them in. More riot vans were arriving loaded with riot police. On the steps of the town hall building were gathered rows of TV cameras and journalists. Photographers were running around in front of the police lines taking pictures of the English hooligans.

Simmo: The pub we were in was soon stormed by the police. They gassed the whole place and Tucker was nicked. They were battering everyone who came out and arresting them

Solo: Some of the lads turned and started to head off down the side street behind the pub, in case the police trapped them and blocked them in. The police suddenly charged across the street to speed them up. The police had now upped the ante from high jinks to complete confrontation. You could see the Belgian riot police were itching to have a go. The police lines reformed to face us. The English started goading the police for confronting them. A white smoke trail looped through the air towards us. The first tear gas canister landed and the crowd started to move back. More tear gas hit the floor and then they charged at us. They steamed into us. A few English decided not to move. They hadn't done anything wrong so had no reason to run. They were clattered to the floor and beaten with batons. Everyone else ran up the only street they could. It was a narrow little side street full of restaurants and cafes. Tables and chairs filled the little street. Tear gas was raining in behind us as we tried to run from the scene. Bemused locals were caught up in it as tables and chairs were sent crashing. Screams from the terrified locals filled the air along with the shattering noises of breaking glass competing with the shouts of English lads trying to regroup and get organized. The police pursued us for a while then stopped. We gathered up at the top of the street. Some of the more innocent England fans had continued to run further up the hill and get away from the chaos. Minutes later they ran back down to us. They'd been confronted by groups of Turkish youths who were also heading for all the noise. The Turks were brandishing blades and had blatantly mugged and beaten a young English couple in the full view of the police. Word spread fast about the mugging. More tear gas canisters dropped into the street and we took off further up the hill. Anyone who looked like a Turk was now fair game. Shopkeepers, bar owners, taxi drivers. There were so many groups of English running in from different directions that the police couldn't keep track. They pulled out and left us to it for a while. The afternoon was giving way to evening now and the sun had gone down.

Even though the place was being wrecked, a bar called the Fiacre Bar was still open and serving beer. This seemed to become the focal point for everyone. It was clear that the confrontation had come out of nothing. There was no trouble until the Belgian police started firing tear gas. The Germans were nowhere to be seen. The Turks were only now putting in an appearance. A few Villa lads were standing together, but a lot of us were missing. The British police were standing across the street from the bar armed with video cameras. They were filming everything and everyone. Journalists and TV camera crews were getting it all too. Things had just started to settle down when suddenly hundreds of riot police flooded in to the area from all directions and completely blocked off every exit to the surrounding streets.

There was no possible way to leave the vicinity. Suddenly there was a surge backwards as everyone tried to get into the bar itself, but it was already filled to bursting point. The police came in and they came in hard. The first English to be on the receiving end were beaten to the floor. The police moved forward and were flattening anyone before them. Pepper spray was fired into the faces of anyone who tried to protest their innocence. That's why the English lads retaliated. Glasses were thrown. Tables and chairs were launched across the street. The place was lit up by TV cameras, flash photography and blue flashing lights. The police laid into anything that moved. Even women weren't spared a pasting. It was carnage. It was a zero tolerance operation at its very worst. They'd been given free licence to round up all the English and clear the streets at all costs. It became increasingly apparent that the police were out of control. We made a break for it and charged at a gap in the line that had appeared in the chaos. Bruno was collared by a couple of Robocop's. He was struggling like hell with them. More riot police swarmed round him. They'd got him round the neck and were trying to wrestle him down. Steff had been nicked and was cuffed up on the ground. The air was thick with the smell of teargas and pepper spray. We managed to break through the lines and ran off up the street. We turned and watched. The English at the bar were overwhelmed. Everyone was being cuffed and dragged to be sat in lines, one behind the other. There was blood everywhere. More and more lines were formed. There must have been hundreds arrested. The bar itself was still full. The lads didn't want to come out. The police pumped the place full of tear-gas. The doors burst open and everyone started to spill out, blinded, choking and spluttering. They were hit over the head and beaten to the floor. We were spotted at the top of the street and a big group of Robocop's came charging up after us so we took off. We ran for ages. We had no idea where we were going. The small narrow streets were a just a network of rabbit runs. Other groups of English were also being chased around the city. We kept on the move but were relentlessly pursued through the streets. For hours, the streets were filled with drifting clouds of white tear gas. English stragglers were being picked off by the Turkish gangs. They were now on the streets in greater numbers. As the English and the OB played cat and mouse the sirens continued constantly well into the early hours of the morning.

Simmo: The next day we left the hotel, Tucker had been nicked so Clinchy borrowed a couple of items of his clothing. Well Tucker didn't need them. Tucker was on his way back to the UK on some transport plane. Tucker never forgot that, it proper did his head in. He'll often say when Clinchy walks in a pub, 'Hey, is that my jumper?' or 'Hey! I recognise that,' even eight years on. We found a bar and were drinking with Spurs. We'd heard that Blues and Leicester were in Brussels and apparently were looking for any Villa who might be here. We bumped into Pete. We went looking for the rest of our lot. We found some Blues in a bar, there were ten of them. We walked over, the three of us. 'What you saying lads?' said Clinchy. 'We hear you're looking for us?' said Pete. They didn't want to know, they proper bottled it. We stayed at this bar for a while. We could see something was happening down the road. We ran towards it. We bumped into a right mob coming up the road. It was the England fans coming back from Charleroi where England had been playing. The police were starting to get stuck into the English fans, for nothing really. We plotted up at a bar with a load of English. The police surrounded the place and eventually threw tear gas inside. Everyone was choking and running out the front here they were being beaten and arrested. The owner of the bar was an Englishman. He threw wet towels to some of us and told us to get down the cellar. When we got down there, there was another ten England fans down there. He just told us to stay down there out of the way and to help ourselves to beer, fair play to him. We had a laugh down there until everything had cleared upstairs. We were stuck for getting home, Tuckers car was in Dover but he had the car keys on him. We were going to struggle getting home. Fowler rang and I told him. He arranged for me and Clinchy to fly business-class back to the UK.

England Vs Spain Friendly Int. Villa Park 25th February 2001

Fowler: The weekend before this game Villa were playing at Derby. We'd travelled to see them play. We were in this pub after the game. The old bill came in. They were trying to give Screwdriver and me letters. The letters were orders preventing us going to the England versus Spain match at Villa Park. We were having none of it and we wouldn't take the letters from them.

Screw: It was funny. We left through the back doors of the pub and down the road. The police were in hot pursuit trying to make us accept these banning orders. We wouldn't accept them.

Fowler: They followed us all the way to Derby station. I got hold of my solicitor on the phone. He was telling me not to accept the letter. He told me I didn't have to, so I didn't. The police followed us onto the train. We got off at Burton. We plotted up in the one pub with the police outside. I had this phone call. A bloke on the other end of the phone said he was Burton Albion's main lad. He said they were trying to get something together. 'Fucking Burton?' I said. 'Listen mate we're fucking Villa Hardcore. I wouldn't fucking bother if I was you, but I'm telling you, if you fucking turn up we will waste you!' The cheeky cunt! Imagine Burton Albion landing on Villa Hardcore? He had to be joking! He put the phone down. We heard nothing else.

Baz: For all the lads the England Spain fixture was an interesting prospect as hopefully various mobs from around the country would be showing up in town and we knew we could put on a good show as we always managed to at away games with England. The first game at Villa Park was on a wet Wednesday night. I think it was Sven Goran Eriksson's first game as international manager. I was out of work at dinnertime and headed to the Trocadero in Birmingham city-centre close to New Street. As the afternoon wore on we started to grow in numbers and for a week day friendly international I would say we had a good hundred in the pub by six o'clock. Personally I hoped that blues would be out in large numbers. The old bill turned up with PC Kelly pointing out the who's who to his spotter mates from other forces.

Fowler: We marched down towards Villa Park with a massive police escort. There must've been 150 of us. We merged in with the crowds as we neared Villa Park. I noticed I had some police following me. When I stopped they stopped. I thought 'fuck this, I'm going back to the pub. I decided to head back to the Adventurers. Some of the lads including Screw, Luddy and Tucker were in there. I'd just ordered a drink. The old bill came flying through the doors. They arrested Screw and took him out. Then they arrested me. I asked the one copper why I was being arrested. He told me we weren't being nicked, 'we're just holding you until the match finishes.' They took me outside the pub Screw was rolling around on the floor with two of them. 'Relax Screw! We're not getting charged!' I told him. 'You might not be getting charged Fowl but I fucking am!' He shouted back to me. They took us to the station and put us in holding cells until the match had finished.

Daz: We were walking up towards Villa Park. We were pretty spread out by this time. There was a group of lads in front of us singing 'shit on the Villa.' We just steamed into them with no warning, nothing. We just hit them. They scattered. We got hold of a few and clumped them. They were crying. The one said to me, 'We were only having a laugh mate,' Crying he was, 'You don't sing that here and get away with it,' I told him.

Baz: We left the pub. We probably numbered about one hundred and fifty. By now the old bill had landed on us big time with more riot vans than I'd seen before. They escorted us all the way to the ground. They started getting really aggressive and pushing people about. I don't think they had expected us out in such big numbers. We didn't see any other firms that night even though different people were on the phone to some of our lads saying they were here and there. Our spotters were telling us a different story. I felt it was a real let down and was gutted that no one had made a show in Birmingham still at least we had.

Clinchy: A few weeks later we were walking down from the Adventurers towards Villa Park; there were a handful of us which included Fowler, Baker, me and a few others. A police van drew alongside us and slowed down, they were shouting out of the windows to us, 'Where's your mate Screwdriver? We stitched him up good and proper!'

England Vs Finland Euro Champ. Qualifier Anfield 24th March 2001

Fowler: We had a good mob out for this one, it was quality. We took around 30-40. They were all sound lads, all game. We were meeting Sunderland up there. They were supposed to be taking a mob. When we caught up with them, some of their lads said, 'Fucking hell, we saw you coming round the corner. You're all big lads. We've got mainly youth with us'. We know a couple of Sunderland really well. One of them, Steve Mac has just been on holiday with us. Another of them, Little Joe has been away with us on a few occasions, they're cracking lads. A Stoke geezer kept on ringing me. I can't remember who as I'm hopeless with names. I went round to have a drink with them. Stoke had loads out for this one. They're good lads Stoke, never had a problem with them. Villa haven't played them much but most Villa lads have respect for them. During the game we were in a city-centre pub with Sunderland. Sunderland were saying, 'Newcastle are up the road in a pub drinking with Forest.' I told the Sunderland we'd go up with them and have a look. Steeley came up with me, just the two of us and a few of the Sunderland following at a distance behind us. We walked up to this pub. I walked up to the door. They saw us coming and there was a commotion in the pub. One of them came to the door and opened it just as I got there. Without saying a word I smacked him. In their book, the Forest book they say it was a glass. It wasn't a fucking glass it was a punch. They were in a pub, they had the glasses. I'd just walked up the road. Anyone who knows me knows I don't carry. I've used stuff at hand but I've never carried anything. As I hit him he staggered back and I shut the door and held it. I'm holding the door and they were going mad inside the pub trying to open it. I could only just manage to hold it shut. Sunderland were hesitant. I shouted 'Fucking hell Sunderland! This is your row, come on!' I turned round and let the door open. It was the same geezer at the front. As I opened the door I stepped back and twatted him again. I put him on his arse again and shut the door. They were going mad in there. I was struggling to hold the door. I was laughing and this was making them madder. Steeley shouted to me they were coming out of a side-door. I said to Steeley, 'Don't fucking run!' He replied, 'Fowl, I ain't going anywhere!'

Steeley: As soon as we walked up to the doors of the pub you could see them looking at us watching us approach. The one came to the door to meet us. Fowler and I walked up towards the door and the Sunderland to be honest were holding back a little. One of the lads inside came to the door looking cocky and Fowler just sparked him. He fell back. Fowler held the door as his mates tried to get out. They started coming out of a side door and I went to meet them. We were trying to encourage the Sunderland to come over and join us. There were two of us fighting with seven of them outside the pub. Suddenly the police started to arrive. Fowler shouted to me to do one. We ended up in a sheet music shop trying to look casual as the police flooded the area.

Fowler: I wasn't taking much notice now what Sunderland were doing. I'd got the red mist by this point. We heard sirens and the old bill start to land. Steeley and I did one. We ended up in some record shop pretending to look through the CD's. Forest's lads go on about this incident. They say someone threw a glass. It's bollocks. I smashed him. No-one threw fuck all. Soon after we were walking down this road and landed on a boozer. I was standing outside having a look. I noticed Everton were milling about. Fucking Everton what a joke, they really are fuck all but love to give it loads. I clocked them and they clocked me. Our lads in the pub knew what was going on. I was telling them to stay where they were. 'Don't let them know how many of us there is, if they do they'll fuck off,' I said. I was going to the Everton, 'Come on you Scouse cunts!' They now fancied their chances. They thought there were only a handful of us. They started to bounce towards me. Just as they got closer, our lads piled out of the pub. They steamed towards them throwing stuff. Everton just turned round and ran off, pathetic! The thing about me is I don't lie if I get turned over. Cunts like them they'd never admit it in a million years! Could've been us getting turned over, so what? We'd admit it, like it will hopefully come across in this book, it happens. To hear or read some peoples accounts it never happens to them. They must be very, very lucky that's all I can say, or simply bullshitting.

Stan: We had it with Huddersfield on the night in Liverpool. They were walking down a road which we happened to be walking down. There were two small groups of us. I remember they had the same black lad with them that we'd met on the train to Poland. He and Screwdriver exchanged a few punches before the old bill came and broke it all up. The police chased us on horseback and we all ran into a pub just up the road.

Germany Vs England World Cup Qualifier Munich
1st September 2001

We were now very well known to West Midlands Police. They were on first name terms with most of us. We were also well known to British Transport Police and they seemed to have taken a real dislike to us. We had outsmarted them time and time again and I think they were getting sick of it. One of our fringe players was an electrician and he had been working at Lloyd House, the West Midlands Police Headquarters. He reckoned he had seen big pictures of a lot of us with our names underneath on a big white board in there. We were obviously a target for them by this point.

England were due to play Germany in Munich in a World Cup qualifying match. As usual we decided we would take a firm out for the game. We knew that there would be no chance of us flying direct to Germany as they would be looking out for us and possibly turn us back on landing. We also knew that they would stop us and turn us back if we even attempted to fly out from Birmingham. So we purchased flights to Prague from Heathrow. We had a cover story that we were going to Prague for a stag-do and had no intention of going to the match. We knew there was an over-night train from Prague to Munich where the match was being played. We intended to get on this train and travel in the hope of getting into Munich unmolested by the police. We drove down to Heathrow in a convoy of cars. We parked up and entered the departures terminal. Straight away we were approached by the Metropolitan Police. They asked us our names and where we were going. The stag-do scam amazingly worked. They let us carry on our way. We flew out to Prague and had a jolly up the night before. Most were a little worse for wear the next morning. A few more of our lads met up with us. They'd caught a flight on the Friday from Birmingham. One of them, Pete, was stopped and asked in a sarcastic manner if he was also going to the 'stag-do' he said 'Of course!' He was allowed through. I think they already knew the horse had bolted by that point. We boarded the midnight train to Prague. Once on the train we settled down for the night. We were interrupted continually by the Czech police. They were touring the train at certain stations. They were fining people for the most petty of things. Feet on a chair, so many Czech crowns fine, sleeping in a luggage rack, so many Czech crowns fine, breathing, so many Czech crowns fine. Most foreign police are up to it. In Western Europe they beat you up. In Eastern Europe they beat you up, and then they fine/rob you. Rumour after rumour was sweeping the train. They were saying that people were simply being turned straight back at Munich train station. Fowler was a prime target for England police spotters at that time. He grabbed a taxi from the last but one station before Munich with a couple of lads.

When we got to Munich we were amazed. After all the hype by our press about the reception we were going to get from the Polizei, the station was deserted. We filed out in shock expecting the police to jump on us at any moment. They simply did not appear. There was still nowhere open so we plotted up in a McDonalds and most of us caught up on some sleep sprawled across the plastic benches. Mark B and a couple of the boys had a walk around to see what was going on. The city was starting to get busy and they returned saying they had seen PC Kelly who had asked them where we were. They had shaken him off. They said there were a few bars or Beer Keller's opening up by this time. We decided to travel down to the main drag and set up shop in one of these. The place was half empty when we got there. We soon filled two or three long tables and ordered the drinks. There were a few people scattered about in there. New arrivals were suspected of being under-cover German or English police. We saw one blatantly talking into a radio in the top pocket of his denim jacket. We took no notice. We were doing nothing wrong, not yet we weren't anyway. The bar filled up, a lot of English came in, and a lot of Germans. We were sitting close to a group of Luton. We spoke with them with no problems. As the beer flowed the singing started. To our surprise our songs were answered by a large group of German fans at the front of the place. They were dressed in a typical Germanic fashion. Mullet hair cuts, bleached denims and football shirts. Once the 'There's only one Bomber Harris!' song started things got livelier. With obvious 'Dutch' courage the Germans answered with a song about Winston Churchill. That was all it needed. If I'm honest we were waiting for that point. We didn't need much of an excuse anyway and being closest to the Germans I was first in. They were halfway through a song about Churchill. Bang! I hit the one nearest me. That's all it needed, the place went up. A huge litre glass pot grazed my head as the English rose and pelted the Germans with missiles. The ones at the front, me included just waded into them. The Germans scattered everywhere. Holes were appearing in the windows. Some of the Germans jumped through these holes in the windows to safety. Some of them trapped inside took one hell of a hammering. This only stopped when riot police stormed into the bar. They started beating up everyone with their riot sticks. We had a bit of a go back. After a while some of us thought 'Fuck this!' and jumped out the same holes which the Germans had utilised a few moments earlier. We flooded out onto the street. We were greeted by a hail of flashes from the press who were outside. We walked away quickly from the incident. Around the town there were lads everywhere. There was loads of English and we walked in a circle and ended up back at the same beer Keller we had smashed up. We went back inside as though nothing had happened. Things were getting back to normal and they were serving as if nothing had happened. There were more English in there by this time. We walked in and I heard someone say, 'There's Fowler and Villa Hardcore.' I felt a buzz when I heard that. We were recognised on the England scene by this point. We were associated with travelling in numbers to watch England play and having it.

It didn't take long for exactly the same thing to happen. We were over confident by this point and we thought we could just take the piss. We'd smashed the Germans, wrecked the place, then simply walked round the block and walked back in as if nothing had happened. Some of the Germans got lairy at the front - we simply steamed into them again. Everything went haywire again. We ran straight into the middle of them hitting anything or anyone that moved. The police were already outside at this point, due to the earlier trouble. They ran inside battering everyone in sight. I jumped straight through one of the holes in the window which we had made earlier. It was a hail of flashlights again as I emerged onto the street.

Mark B: After it had gone off and the police had landed I somehow got mixed in with the German fans. How I got away with it I'll never know. I was standing in the middle of them holding just the handle of a stein glass. Minutes before I'd been bouncing the glass off one of their heads. They thought I was German.

Screwdriver: I was in the toilet when it all kicked off. Ginge was also in there. I could hear something. 'Is it going off Ginge?' I asked. We made our way back inside and it was mayhem. We entered just at the same time as the German police. They steamed us. I went down with the police hitting me. They carried on hitting me and I remember seeing Bruno who I pulled in front of me to shield me from the blows. He never did thank me for that!

Fowler: After it had gone off in that Beer Keller some of us were trapped in there and couldn't get out. This one copper told Jez and me to sit down and stay where we were. The woman behind the bar was sticking up for us. She was saying 'No it wasn't them! They didn't do anything,' I turned round to Jez and said 'We're sweet here they're not going to do anything!' As I said that, they swamped Jez. They handcuffed him

and dragged him outside. They took me out but I wasn't handcuffed. As I walked out I saw Deakin lying on the floor outside. He was all smashed up.

Tucker: Fowler was going, 'Sit here, sit here and keep quiet they won't think it's us.' They came straight over to us and nicked the lot of us.

After the confusion which followed the second fight a lot of the lads had been roped in. I couldn't spot anyone I knew in the vicinity outside. I was basically on my own. I had a look round to see if I could find anymore of the lads who hadn't been lifted. I met a couple of Stoke lads. They were sound, Stoke always are with us. We made our way down to the ground.

Fowler: They took us to a police station, it wasn't far away. I thought I've got no problem here, that bird from the bar said I'd done fuck all. Obviously we had done something. We'd kicked fuck out of the Germans, but the old bill weren't to know that. We were standing in the police station. There was this cell full of Germans. They were snarling at us. It was probably their lads. They said something to me and I replied. One copper said to me, 'You! You! I put you in there!' I said, 'Fucking sound! Put me in there then!' Jez is looking at me as if to say, 'Shut the fuck up Fowler.'

Screw: They took us to this police station and took us inside, as we got inside there was this big cell and it was rammed full of Germans. They were all drinking beer and mouthing off at us. I told the copper if they were allowed beer in that cell I wanted to go in there. He thought I was joking, I wasn't.

Fowler: They put me and Jez in some big prison van. 'You two!' they were going, 'Big jail for you, you're in very big trouble!' 'Yeah, yeah whatever mate,' I was going. We looked out the windows of the van and we could see Clinchy being dragged across the yard. He had been nicked as well. Jez and I are banging on the windows of the van shouting, 'Clinchy! Clinchy!' 'Is that you Fowl?' shouts Clinchy, 'Here mate, put us in there with them will you?' They put him in the van with us. Eventually they put us all together in one big cell. Tucker was being really smart with them, taking the piss. They gave us some bread and water. As they did that they took Tucker and Screw out. Tucker was going, 'No mate! Don't move us! Not just as the foods arrived!' They just put them in another cell and fed them in there. They then brought Deakin in. He was bandaged up and not looking too clever. Mind you he had improved since I had last seen him unconscious on the floor outside the Beer Keller. They came in with a big list and started calling our names out. They called everyone's name except Deakin. I started winding him up saying, 'Oh Deakin, you're in trouble. They must have you down for something major!' 'What do you mean Fowl?' he said. He was shitting himself. I had to tell him I was winding him up.

It was mayhem round the stadium. England fans without tickets were trying to get into the stadium and trying to turn the ticket touts over. The Polizei however had seen enough. Some of us were forced back into the city-centre and ended up watching the match on a screen in a local hotel. England won the match 5-1 and I celebrated with a mixture of Stoke, Chelsea and a couple of other clubs. After the match I met up with Alcoholic Andy and Mark B. We hung around the station waiting for more of ours to reappear. Mark said he thought they'd all been nicked. A large group of England gathered near the station bar celebrating our win. The old bill had ringed them. They had riot shields and dogs. They were just itching to get stuck into the English you could sense it. I had had enough. I was battered and bruised I just wanted to get home. We jumped on the train and headed back to Prague.

Fowler: We all got released. The landlord or bar staff had told them it wasn't us. It was 4am. There wasn't a train till later on. Luckily one geezer who had been released with us had a hotel room. We all piled in there. Roughly about 10 of us all piled in this little dingy room. We caught the train the next morning and headed back to Prague.

World Cup 2002 May 31-June 30th Japan and Korea

Fowler: We'd booked a two week holiday in Thailand. We planned to get some flights from Thailand to Osaka. Pete, Steve Baker, Simmo, Bruno, Jez and I were over there. We got to Osaka at 6am in the morning. The flight doors opened. No sign of any old bill. The place was deserted. I remember thinking brilliant! We've done it! We got on the escalators. As we were coming down there sitting at the bottom was PC Kelly. He was with some other old bill. He saw us. He was shouting, 'You've got no chance Fowler! You've got no chance!' He sounded like Blakey from On the Buses. Pete and Simmo tried to do a sneaky one but they were all over us, with the Japanese police.

Simmo: They didn't know what to do with us. Once they'd arrested us they took us into some room and we were in there for hours.

Fowler: We had one copper for each of us. The one was going to me, 'You! You have done nothing wrong! You're okay!' I was grinning at Jez. He was shaking his head as

if to say, 'You jammy bastard.' They then took us to get our bags. They started walking us toward passport control. They checked us through. We put our bags through the x-ray machine. I was thinking they were letting us through. We gave them our tickets and they waved us through. We were stunned. As we walked through they jumped on us again and re-arrested us. I was going, 'What are you doing you silly Jap cunts?' They took us back to where we have just come from. They then told us that we had to pay to get locked up! It worked out at around £10 each to lock us up. 'You're joking aren't you?' I asked one of them. 'You expect me to give you a tenner to lock me up? Are you mad? I don't mind paying for a hotel, but I'm not paying for my own fucking cell!' They looked at me as if I was mad. I looked at them as if they were mad. We said, 'Right, we'll pay you, on the condition you get televisions so we can watch the England versus Nigeria game.' They swallowed it. 'We also want food!' 'No problem!' they said. They took us down to the cells. They wheeled in a television for us to watch the game. They tried to put us in the cells, 'No mate, leave the doors open,' one of us said. So they left the cell doors open and just locked the one on the outer perimeter. We had the run of the place. We started to watch the game. We watched the match. Afterwards Simmo, Pete and I were playing cards. Baker was croaking. He was bitten by something in Thailand. He was doing the dying fly in his cell.

Simmo: They couldn't have treated us any better to be honest. We had them bringing us McDonald's. They brought in a television so we could watch the football. When we were due to fly out they took us into the main terminal. We had these little buggies waiting. They took us in those. The Japanese were taking pictures of us. They even let us stop off and buy some beer from a shop in the terminal building. We flew back to Thailand via Singapore. They even had an escort waiting for us, complete with buggies, for the connecting flight in Singapore.

Fowler: The next day they escorted us back to departures and we think we're getting deported back to Birmingham, but no, they deport us back to the country we've come from. So we were packed off back to Thailand to continue our holiday, brilliant. It's all over the papers and the television but we went back to Thailand and continued our holiday.

Kavos June 2003

Gregg: It was as much about having a laugh as having the row for me. The holidays and weekenders were top drawer. Like the time in Madrid when we nicked a taxi. The driver got out for fags. We drove off in his taxi and then realised we didn't know how to get where we were going. We went back and asked him for directions. Another time was in London when Arsenal came in a boozer looking for us. There were three of us. I took all my clothes off and stood at the bar drinking. I don't think they felt comfortable fighting with a naked man. They were great times. Getting up early to get into a firm's boozer before them was a struggle for me especially after a Friday night. I usually pulled and then I had to then get home and changed into the right clothes for the match. I was without doubt our top shagger at that time. That is why the lads usually wanted to room with me on holidays. We went over to Kavos in June 2003. I shared a room with Fowler. He was under the correct impression I'd be bringing back three or four birds every 24 hours and he could have a quick butchers while pretending to be asleep. Within an hour of landing there he looked wiser than he actually is. I had met a sort from Luton in a bar. I had a kiss and a cuddle in the toilets and came back onto the dance floor in her dress. I left her to come out minutes later in my shorts and tee-shirt.

That was the beginning of the worst trip of my life. An hour later I'd got my clothes back on. We had moved onto the next bar. We had a heated discussion with some lads. This time it was with some West Ham. Clinchy and Baker and I saw them off up the road. I received a bottle over my swede that opened up and it needed nine stitches. We had only been on the island for an hour and a half. I went and saw the local doctor who did a decent job on my head. I promised to go back in the morning with the money. I signed the form as Trevor Francis and put my address as St Andrews football ground in Birmingham. I got back to the digs before Steve. I heard him banging about in the toilet and crashing into the bath. I thought nothing more of it. I got up in the morning ready for another day on the lash. Fowler was still sucking the curtains in, fast asleep. I got ready and had a shower. I put my contact lenses in and went out. Ten minutes later my eyes are stinging like fuck to the point where I couldn't see. I had to go back to the digs. Steve was up and on his way out and mentioned in passing that he 'might have pissed in that contact lenses pot thing that I was holding.'

Fowler: I had been doing something in the bathroom and I knocked this little pot Gregg had for his contact lenses down the toilet. I managed to get it out. I found both of the lenses and I swilled them under the tap and put them back hoping he wouldn't notice.

Gregg: I was now half blind with nine stitches in my bandaged up head. My eyes were full of Fowlers piss. I had to go to another doctor at the other end of Kavos High Street who gave me some eye drops. For three days I was stuck in the digs. I was blind and had a banging headache. I even put it on the big fat Geordie bird from the block opposite on the snide. I was only after some company. Even she blew me out. Those prats were coming back at all hours, shouting and bawling. Some of the ugly fuckers even had birds in tow. I was fuming. Every night Steve came crashing through the door, waking me up. He'd whack the loudest fan in Kavos on. Within minutes he'd be snoring like an old dog. His snoring was so loud it kept me awake all night. It was hell on earth. It couldn't have been worse. Then one night Tucker stuck a fire extinguisher through the door. He covered the room in white powder. The dopey holiday rep thought I'd done it myself and tried to chuck me out. The doctors of Kavos then got together. They came banging on my door with a crowd Greeks demanding their money. I was on my Jack Jones as everyone was out on the lash. I couldn't sleep down to this angry firm of doctors banging on my door. I had to block the door and climb out the back window. I had crash in the room next door. You look back and you laugh, but at the time....

Chapter Six: Villa Hardcore. Mud Sticks

On January 12th 1998, just before the World Cup in France, the Daily Mirror ran a feature which included a couple of familiar faces.

20 THUGS WHO ARE OUT TO WRECK THE WORLD CUP! A MIRROR INVESTGATION

These are the British football yobs who could wreck the World Cup in France - named by The Mirror today in an attempt to head off disaster. Police believe each of the 20 hooligans is an organiser of violence. But they are powerless to stop them travelling to France for the championship in June and July.

The paper printed 20 pictures of allegedly 'known' football thugs with short descriptions underneath of their activities. Two Villa fans were named and their pictures published in the article.

**** ****** heads a 30 strong mob of notorious Aston Villa yobs. Cops say the firm is among the two worst on the international front. Villa yobs are divided into right-wing racists and a Loyalist division.
**** ***** is a skinhead viewed by police as a key 'organiser of violence' and a threat to security during the World Cup. The active loyalist is a sidekick of **** ****** at Aston Villa - one of the key 'firms' on the England travel scene. He was in Poland in 1997 and involved in violence after the game.

They labelled Villa Hardcore as one of the two worst football firms who followed England abroad. We were a key firm apparently. If you knew anything about the England international scene it was hard to believe we were key to some sort of right-wing plot. We were very prominent and had been taking firms of differing sizes to England matches. We could hardly be described as a key firm in organised extremist violence. We didn't mix with other teams for starters. We were simply football hooligans. They were looking for something which wasn't there. We were also labelled with having a 'racist' and 'loyalist' divisions in our firm. It was utter rubbish of course. At this time we were well on our way to peaking as a firm. We had large numbers of lads. It was a cross section of mainly British working-class. Identifying two individuals who may or may not have been involved in politics of some sort the paper managed to label us as a 'racist, loyalist supporting right-wing football hooligans'. Now get me a hundred British working-class people in a room. Then tell me that a handful won't have right-wing sympathies. On the other side of the coin a small number will have left-wing allegiances. The main body of people will be somewhere around centre politically. That's if the majority take any interest at all with the apathetic electorate of today. It was the same with us. If some people had extremist views the rest of us were by and large ignorant of the fact. We followed England, maybe sang certain songs. We were patriotic in the main that much is true. In some people's eyes, especially the left-wing media, that makes us all NF supporting fascists. It wasn't the truth and we had many affiliations within our group, white, black, Asian, Catholic and Protestant. You name it we had it, it suited some to promote this myth however. As for the loyalist accusations, again Birmingham has had a large Irish community settle over the years. It would be naive to presume all of these were Irish Catholics and that a few Irish Protestants hadn't settled here. We were under-represented, for a Birmingham organisation, from the black community. This was for reasons stated previously, when the Zulu Warriors gained momentum and Afro-Caribbean lads joined them en-masse. This article in The Mirror would polarise the situation ten-fold. At the time we didn't realise it. Some of our lads, such as Reidy, who lived in South Birmingham received phone-calls. 'What's this about you lot all being Combat 18?' Several of the lads received similar calls. Obviously we denied it, it wasn't true. Some people, Blues especially, they used it. They used it to cause trouble at Villa. They'd approach some of our black lads. 'Why are you hanging around with the racists?' would be the usual question. It was like a gift for Blues, courtesy of the British shock-press. They hadn't been able to cope with us for a few years. They were reduced to drinking in a small part of the city centre on the East side of the city. They rallied troops with promises of fighting the racists. We became the right-wing racists in their propaganda. They would ring round when they found we were drinking in town. They would add to their numbers by dragging loads of black lads into with promises of smashing the BNP. They distributed leaflets with our lad's pictures on. They wrote to the local press claiming that we had shipped in Combat 18 members to help us against them. It was all rubbish of course. It was just an excuse to explain them getting turned over by us. Some of our lads were black as I've said before. They are lads I had and have known for years. They are very good friends of mine. The same can be said for a lot of lads my age. We mostly all grew up in multi-cultural Birmingham. Organised racism within our firm was never going to prosper in those circumstances.

Big Tony: I want to say one thing about this, the Combat 18 rumours are bullshit. I am black. Fowler is a mate of mine. He has other mates who are Asian and black. I know he isn't Combat 18. I know he isn't racist. Like I said he is just my mate.

Manchester United Vs Aston Villa Premier League 1st May 1999

Quite a few Villa gathered in New Street station. A lot were Hardcore. We were on our way to the game between Manchester United and Aston Villa at Old Trafford. Mr A and Mr B entered the station complex. The station was quite busy as it usually is on a Saturday morning. They passed one or two scruffy looking individuals and approached Mr C, who was near our group and who had some tickets for them. Mr C has one or two innocent looking males standing by him. He takes little notice of these. He greets Mr A and Mr B. As he does three of the people around him and the two or three Mr A and Mr B had passed, pulled out chequered caps and more noticeably guns. 'Right! MI5, Scotland Yard! On the floor! On the floor now!' they screamed. The lads were incredulous, 'You've got the wrong people! We don't know what you're on about mate!' they remonstrated. The police had formed a semi-circle around them. They were having none of it. They were all bundled out of the building.

Mr B: I wasn't paying much attention really. I had a bit of a hangover. All of a sudden this bloke standing in front of me turned round and whipped a pistol out of his pocket. He was pointing the gun at me shouting, 'On the floor, on the fucking floor now!' I looked round and Mr C had a similar bloke pointing a gun at him and yelling at him to get on the floor. More plain clothes police ran from what seemed to be everywhere. They all had those baseball caps with the check pattern along the side. They wrestled me to the floor and handcuffed me.

Mr B: I remember seeing Pete walking in the station whilst I was being taken out. He'd just bought a burger. He was in the middle of taking a bite when he clocked what was happening. I shouted to him to see if he wanted my ticket. He threw the burger away and did a sharp about turn and left the station. It made me chuckle at the time. I still didn't know what was going on. I thought it was football related. They dragged me into an unmarked Volkswagen Golf which was parked outside and drove out of Birmingham city-centre straight onto the motorway. I asked where we were going. They told me they couldn't take me to a local police station as they were all full of shoplifters. They were taking me somewhere else. I thought to myself that's strange. It was only 9am they wouldn't be full of shoplifters that early surely.

At around the same time Mr D was travelling down Bunbury Lane towards Cotteridge in West Birmingham. Mr D has two friends with him. They were travelling to a pub in Kings Norton, the Navigation Inn. Mr D in the front passenger seat tried to use his mobile phone. He found he had no signal.

Mr D: I turned to the lad in the back and asked if he'd got signal on his mobile. He pulled his phone out. He hadn't got any signal either, I thought that was strange. We found out later they'd jammed the phones. About the same time a car pulled up beside us. It was a single lane road so we thought he was a bit keen. It was full of blokes, they looked into our car. At first I thought it was Blues. They pulled on chequered caps which the old bill use and sped off in front of us. We said to each other that something must be going on. The car which had overtaken us screeched to a halt in the middle of the road. Armed police jumped out of both cars. They also ran out of gardens at either side of the road. Another car with armed police also pulled up with a screech behind us. They smashed the window and dragged me out by my neck. They pulled the other two out of the car. They were screaming, 'Scotland Yard! Anti-terrorist branch! You're all nicked under the prevention of terrorism act!' The one lad with us was complaining. He wasn't going to lie on the floor because he had new trousers on!

A controlled explosion was carried out on my mate's briefcase in the boot of the car. All he had in there was a packed lunch. They'd blown his sandwiches up.'

I was taken to Halesowen police station. They kept on driving round Birmingham. I presume they were trying to disorientate me. I know Birmingham like the back of my hand, they were wasting their time. We got to Halesowen police station. I was taken in front of this Chief Inspector or something. He had all the ribbons and medals on his uniform. He opened a big folder where a piece of paper had been left to mark the page. He said to me, 'You are being held under the prevention of terrorism act 1989. You will be held here and questioned.

Mr B: Eventually we arrived at Halesowen police station. They took me inside and I was taken to the desk. They had a large file. They were quoting a lot of things I'd done in the past, quite a few which I'd been arrested for and not charged. 'You've been a lucky bastard haven't you Mr B?' one of them said. 'Well your fucking luck has just run out son, you're going to get 20 years for this!' 'What are you on about?' I said. I had no idea what they were going on about. They sat me in the reception area for what seemed like ages. I couldn't think what they could be holding me for. I asked one of them what was happening, 'Do you realise how much trouble you're in?' one of them replied. 'Do you know how difficult it is to get a ticket for Manchester United?' I asked him. I was still taking it as a joke, which was a mistake in hindsight.

Mr C: When we finally got to Halesowen nick I was informed me that I was being held under the Prevention of Terrorism Act. He told me I was going to be charged with conspiracy to cause criminal damage. I thought this it was a bit heavy for criminal damage. He then added that it was criminal damage with explosives. To say I was shocked is an under-statement.

Mr D: I was then taken past a room which had all our pictures on the wall. It wasn't just the four of us who had been arrested. It was all the Hardcore lads taken at various times and outside various pubs and grounds. One copper with a London accent was asking the main man with the ribbons to transfer us to Paddington Green police station in London. The West Midlands officer was having none of it. He told him we'd be held there. Our clothes were taken away and I was issued with a white paper boiler suit. I was then taken to a cell which was completely covered in paper from floor to ceiling, obviously for forensics.

Mr C: They refused to tell us what we were supposed to have done. We were denied legal advice at first. They told us we were in deep shit for what we had done. One copper, well I think that's what they were, they could have been Special Branch, he joked with us. He told me they were surprised we hadn't wet ourselves. He said people who are surprised and arrested with guns like that usually lose control of their bladder. I couldn't reply I was too stunned at what was happening to us. In Halesowen Police Station, we were isolated from each other and stripped, given these white paper suits and held alone in cells with the walls and floor covered in paper, I was brought out and questioned four times during the 24 hours we were held there.

Mr B: I was taken to the desk to be formally arrested. The duty sergeant asked who the arresting officer was. He didn't seem to know what was going on. 'You don't need to know my name,' said one of the blokes who arrested me. He quoted him the letters 'SO' followed with some numbers.

Mr A: In the interview they started off with saying, 'You are a member of Combat 18, a far right racist terrorist organisation.' I replied, 'I have never had anything to do with any far right group. 'We know you are a committed right-wing activist and a member of Combat 18,' they replied. 'If I am a racist why have I got an Asian solicitor?' I said to them. They ignored this obvious irony. 'We believe you have been attending football matches and using this as a pretext to plant bombs around the country.' I was stunned. Then it hit me. The day before a bomb had gone off in London. A gay pub in Soho had been blown up. It was linked to two other bombs that had gone off earlier that month, one in Brixton and another on Brick Lane in London. I was worried now. They said they knew we were guilty and some of the others had admitted it. They told me that we were looking at 20 years in prison each. They accused me of planning to bomb the Lozells Road in Handsworth. It was madness! My favourite Indian restaurant is on the Lozells Road. I kept on denying it, what else could I do? I was innocent. I'd never been a member of the BNP or the National Front, let alone trying to bomb the shit out of innocent people. I'd grown up in Birmingham for God's sake. Yes I was patriotic, but I'd defy anyone to grow up in 60s/70s Birmingham and be racist, it's almost impossible! I have black friends, they couldn't believe what had happened to me either.

Mr D: They started firing these ridiculous accusations at me. 'Mr B is the master bomb maker isn't he?' I replied, 'Mr B struggles to tie his shoelaces never mind anything else!' they continued, 'You were part of the team which were going to plant the bomb, one of your targets was St Andrews (Birmingham City's ground not the golf course) wasn't it? This was getting ridiculous now. I was getting pissed off. I replied, 'Mate, it's a cracking idea that, bombing St Andrews, but sadly, it wasn't one of mine.'

Mr C: They gave me access to a solicitor. He looked like a spotty little kid. I'd asked for Rumpole of the Bailey and he turned up. He came in and said 'Hello, how are you?' I looked at him open mouthed and said 'Er, not very well as you can imagine,' He just told me to say 'No comment' to everything they asked me. He looked like a spotty little kid and he was as annoying as one. He was annoying the police who he constantly pestered telling them they couldn't do this and they couldn't do that. That's when the worrying kind of stopped. I had someone who knew their stuff on my side.

Mr B: The normal coppers were alright to be honest, they were fetching me fish and chips and food from local shops. I didn't realise how much trouble I was in until the Sunday morning. The copper in charge of the cells had a newspaper. I asked him if I could have a quick look. I wanted to know how the Villa had got on. It had in big headlines on the front. It said that a youth aged 23 had been arrested in connection with the nail bombings which had taken place recently. I said to him 'Fucking hell mate, he's in a lot of trouble isn't he?' 'I should say so,' said the copper. Not long afterwards I was taken to be interviewed. It was then that I realised it was me the paper had been referring to! My solicitor came to see me before the interview, 'You know the score here don't you?' he asked, 'Yeah mate, no comment all the way,' I replied, 'If I were you, I'd be as helpful as you can, this is very serious,' he told me.

They interviewed me. They told me I was in New Street station that morning to carry out a bomb attack. I was stunned by the stupidity of it all. 'Mate, I was going to Man United! If I was going to bomb New Street station do you really think I'd be standing in there?' I asked him. They then accused me of being some kind of master bomb-maker.

I laughed at that. 'To be honest mate I can't make a sandwich without hurting myself, never mind make a bomb,' everyone in the room smiled at this, except me. They were trying to tell me I was the brains behind the operation. Anyone who knows me knows how ridiculous that is.

Mr A: They questioned us for ages. All of a sudden their attitudes changed. They seemed to know they'd made a mistake. They started to offer me drinks and were telling me we wouldn't be held much longer. Then we were released. They kept our clothes. I've tried to take legal action against them since, but to no avail. I know it's still on my police record. I've had it mentioned by police since. I've even heard them say 'Here comes one of Villa's nail bombers!' at an airport while I was on my way to an England match. Some of it has obviously stuck and it's not right. It was all lies. We were all released without charge. We were told they would be contacting us again once our clothing had been analysed. All our houses were raided and trashed. They had ripped the floorboards up. Our families had been terrified. No more action was taken. I have never received my clothing back. I was annoyed because I was wearing a cracking pair of trainers.

Mr B: At one stage they were going to take us in front of a judge to get permission to hold us for longer. They wanted to transfer us to London. I was really starting to worry, this was bigger than I could have ever imagined. While we were held they raided my Mothers house. They ripped it to pieces. They started on the Saturday and left armed police on over-night guard and came back on the Sunday. My Mom was selling the house at the time. I think they knocked about 20 grand off the value in one foul swoop.

During this operation houses in Northfield, Rubery, Weoley Castle, Aldridge and Sutton Coldfield were raided. Unknown to the group in question on the 30th of April, the night before the arrests, a man was arrested for the bombings of Brixton, Brick Lane and the Admiral Duncan pub in Old Compton Street central London. David Copeland admitted the bombings and was sentenced to life imprisonment.

Nosey Parkers 2000

Kas: There was a bar in Digbeth called Nosey Parkers. It was used by Blues a lot. One night I was around there with a bird and decided I'd pop in for a drink. I went to the bar for a drink while this bird sat down at a table. While I was waiting at the bar five Asian blokes approached me. 'You're Villa,' one of them said. 'Yeah that's right mate I am,' I replied. He continued, 'You're Asian, what the fuck are you doing hanging around with

Fowler and the rest of those Combat 18 cunts?' 'They ain't C18,' I replied. I knew that it was on top but I wasn't going to disappear and leave the bird. I sat down with the drinks and they went back to where they had been sitting. I went to the toilet. As I walked into the toilet I was grabbed from behind. The five of them had followed me in and were now dragging me into the cloakroom. There was a stair case they were trying to throw me down. I was fighting back but there was too many of them. I was bleeding they had cut my head open. I managed to run out. I ended up in hospital and had 15 stitches in my head. The annoying thing, there was other geezers in there who I knew. If they had known what was going on it would have been a different story. But they didn't, they couldn't see what was happening. They were boasting about it afterwards I heard. That's Blues for you eh? They did one Villa fan, on my own and it's a result for them.

May 18th 2002 the Sting, the Sunday Mercury

We had always had lads who had sent spoof letters to the local papers. The letters section in the Birmingham Evening Mail was always a favourite. They seemed to print anything. It started out with genuine letters being sent in. The author would sign it as one of our lads. It was an in-joke. One of the lads would be reading the letters column and see their name at the bottom. Mostly, at first they were signed from Steve Baker. He knew nothing about them until he saw them in the Mail or was told 'he'd' written another one. It was just a bit of a laugh. Most were about the Villa, but it was evolving. One letter read:

No time for John! A letter in your column last week stated that we should give John Gregory more time as it took Alex Ferguson 12 years to get to where he is today with his team. I would not give Gregory another 12 hours!

S Baker, Birmingham.

Another read:

Well done John Gregory! Finally getting Benito Carbone to sign. Now watch all the moaners come back in their droves. I suppose then the letters pages will be full of those people moaning that they can't get into the ground. Well, that's their fault. They should've renewed their season tickets and have faith in the best Villa manager in recent times.

S Baker, Birmingham.

I Windrup was a regular contributor to the letters page. I Windrup, it comes up as wind-up on spell-check. They didn't spot it. He wrote on one occasion that he thought the club should:

Price the idiots out of football! Many people have complained about the price of admission to football matches but I think the prices are too low. I recently had the misfortune of sitting through 90 minutes of foul and abusive language. (The author of the letter was known for his foul and abusive language at matches) It is high time we priced these morons out of the game and got back to the days when the elderly and families could enjoy a match in comfort.

I Windrup, Stratford.

All Change! I recall that many years ago Leeds United changed their kit to all white in an attempt to achieve the successes of Real Madrid who did so well in those colours. Perhaps Villa should change to the red and white of treble winners Manchester United. They could retain some of the claret and blue in the trim to appease the die-hards.

I Windrup, Stratford

It was amazing the Evening Mail believed it all, that someone could think like that. We had loads of letters printed. It wasn't just the Mail however. The letters received angry replies from fellow Villa fans on the subject. It seemed they would print anything. The media, especially the local press had a different attitude to the Hardcore. Some of them seemed to have a grudge against us. In the summer of 2001 a journalist wrote a piece of fiction saying that we had plans to attend an England-Pakistan cricket match and cause trouble there. It was untrue. We had in fact booked to go to Crete while the cricket match was being played. The England football team was playing Greece in a Qualifying match. They'd obviously believed the rumours which were circulating about us. They had picked out the next sporting event where trouble might occur and blamed us for it before it had even happened. To be honest I got the raving hump about it. They were lies. They were keen to bracket us as racist right-wingers who wanted to incite racial aggravation wherever we went. Some of the lads were now using the internet, there was a bit of a football lads scene starting on the net. We had our own website which had a message board. We'd noticed that a couple of times what had been posted on the message board would find its way into either the Sunday Mercury or the Birmingham Evening Mail. You'd get allsorts of comments on this message boards. They were usually the 'we're going to smash you' bollocks from other teams. One day a poster appeared on the Villa Hardcore message board. He called himself 'Shaka Zulu' and talked of a gang called the Demolition Boyz from Nechells in Birmingham. He claimed this mob followed Blues and would be waiting for us at the next fixture between the two clubs. He mentioned a Bristol Branch and a meeting they were going to have. The post also mentioned members such as Cridgey, Mossy and Baggy. Some of our lads on the net jumped on this a bit. They started posting on the message boards as 'Mossy' and 'Cridgey'. They'd post outrageous claims but also would occasionally add a reasonable sounding post in order to make them seem genuine. They were basically making fun of the original post on our board by 'Shaka Zulu'. These posts gradually developed. A new character was invented, 'Nechells Neville' spokesman for the BCFC Demo Boyz. Other posters gradually joined the fray. People started posting as 'Jermaine, Tito and Randy.' The lads were just having a laugh. They were bouncing posts off each other just taking the piss really. The posts became more and more ridiculous and bizarre. A scenario developed, 'Cridgey' and 'Baggy' became crack dealers from Bristol. They also raised funds for Loyalist prisoners in Ulster. Nechells Neville was a budding DJ and had composed a reggae version of 'The Sash my Father Wore'. Jermaine was a younger member of the crew. He had recently got the sack from a fast-food chain. He had been sent to work for the 'Bristol Branch' in a desperate attempt to put him on the straight and narrow. If a blatantly stupid post was made, people would say, 'That's someone imitating the Demo Boyz!' They would ask for the real 'Cridgey' or 'Mossy' to come on the board and have their say. People really started to believe the Demo Boyz existed. You even had Villa lads who knew about it replying in anger to a Demo Boyz post. It added to the illusion. We realised that although a lot of people had sussed it was a wind-up some people were starting to take the Demo Boyz seriously. There was trouble at an Aberdeen versus Glasgow Rangers match one Sunday. Some Aberdeen had gone onto the pitch and attacked Rangers fans. The Demolition Boyz immediately went onto the internet and claimed responsibility for the trouble. Someone claimed that the Demo Boyz had been at the match. They had been major players. After all they had links with far-right groups, a reggae version of the Sash and often travelled the country supporting Rangers, Linfield and Chelsea. Obviously we thought we'd gone too far. The Demo Boyz was shelved because it was thought it had run its course. The scenario was just too ridiculous. No-one would buy all that surely even the dimmest of internet posters were cottoning on now. We didn't reckon on an eager reporter at The

Sunday Mercury. He bought the story hook, line and sinker. The next Sunday the Demolition Boyz had a three page spread in the Sunday Mercury.

Birmingham City hooligans travelled more than 400 miles to riot at a match in Scotland the Sunday Mercury can reveal. The thugs are thought to have joined a mob of English supporters with right-wing links at the Rangers FC game with Aberdeen. One chilling website a message bragged about joining their so called 'Weegi' cousins to take part in the disgraceful scenes which blighted the Saturday night match at Aberdeen's Pittodrie ground.

The live televised match was stopped after 20 minutes when fighting broke out. It was the worst case of football violence seen north of the border in 20 years. The Sunday Mercury has now discovered sick boasts on an unofficial hooligan website which claims members of the Birmingham City Demolition Boyz, a notorious hooligan gang, were also at the match. One said, 'Just watched the Rangers Aberdeen match on telly and saw my mates on TV - it's about time us Blue-noses showed we still have teeth across the border. The Sunday Mercury has now discovered sick boasts on an internet website which claim that members of the Birmingham City Zulu's, a notorious hooligan gang, were also at the match. One message says that a breakaway crew of Zulu ruffians called the Demolition Boys were involved in the horrific scenes. 'Just remember where you heard it first, BCFC Demolition Boys.' It goes on to explain: 'This season has seen the re-forming of the original Demo Boys - one of the most active elements of Blues fans. We were around before the Zulu's started and since reforming we have certainly left our mark.' The most chilling message though is one which asserts the travelling yobs may have links to far right-wing organisations and Northern Irish terror groups. It states, 'Yeah quite a few Blues go up to see Rangers. I was given a key-ring saying Rangers RSC and Birmingham Loyal! No surrender!' We have forwarded this information to Grampian Police who have launched a massive investigation into the trouble and 30 officers are now trawling through hours of CCTV and television footage frame by frame. The police last night thanked the Sunday Mercury for passing over the information. 'We have not got any information at the moment regarding Birmingham fans so we would be interested in seeing what you have. If this stuff shows they were involved in or planning violence we would like to look at it. We will also contact West Midlands police.' A spokesman for West Midlands Police said: 'We are liaising with the police in Scotland, but we have no evidence that people from Birmingham were involved in this particular incident.' A spokesman for the National Criminal Intelligence

Service said it did not cover Scotland but added: 'We keep an open mind but are very interested in receiving any intelligence which will help us keep violence out of the game.' Ellis Cashmore, a Professor in Culture, Media and Sport of Staffordshire University said: 'You could not get any further away from Birmingham - but perhaps that is the hooligans intention. They know they will be heavily policed in the West Midlands and so they have picked a location where they are not so well known. It's almost a displacement of hooligans - you can even fly to these matches. We have a World Cup this year and perhaps they will fly there. Perhaps we have entered the age of the jet hooligan.'

Misinformation, that's what it was. If you say something enough times people will start to believe it. We had experienced that ourselves with the accusations people, the press and the police included, had been aiming at us. We had turned the tables. It's something which still goes on to some extent. As a derby day approaches people will be coming up with ideas how we can wind the press up. It has to be pretty good to get in these days as they have now become wise to us.

Chapter Seven: You Know the Score - We're Villa Hardcore

Aston Villa Vs Sunderland 1st February 1997

Sunderland were back in the top flight. Always a tough proposition up there but they hadn't really shown at Villa since the very early 80's. It was the usual crowd in the Peg. The usual crowd bar me and Jonesy. We were doing the door at the Witton Arms. The Witton was solely for away fans really those days. They were charged a pound to get in for a drink before the match. Jonesy and I would do the door, occasionally Steamy would lend a hand. We managed to do both sides of the pub on our own. They now employ a team of bouncers to do the same job.

Tucker: I knew Sunderland were in the Cabin. It's just over the road from the Square Peg. I went in and had a look. There was a small firm of them in there. As they left the pub I followed them. I was on the phone to the lads in the Peg. I said, 'Lads, stand behind the doors in there. Let them come in, they don't know what they're walking in to!' The lads couldn't wait though. As Sunderland turned the corner the lads emptied the pub. Sunderland shit it, they didn't have the numbers. We chased them everywhere. We caught a few of them. Some of them ran into a jewellers shop and tried to vault the counter. We had to stop slapping them in the end. Nobby was running around saying, 'Leave them now, we're not Blues!' That hit home. They'd had a slap, anymore would've been bullying.

Dandy: We spotted them coming. We went out to meet them. It was a strong showing for us that day. We flooded out. Sunderland clocked the numbers coming out to greet them and stopped. Some stood their ground. The others were on their toes. We flooded out and literally engulfed them. Some were chased into the adjacent shops with Villa fans in hot pursuit.

Stan: When we emptied out of the pub they didn't hang around. Some of them tried to stand but they were eventually on their toes. I remember some ran into a shop. I followed them and one stood in front of me. I chinned him. I remember Skinhead Neil running around shouting to us to leave them alone as they'd had enough. We stopped and let them fuck off.

Tucker: After the match a mini-bus was passing the Vine, it was the same lads although we didn't realise until afterwards. It got stuck in the after match traffic and it was smashed up. They managed to drive off in the end. That was bad luck we thought, bumping in to us twice in one day. We then travelled up to town. We were in the Square Peg. There were about 40 of us. Guess who came round the corner again? Yeah, it was Sunderland. A lad called Little Justin was with them, I've met him since. He asked if I remembered him, I did. They came back for another pop at us. We mullered them. We chased them all over the town. Some of them ran to their van. We totalled it, we wrote the van off. We were then going to go up to Mere Green for Screws leaving do. We saw Sunderland in some sort of police escort being led into the station. We got to know Sunderland really well after that. A few of them are in regular contact with us. Fowler and I were invited up for the Sunderland-Newcastle local derby game and one of them recently flew over to Spain for my 40th birthday party, good lads.

Danny Hutton: You can't knock Sunderland that day - they had 3 goes at us. There were 3-4 vanloads of them. They had a pop at the Square Peg in the morning. They landed at The Vine on the Lichfield Road after the match. Then they came back to the Peg on the evening to have another go! Fair play to them. I remember when we chased them the third and final time, shoppers were scattering everywhere as we piled out of the Peg. We chased them down towards Moor Street train station where they had parked their vans. We totally trashed the vans. They were certainly in no state to be driven back to the North-East.

Nottingham Forest Vs Aston Villa 22nd February 1997

We took two vans to Nottingham Forest. We'd had trouble there the last couple of seasons. In my opinion Forest must be one of the most over-rated firms in the country. They have never made the 50 mile trip to Villa Park as a mob. We've had it with them in Nottingham and away with England a few times but they'll only come for it at home if they outnumber you. I had my nose broken for the first time in Nottingham in August 1989. We had visited Nottingham the season before and had a battle with them during the match. We intended to do the same thing again. This time however the police were ready for us.

Big Tony: We had about 80 in Nottingham city centre. We were walking round during the match. I was with Liam. Liam and I walked down a one-way street in the city centre. All of a sudden Forest turned the corner. It was a small mob of them. I think

they were avoiding our main firm. We stood and they jumped on us. Liam ended up having his head put through a car window. They gave us a kicking.

The year before that we hadn't gone to the match and had hung around outside pubs in the area. We had bumped into Forest on a bridge near the ground and one of them had jumped into the road, pulled a knife and shouted 'Come on Villa, do you want some of this?' Unfortunately he'd forgotten his highway code and was immediately run over by a car. The driver hadn't expected some knife wielding lunatic to jump out in front of him with his back turned. As soon as the car hit the Forest fan we were on top of them. Screw ran in with this screwdriver that Fowler had found and we steamed them. Obviously ignoring the casualty who had been run over, we chased Forest down the road. People might rate Forest, or might have rated Forest in the past; we don't however. They've never showed once at Villa Park. When you see them in Nottingham or with England they've always got Mansfield and a host of other clubs tagging along with them.

Screw: I'd got my nickname 'Screwdriver' from the same game the previous season, Fowler had given me a screwdriver he'd found in the toilets on top of a condom machine. I'd run into some Forest on a bridge not far from the ground and used it while the game was on. I also got arrested that day. I head-butted someone. I received a £300 fine for that.

We landed in the city centre. We parked up the two vans. I was driving one of them. I wasn't drinking at the time due to training. We walked round looking for Forest. A few of our lads who had travelled independently in cars or on the train approached us. Forest were round the corner in a pub. They had a full pub. Numbers looked to be in their favour. That didn't deter us. We headed straight for them. As we neared the pub we were met by the police. Flynnie our football intelligence officer was with them. One of the Nottingham police shouted, 'Right, you lot! That way, now! We're not having you Villa bastards causing trouble here again!' They marched us in the opposite direction and put us in a pub near to the canal area. No-one, not even normal punters were allowed to leave the pub once we were in there. Gradually some of our stragglers and any loose Villa they could find in the city-centre were brought to the pub. We stayed there until kick-off. We were escorted to the ground. We tried our old trick, 'We're not here to go to the match mate. We've just come for a drink.' We tried this the year before. That had led to the knife-wielding Forest fan getting run over. We had toured the local pubs during the game. They weren't having it this time. The old bill issued an ultimatum, 'You either pay in and watch the game or we're going to arrest the lot of you!' Well not much choice there then. We paid into the ground and watched the game. It was an uninspiring 0-0 draw. We decided it was too easy for the old bill to keep tags on us if we stayed together. We decided to split up and meet back at the pub by the canals. We had a few drinks and discussed what our next move would be. The police had surrounded the place. We decided it was pointless us staying in Nottingham. They had got some lads out but with the number of police surrounding the pub we were not going anywhere. The police had decided we were not moving anywhere unless it's on the M42 back to Birmingham. 'Leicester is just down the road. They've got Derby today. They'll have some boys out. Let's go and row with them!' said Oldie. I approached Spit the Dog (PC McMahon, our other intelligence officer). I told him we'd had enough and had decided to cut our losses and return to Brum. 'You aren't going anywhere without us, not even to fetch the vans. We'll take you,' he told me. The other driver and I were taken to fetch the vans. We headed back and pick up the rest of the lads back at the pub. We're escorted out of Nottingham with a full police escort, lights flashing. 'They'll follow us all the way back to Birmingham!' someone said. They didn't. As soon as we hit the M1 they left us. We were on a straight road to Leicester.

Fowler: They always get hold of us at Forest. It's a waste of time going really. Their police always seem to find us and hold on to us. Oldie said, 'Hey Fowl, Leicester are playing Derby today!' I said 'Fuck it, that's what we'll do. We'll go and land on Leicester!' We headed towards Leicester. It wasn't far down the motorway. The old bill escorted us out of Nottingham. They thought we were no longer a threat. We were thinking 'Bollocks to you, we're off to Leicester!'

We landed in the city centre. We were buzzing with excitement. We plotted up in a pub near the post-office sorting centre. Fowler, Oldie and Steeley went to have a scout around and see what the score was with Leicester or Derby. They returned and told us that Derby were long gone. They had been escorted out of town. Leicester were in large numbers at a pub in the city centre.

Fowler: We went down to one of their main pubs to have a look. We came to one pub and I walked in and had a look. When I got in I thought 'Bingo!' It was full of lads. I went back to the pub where the lads were and said, 'Right, let's go, we know where

they are!' I saw some cuttings from the local paper after this incident which Oldie had saved. The Landlord of the pub said, 'All these lads were sitting in my pub. Someone popped their head round the door and said 'Right we're off!' My whole pub got emptied, pool balls, chairs, the lot!'

Steeley: I walked down to the pub with Fowler and Oldie to have a look. We knew we were going to do it whatever we found down there. It was still better to go and look to see what we would be dealing with. It was packed when we got there. We looked through the windows. It was full of lads, all their firm.

'We're mad going there!' said Oldie 'There's a pub full of them, they've had a local derby and they've got all their boys out!' Fowler was having none of it, 'Look, we've come for a fight and we're going to have a fight. No-one here will run. We can more than match them. We have the element of surprise. Who will be expecting Villa to turn up? This will fucking hurt Leicester' Bruno had an ashtray in each hand, he opened his arms and exclaimed, 'I don't want to hurt them, I want to fucking kill them!' While saying this he brought his arms together smashing the two ashtrays into each other. 'Fancy smashing them before we even get there Bruno,' said Fowler rolling his eyes. We all piled out of the pub and into the vans. We skirted our target, which was on a pedestrian area. We parked close by. You could almost taste the anticipation as we got out of the vans. The city-centre was still relatively quiet. Fowler led us down the road to our target. You could see the flashing lights of a disco and the shadows of people inside. They were totally unaware of what was about to happen. There was no-one outside, no doormen. No-one noticed our approach. There was some hesitation when we got there. We knew we would be vastly outnumbered and some people stalled. They still hadn't noticed our arrival. Fowler took control. 'Come on are we Villa Hardcore or what?' he asked us all. He walked into the pub followed by the rest of us.

Fowler: I walked straight in the door and chinned the first lad I saw, I shouted 'come on! Let's fucking have it!' I remember them panicking. One of them shouted 'Fucking hell! It's Derby! Derby are here!' I shouted back 'Come on! We're fucking Villa!' The whole pub came at me and the lads who had gone in there. Obviously only a few of us had got in there. The rest we're still outside trying to get in. Now we've got a full pub attacking us. Glasses, bottles and chairs came flying at us. We were forced out of the pub. I remember one big geezer running towards me. I was gone by this point. I put him straight on his arse. Brilliant, the best thing about that is, when we landed there, Leicester weren't playing anyone shit. They were playing their local rivals. We, Villa

Hardcore, had landed there with 50 lads tops? We still landed there, Forest didn't land there, Derby didn't, but Villa did, brilliant.

Steeley: I went in the doors behind Fowler. He chinned the first geezer he met. A few of us followed in shouting and throwing stuff at them. They backed off at first surprised. Then they hit us with everything. They threw everything at us and we had to back off out of the pub into the street.

'Come on! We're fucking Villa! We shouted as we hit the people nearest to the door. They didn't know what had hit them and were forced back as we surged through the door. Everything came at us. Glass was flying around and you just had to shield your head and go forward. We were picking up stools and throwing them at them. There were loads of them though and we were backed out of the pub. They outnumbered us with what we'd got in total, so they certainly outnumbered us inside the pub as only a fraction of us had managed to get in there. They surged back towards us, 'Come on Derby, we're Leicester!' They still thought we were Derby. Sheer weight of numbers and their easy access to missiles forced us back into the road outside the pub. A pitched battle ensued as they tried to get out the pub and we tried to stop them leaving. We were slowly being forced back. In the end they flooded out. Fights were taking place all over the place. They were coming round the sides of us and all I could think of was the vans. I was thinking we'd have to get out of this as it was really on top. They outnumbered us two to one but we were giving a good account of ourselves. Police started to arrive in bits and drabs but couldn't get a grip on the situation as we were all spread out by this point. The police appeared to be dressing themselves and were in shirt sleeves. They'd been changing shifts. When they'd packed Derby off on the train they thought their work as far as the football went, was over for that day.

Simmo: I remember as it was going off I was put straight on my arse. I didn't see who did it. I was lying there trying to get up I could feel a couple of people grabbing at me One of our lot steamed into them and I managed to break free. When I turned and looked it was old bill that had got hold of me. I was lucky to get away.

The Police weren't really arresting anyone. They were simply trying to spli the two groups up. We were slowly but surely getting backed away from th pub by sheer weight of numbers. We must have been outnumbered 3-1 and th Police were in effect keeping us there by not allowing Leicester to get too fa into us. 'Go and get the vans Luddy! Get them ready to roll. We might have to do one here!' said Fowler. The other driver and I ran into our respective vans and started the engines. We noticed a few Leicester had come round the long way. They were approaching the vans with red and white striped planks borrowed from road works. I jumped back out from the van. Stan was the nearest I could see, I shouted him. The vans were our only means of escape. Stan and I ran at the lads. They had around 40 stone of Birmingham's finest coming at them and they shit themselves. They dropped the planks and ran. I got back into the drivers seat. Stan ran and opened the back doors. A motorcycle copper arrived at the side of the van and screamed at me to move the van. 'I'm not leaving my mates,' I told him. 'Move the fucking van, now!' he ordered. He hit me on the arm with a truncheon, 'I'm not leaving my mates!' I replied again. He hit me again. 'Move the fucking van, now! It hurt. 'I ain't leaving my fucking mates! You can hit me all you fucking like!' I shouted at him. He shook his head and gave up. They'd managed to force the other driver to leave the scene. Now it was my van which was our only means of escape. The fight was still going in the road. More and more Police were now arriving and separating the two sets of combatants. 'Villa, Villa!' the lads in the road shouted. They certainly knew who we were now. I was in and out of the van screaming at the lads to jump in. The police managed to force Leicester back down the road towards the pub. I reversed a short distance into our lads. They all jumped in the van. We were made to follow the police. We drove round and were escorted into the train station. The other van was there waiting. They took our names and asked us why we were there. 'We've just come for a drink that's all mate' we said, 'we walked into the wrong pub obviously.' They swallowed that and let us go. We divided up into the two vans and were now escorted out of Leicester back to Birmingham. The next morning Jonesy rang. 'Fucking hell, some Villa had it off in Leicester last night,' he said, 'I've just seen it on Ceefax.' He was gutted when I told him it was us.

Leicester City Vs Aston Villa 9th August 1997

Gregg: This was the first game of the season I think. We were in poor order. People were still on holiday. Fewer than 30 of us turned up to travel to this match. Still, sometimes its better travelling with 30 you know well who won't let you down rather than bigger numbers. I knew Leicester would turn out for this one. They always turned out for us and us for them. We stumbled across a fantastic football pub. It was raised

from the road with a balcony overlooking the road. Anyone coming to it had to come up the hill towards us. If Carlsberg did football pubs when you are outnumbered this would be the one. We were in this boozer for an hour and there are three lads in there. They're Leicester and one of them was on the blower to his Leicester mates. We approached them. 'Go and tell your lads we are here. We're Villa. We're here and we want it.' Within fifteen minutes a car drove past with a mixed race lad hanging out of the window. He shouted, 'We'll be back!' Well we'd have been disappointed if they weren't coming.

Jonesy: We landed at a pub called the Crows Nest. It was a pub on a main dual-carriage way which leads into Leicester proper. It was about a mile or two away from the ground. Four of the lads had tickets and they left us to go to the match. The rest plotted up in the pub. Phone calls were made to the Leicester Baby Squad to let them know of our whereabouts. The lad on the phone informed us that majority of their lads had gone to the game. He said he would be back in touch when the match finished. He would see what he could sort out. It was a beautiful sunny day and the pub was quite busy with locals. Most of us were standing outside on a patio area, which surveyed the road because it was higher up. We could see virtually the length of the road which we presumed the Babies would take to get to us.

At approximately 5-30pm the Leicester lad rang up and said he was popping up the road to have a look at what we'd got. He came up with another lad. Oldie and Fowler had a chat with him as he approached the stairs which lead you to this patio area. 'Fucking hell!' he exclaimed, 'Is this is all you've got? He shook his head as he looked at the 30 or so of us. Oldie in a slow and measured tone said, 'What you see is what you get. We're here for one thing and one thing only. I think you know what that is.' The Leicester lad smirked and said, 'Fine, give us half an hour and we'll be back.' We spent the next fifteen minutes or so preparing for their arrival. Fowler, Steff and Steve Baker had a slow walk down towards the pub where Dolby said they were. The rest of us just found as many missiles as we could. We knew we were going to be massively outnumbered. That was all part of the buzz with the Hardcore.

Simmo: I was reading a paper at the bar. Clinch, Baker and Fowler had gone down to have a look. I remember they came back in a hurry. They were swiftly followed by Leicester. 'They're coming! Leicester are coming!' I could see that, they filled the fucking road.

Tucker: There must've been hundreds of them. They were like ants! Fowler went round everyone, 'Right everyone stick together. If we run we're fucked. Everyone stand your ground!' Greg and Big Dean cleared the few Leicester fans out of the pub, we had to. We couldn't have them helping their mates when it started by firing into the back of us. A few wouldn't move. They were slapped and they moved then. Skinhead

Neil had gone to a local shop and bought some lighter fuel. The type you use with barbeques. He sprayed it all over the floor saying he was going to light it and make a wall of flame when Leicester arrived. He didn't think, obviously that it would evaporate by the time they got there.

Jonesy: We couldn't believe it; we could see them, 100 to 150 Leicester. It wasn't long before we could hear them either. 'B...S! B...S!' they chanted. It didn't take them long to get nearer. They started to cross the road and jump the railings which divided the dual carriageway. Some of our lot, Fowler, Big Dean, Nostrils and a few others made their way down the steps to meet them. Missiles, bricks, stones, bottles and road signs fill the air. A couple of our lot were caught full on by these. Big Dean had blood streaming from a head wound. 'Come on we're fucking Villa! Let's fucking have it!' we shouted. The missiles were still coming. The favour was being returned by the majority of the Hardcore on the elevated patio area. Some of their firm weren't keen on it. They split into two. The ones who did fancy it were game as anything. The two firms clashed. Leicester by sheer weight of numbers forced us back up towards the pub. Seeing this, the Leicester who were in two minds whether to join in, now streamed forward. At the top of the stairs we desperately tried to make a stand. Skinhead Neil was spraying lighter fluid onto the floor and trying to ignite it.

Simmo: A police car pulled up in the road and it was attacked by the Leicester fans. It reversed at high speed away from the hail of missiles which were raining down on the roof and bonnet. They swarmed forward into us. Big Dean had claret everywhere. They were all around us. Danny Hutton picked up a bin to throw and a load of bottles fell out. We all threw them but we couldn't stem the tide. We were pushed back into the pub. We managed to shut the doors. Someone tipped a fruit machine over in front of the doors to stop them being forced open. They were hammering the doors trying to get in at us. The windows were being put through. A massive chunk of concrete came through one of the windows.

Tucker: We were split either side of the pub holding the two sets of doors. I remember Skinhead Neil was holding the one door. He shouted, 'Fucking hell! Are we Villa or what? Let's get out into them!' He opened the doors. We all ran out, literally steamed into them. We had tables, chairs, bottles the fucking lot. They were shocked. They were tripping over themselves to get away. It was the ferocity of the whole thing as we ran into them.

Jonesy: They were on the patio area but slowly and surely they were backing off down the steps. Someone produced a chair and it was flung at the ones now remaining on the steps. They were forced down. Simmo emerged from nowhere and steamed into them. Other Villa followed. We steamed down after them. We were taking advantage of them being on the back foot now. Skirmishes broke out in the road as both firms desperately tried to gain the advantage. Fowler was standing in the middle of the road beckoning any of them to have a pop at him. The sound of police sirens filled the air. The police entered the area and we backed off up the steps. We were laughing. Insults were hurled from either side as the police divided us. The Police started to baton us forcing us back into the pub. They surrounded it. Leicester were treated in a similar fashion and made to disperse by the police. The police started asking questions, 'we were just here having a quiet drink and we were attacked,' that was the uniform excuse. Amazingly the landlord of the pub backed our story up. 'Yeah they were just having a quiet drink when Leicester fans arrived,' he confirmed our story. They made sure the area outside the pub was cleared. We had 4 or 5 people seriously injured. They were cuts from missiles mainly. Oldie's phone rang. It was the Leicester lad from earlier. 'You did well there Villa' he said, 'If you'd have had anymore you'd have done us,' 'We did do you!' said Oldie. Once our details were given to the old bill they escorted us out of Leicester in a convoy of cars and police vans.

Simmo: When the old bill landed we'd forced Leicester back onto the road. They were definitely on the back foot by the time the old bill landed. The police set their dogs on us. We all scattered but they managed to round us all up. I remember about 20 Leicester on the other side of the road. They were clapping us as the old bill held us there. It was on the ITN main news that night; they were calling it a riot.

On the following Monday the Birmingham Evening Mail reported;

VILLA FANS ARRESTED IN CLASHES
By Ross McCarthy

Police arrested 21 Villa fans after violence erupted following their team's opening day premiership clash with Leicester City.

Three Leicester supporters were also arrested and three people were hurt when the rival fans smashed pub windows and hurled street signs during violent clashes which lasted for about 10 minutes.

Police, who are appealing for witnesses, said trouble broke out at the Crow's Nest pub in King Richards Road, Leicester, shortly after the game which the home side won 1-0.

Street signs were ripped from lampposts and other street furniture was wrecked, said a police spokesman.

Detectives believe the incident may have been photographed by a member of the public and are appealing for him to contact them.

RELEASED

Detective Sergeant Stuart Prior said three people who were drinking in the pub received cuts. He confirmed that none of those involved in the clashes were injured. Those arrested were aged between 17 and 30 and have been released on police bail after being interviewed on suspicion of violent disorder, he said.

'It was serious disorder which lasted about ten minutes. The pub suffered extensive superficial damage - windows were smashed and stools broken.'

The Express and Star Monday 11th August 1997:

VILLA FANS ARRESTED IN STREET PUNCH-UP

Aston Villa fans clashed with rival supporters in a violent street brawl after the Birmingham team lost 1-0 in the first game of the season. Twenty-one Villa fans and three from Leicester City were arrested after Saturday's match.

Pub windows were smashed, and three people injured when a ten minute battle broke our shortly after the game ended. The trouble flared at the Crow's Nest pub close to Leicester's Filbert Street ground. Detective Sergeant Stuart Prior, of Leicester Police, said street signs were ripped from lampposts and other street furniture was wrecked. He said three people who were drinking in the pub suffered cuts but those involved in the clashes were not injured. 'It was a serious disturbance which lasted about 10 minutes,' he said. 'The pub suffered extensive superficial damage - a couple of windows were smashed and stools were broken. Three drinkers in the pub were cut but their injuries were not serious.'

Those arrested were aged between 17 and 30, and have been released on police bail after being interviewed on suspicion of violent disorder. Det Sgt prior added that officers would consider bringing charges after statements had been collected from witnesses.

Crystal Palace Vs Aston Villa Premier League 8th November 1997

Fowler: We were down in London. Villa were playing Crystal Palace. We were in Euston. People were arguing where we should go on the way to the game. Someone had mentioned earlier to me that Carlisle were playing Millwall that day. I said' Fuck the Villa game. Let's go to Millwall and look for Carlisle. We're going to Millwall!' The rest of them looked at me as if I was mad. Around 15 of us decided to head down and have a look round Millwall.

Simmo: No-one wanted to be there. It was mentioned on the train. Fowler told us all we were going, so we went. I'd be lying if I said we were keen.

Fowler: We caught the tube and got off at London Bridge station. We walked down towards the ground. We got to this boozer. As we approached some geezers came out. I walked up to them and said, 'Are you fuckers Carlisle?' 'Nah mate, we're not Carlisle,' the one replied, but not convincingly. We filled them in. There were about ten of them and they did one down the road. We were on a bounce then. All of a sudden two old bill appeared out of nowhere. They grabbed hold of me. They were Carlisle police. Carlisle's police had spotted me and grabbed me. 'Fowler, Fowler!' they were shouting as they grabbed hold of me. Some of the Villa lads were going, 'Come on! Let's do the old bill!' I was thinking, no, no, they know exactly who I am! Please lads don't do 'em! I was mouthing to Tucker, 'no, no!' Luckily he sussed what I meant. More police arrived and they fucked us off back to London Bridge tube station. We heard Millwall were well pissed off at us that day but we didn't intend taking the piss with them. We just went there because we wanted Carlisle.

Aston Villa Vs Middlesbrough Premier League 23rd August 1998

We didn't know but Middlesbrough lads had targeted this game as a tribute day to one of their lads. Quite a few of them had travelled down from Middlesbrough to Birmingham for the match. Unknown to us a large part of this Middlesbrough group had not attended the game. They had spent the afternoon in the Barn Social Club which is about a mile from the ground. Middlesbrough had never really travelled to Villa Park in numbers before. Up there they were a different proposition. Their old ground Ayresome Park was a really grim place to visit in the 70s and 80s.

Screwdriver: We were undecided whether to go down or not. We stood on the old ASDA car-park for a while deciding. We'd heard that they'd got a massive firm out. It numbered 200+ people were saying. We decided to go down and have a look.

There were two mobs of us that day. Some of us were coming from the ground. Others were heading down the backstreets of Witton to get to Witton Island. As we passed Witton station they'd got all the Boro fans in a long line queuing up to get onto a train. There was a large police presence around them stopping us from getting at them and vice versa. There must've been 20-30 of us floating about around this queue. The old bill started to charge into various groups of us trying to shoo us away from the station. We walked on down the road towards the Yew Tree pub. We saw it going off literally 100 yards in front of us. We ran down towards it and got involved.

Screwdriver: We walked down the back streets to get to Witton undetected. We turned left to go up to the station. All of a sudden they were in the road in front of us. I knocked the first bloke who came to me clean out. I broke my finger in the process. Fowler was getting stuck in. He chinned another. They outnumbered us but they were on the back-foot. They were dragging their lads who had gone down away from us. We were also getting steamed by other Villa fans who didn't realise we were Villa. For a few minutes it was madness.

Jez: As we walked down we could see lads coming towards us, not in an obvious mob. All of a sudden it's gone off near a bus stop on the left hand side of the road. A shout went up and it was suddenly going off in the road. We ran to get to the front and so did the rest of the Boro who were coming up the road. It was the best toe to toe punch-up I have ever been involved in down the football. It went on for a while.

Mark B: As we walked past the Boro fans waiting for the train a few words were exchanged. The police were just trying to fuck us off. We walked past a van load of old bill, they just let us carry on. We found out later they were well aware that there was a big mob of Boro drinking in the Barn Social Club. I think they let us carry on thinking we'd bump into these Boro and they'd teach us a bit of a lesson. They didn't. When it went off down the road they let a number of Boro break off the back of the queue for the train to join in the fight. When it was going off they took their time coming down. It's obvious what happened that day. The police tried to set us up.

Jez: They were game and so were we. It must have gone on for five minutes. The fighting was all in the middle of the road. The old bill didn't bother rushing down from the station. I think they knew the Boro were down there and thought we'd get a bit of a kicking. They literally hated us by this point for the trouble we'd been causing at Villa matches. The one thing I remember is a Judas punch Mark B gave one of the Middlesbrough main lads.

Mark B: I'd steamed into them and found myself in the middle of their mob. Our lads were still running into them so they'd forgotten about me. I was trying to get back to our lads when I saw the one standing right at the front beckoning our lads on. I ran towards the Villa making out I was Boro and I hit him from the side, a proper Judas punch. He went down like a sack of spuds and I ran back into our group and turned and faced the Boro again for another go.

Aston Villa Vs Leicester City Premier League 24th October 1998

Leicester had to go some to beat our achievement at their place the season before. Leicester are severely underrated. They've always been game at home, or they have for out visits anyway. They've always tried to bring a mob to Villa Park. In 1985 they brought a decent sized firm to Villa and even brought it to us on Aston Park, which very few teams ever did. That day we ran them all the way into Handsworth. We even attacked their police escort as the police brought them back into Witton. I was arrested that day as we attacked the escort at the bottom of Bevington Road. They have always been game and we have always matched their eagerness. For this one I was doing the door of the old Witton Arms before the game with my mate Steamy.

Tucker: What a mistake this was, we seriously underestimated Leicester for this one. It was a birthday trip for one of their lads. They had the numbers out. Two coach loads if I remember rightly, about 100 lads. We shouldn't have gone. We talked ourselves into it, or rather some of us did. I was probably the worst culprit. 'Come on let's go down now, we'll take them with what we've got,' and stuff like that. We simply shouldn't have gone for it with what we had. 20 to 30 of us tops. Then it started, 'Come on it's only Leicester!' That kind of did it. We left the Square Peg to go and meet them.

Greg: I loved matches against Leicester. One of ours knew one of their lads and we managed to sort it out for something like 5 years on the trot. Home and away we had it with them. I loved it. You always new something would go on when we played Leicester. It even went at times when we weren't playing them!

Fowler: We were at the Square Peg. All the lads were slowly drifting in. Some of the lads were going, 'Leicester are here. Come on Fowl lets go down there!' I was saying, 'No, there are not enough of us yet, lets hold on for a bit.' In the end, I shouldn't have but I said, 'Come on then, let's go!' It was a stupid thing to do, one of the silliest things I think we've done.

Greg: Our spotters told us they were in a pub called The Bulls Head not far from the Ben Johnson. Sound we thought, we can get round the back over the waste ground and attack the pub. We made our way down and approached the pub. We got to within 50 metres and out they came. They were game as fuck. Fowler was screaming at our lot to stop throwing stuff at them. He wanted to let them get closer to us. For a good minute the sky was full of bottles and all sorts of objects flying over my head from both sides. The front lines of both sides seemed more concerned with dodging glasses than getting stuck into each other. One twat from Leicester, who was wearing a stupid, floppy eared hat, came at me. He was swinging fucking nun-chucks. He knew how to use them properly as well. He wasn't a pissed up kid smashing his own elbows to bits. He was wielding these in proper Bruce Lee style. I looked at him, I then looked at Fowler. I gave it the old two-step shuffle away from him round to the other side of Fowler. I remember thinking, Fowler he can have the row. I decided that he could deal with Bruce Lee. I'll have the fat kid with the vase.

Fowler: I had said to one of them on the blower, that we were coming but not with tools. No fucking tools I had said and he'd agreed. They came out tooled up to fuck and we had fuck all.

We were probably too honest at times, we'd turn up somewhere with whatever numbers we had and let them know where we were and that we were up for it. No matter what the numbers. We went to Bolton one year. I think it was a Sunday game. We landed at this pub about twelve of us. We didn't know we'd been spotted but the old bill phoned the place. They told the landlord to stop serving. When we got outside half of the Greater Manchester Police must've been out there, plus our two police spotters. I overheard one of the Manc police say as we filed out of the pub, 'Is that all there is?' Flynnie said to him, 'there may not be many of them but they're fucking dangerous!' That made me laugh. We turned up and we had it regardless of who it was we were playing or how many of us there were. One of the obvious disadvantages to smaller numbers was obviously that the police got to know you that little bit better. To combat that we just devised different ways of travelling and different routes. Most of the police don't take it personally. You find that if they just do their job they do it better it most cases. If we knew they were taking it personally we made that little bit more effort to outwit them. In those days they had the normal working-class type bobby attached to you. At the end of the 90s they started to introduce these straight out of university middle-class types who just didn't understand our mentality.

Tucker: I remember the press cuttings the day after. The gaffer of the pub said they were dismantling chairs and tables to take out to use against us. It seemed like they had a never ending supply.

Screwdriver: They thought I was Fowler for some reason. They were pointing at me shouting 'Get Fowler!' I was shouting 'I ain't fucking Fowler!' I remember one of their lads was taking pictures of us on the back-foot. He was laughing as he was taking the pictures of us getting backed off. I just couldn't help but smile.

Pete Mc: They threw everything at us that day. I have never seen anything like it. I remember standing there with Little Dek and Seth. Leicester emptied the pub of all collectables, vases, figurines and Toby jugs. I even saw a yard of ale thrown at us. They had a mega firm out and they done us on the day. Little Dek ran into them and he got clattered good and proper. A few of us stood and tried to throw back what they'd just launched at us. We had no chance the rain of missiles was just too much.

Fowler: We were backing off. We were not running, I stood to the side and I could see our old bill with Leicester's old bill standing across the road watching. This was pre-video camera days. They shouted, 'Stay there Fowler!' I shouted 'Fuck off!' I did one. We got done, what can I say. We did, we admit it and it's nothing to be ashamed of.

Screwdriver: A lone motorcycle policeman mounted the pavement, drove his bike into one of our lads. He was knocked off his bike as he did this, whether purposely or by accident I don't know. He came in the Peg later to identify some of us for knocking him off. Loz was pulled out and I think he was charged for it but it wasn't him that did it.

Jonesy: We were forced back up the other side of the subway towards the fire station. We could see the back of the Leicester mob still coming through the subway. They were chanting the familiar 'B...S! B...S!' Running battles again broke out as Leicester

emerged from the subway. We started to have a go at them. Typically then the police turned up. They managed to get in between the two groups and forced ours back into town. We were fuming, Fowler was going bananas. We had just been done on our own doorstep! They did a number on us, fair play to them.

Greg: Naturally we had an inquest with people falling out. The conclusion was that it was only one o'clock in the day and we still had time to put this right. I went down to see the barmaids in the Bulls Head. They told me the coach was booked one way so that ruled out waiting for them there after the match.

Jonesy: No-one bothered going to the game. We all sat in the Witton Arms during the match. There were around 60 of us. We were desperate to even things up. We decided it was too dangerous to attack them straight after the match because of the police. We decided to go into town straight after the match to try and bump into them there.

Jez: We caught the train up to New Street from Witton. As soon as we got onto the station concourse we saw they were in the Rail Bar. We tried to storm the place. We put the windows through and steamed it. They fought back to stop us getting in but they were shitting it in my opinion. We were so up for it was untrue because of what happened earlier.

Jonesy: There was a few Leicester milling about. They made themselves known. One of their main lads fronted us. Irish Jim with his shovel hands put him straight on his arse. We were still attacking the Rail Bar. Windows were being put through but stiil Leicester wouldn't come out. More police arrived. We were baton charged by them into the station itself. We decided we couldn't get back into the station. We decided to head toward the Bar St Martin, a traditional Birmingham City stronghold. If Blues were in there we'd trash the place if not we'd have a drink and see what happened. Just as we were leaving the station two van loads of police arrived. They baton charged us. We realised they were not messing about, proper West Midlands Police 'Bastard Squad' tactics. They were really steaming into us and we started to have a pop back. They were trying to make us move. When we didn't they were hitting us. A few lads had a pop back and we ran the police back toward the station at first. However more showed up and suddenly we were in full retreat. They nicked a few of us.

Aston Villa Vs Manchester United Premier League
5th December 1998

Fowler: We were in the Briar Rose. When I got there everyone was going, 'Man U are up there Fowl, Man U are up there!' There were about 20 of us. I said to them, 'Man United are going to have a right mob up there, you do realise that?' 'Yeah, yeah,' they were going. 'We'll do them Fowl, we can do them!' So I went 'Right, Baker, you're coming with me. We're going up there to call it on,' Baker was going, 'Fucking hell, why me?' We walked into the pub at the top of New Street called Henry's. It was a big pub and it was rammed with United. There were loads of them. We walked in and walked to the bar. I ordered two halves of lager. I've got this thing about half glasses. If you're in a row in a pub a pint glass just shatters. A half glass is thicker so it doesn't shatter so easily. You can do a lot more damage with a half glass. 'We're in trouble Fowl, they've clocked us!' Baker said to me. I told him to just relax. One of them came over to us saying 'Good day today eh lads? 'What d'you mean mate?' I asked him. 'The football, United winning, good day eh lads,' he replied. 'Sorry mate I don't follow football,' I said to him. He went off and Baker and I went and sat down. You could see them all looking at us. We finished our drinks and went to the door. A load of them followed us out. I turned round and said, 'Hang on lads, what you doing? There are only two of us. Listen, we're Villa, so what? Are you going to land on just the two of us? Is that what you're about is it? Listen there's a load of us down the road, round the corner. Come down the road and let's get it on, in two minutes alright?' They were well up for it. We went back to the pub. I said to the 20 lads in there, 'Right, they're on their way!'

Dandy: 'Fucking hell lads there's about a hundred of them,' Fowler said. 'We'll have our work cut out here! When they come,' he continued, 'get into the road and spread out, make it look like there are loads of us.' I couldn't believe it. I thought he was winding us up at first. There was about a 100 of them. There were fourteen of us and he's called it on with them? It was madness but none of us could back down. We were like that. No matter what the numbers we'd always take it to other side. Fowler, Jez, Baker, Mark B, Fordey, Greeny, CC, Ginge, Skinhead Neil, myself and four other lads waited for them to arrive. Someone, I can't remember who, was watching from the door. They shouted, 'They're here!'

Fowler: A spotter came round for them. I walked down the small hill to meet him. He started backing away, I said, 'What you doing? You and me, we'll have it here now!' He ran back up towards Henry's. We knew they were coming then. Suddenly they came flooding round the corner. They were shouting, 'United! United!' I shouted to the lads, 'Spread out! Spread out lads! Come on!' We steamed towards them. They just turned and ran away from us! As we were chasing them I was thinking, 'Fucking hell this isn't right.' You could see the ones at the bottom of the hill clocking how many of us there really were.

Dandy: United were at the bottom of the road. There was a slight hill leading down to them. We spread out across the road. We threw a load of bottles and glasses which we'd got from the pub and charged down the road towards them. There were loads of United but we ran at them. A few stood but most of them ran. It was dark. The street we were on was dimly lit. It must've looked like there were more of us than there was. We charged at them and they were on their toes. We emerged onto New Street, which was better lit and chased them about 100 yards.

Fowler: The ones at the back were screaming to them to stop running. 'Stand United, stand! There's not that many of them!' They all eventually realised what was going on. They then turned and ran back towards us. We had to back off. It seemed like there were hundreds of them. They swarmed back towards us. We were fighting with them but they backed us towards the pub. We knew then that we had got to get back to the pub.

Dandy: They were all around us. We had to retreat. We ran all the way back up inside the pub. There was a bloke and a bird sitting down by the window. I went over to their table and picked up this massive glass ashtray which was in the middle. 'Hey! We haven't finished with that,' said the bloke. 'You'd better move,' I said to them. 'Why?' said the bloke. As he said that the windows exploded. They swarmed around the entrance to the pub. They put all the windows through. They were battering at the door to get in. Skinhead Neil had wisely locked the door. They were trying to get through the windows which they had put through. We were throwing everything at them to keep them out. The door finally went through and one of them came in. He didn't last long. We were emptying the pub of everything we could throw at them.

Fowler: It's always the same isn't it? Football lads will swarm round a pub. They put all the windows through, great. It takes someone special to actually go in there. The reason being, they know they'll get glassed to fuck. Whoever goes through that door is going to get hurt. You could have ten geezers waiting behind the door. It doesn't matter how many of you there are outside. Whoever goes through that door is going to get seriously hurt.

I saw Jez by an emergency exit at the side. I shouted to him 'What the fuck you doing over there Jez?' he shouted back, 'They're trying to come through here as well Fowl!' That did make me laugh. We were under siege.

Dandy: I picked up a table with Skinhead Neil. Neil and I ran at them with the table to force them out of the doorway. You could hear sirens above all the noise. They started to disperse once the police started to arrive. You could hear them having a bit of a battle with the police further down the road. Funny thing was, when we'd run in the pub it was packed. It was absolutely rammed with people. Now when we turned round the pub was empty. It was totally empty there wasn't even any bar staff left in there. They'd all run out of the back doors which we now did to escape the police. We ran out of a fire exit and up an alleyway which led us onto Pigeon Park. We walked across the park and got into taxis. The next day in the Sunday Mercury it reported the incident. It said the perpetrators had literally vanished into the night. A good little battle that was, even though it went tits up. I think we deserved the credit that night for taking it to United with such small numbers.

Ben Johnson December 19th 1998

Jason: It was my birthday. My brother Dino, a lad called Danny joined me in a pub called the Ben Johnson. We were up the bar sitting on stools. It was the early evening around 7-30ish when we got there. We'd been out drinking most of the afternoon and were well on our way. We were drinking Tequila and a beer called Jaeger-meister which is like rocket fuel. We didn't notice but there were a few Blues in there. About six of them with three birds in tow. We were loud and we had a bit of a sing song towards the end of the night. There were a few people in the pub because there was a private party going on upstairs in a function room. We got invited to party, but we decided to stay downstairs. We thought there was just the three of us left in there and one of the regulars. He was Scottish as I recall.

It was getting late. Everyone had gone upstairs to the party. We were now sitting in an alcove near the toilets. There were a couple of alcoves. We were sitting in one and the regular was sitting in the other. I stood up to go to the toilet. As I stood up I saw a group of six blokes coming towards me. They were led by a black geezer who I now know is Garry Williams. 'You fucking Villa Hardcore are you?' he said as I looked at him. I turned to my brother Dino and said 'Its gonna go off here!' Dino and Danny stood up. Williams repeated 'You Villa Hardcore are you lads? We're Zulu's.' My brother Dino just stepped forward and nutted him. Williams staggered back. They all steamed into us. The Scottish bloke became involved as well. We were brawling with them. We were circled by them. Even the birds with them were getting stuck in. The one bird came flying in with a bottle and the Scottish geezer knocked her out. One of

188

them, Fletch was getting stuck in but Dino leathered him. Dino punched him and he went down. Dino bent down and just bit his ear off. He then spat it back at him. The pub had a dog. As Dino spat the ear out onto the floor the dog ran over. It picked up the ear and ran off with it. It was still going off, there as blood everywhere. We were penned in and couldn't go anywhere but they were the ones who were leathered. They were backing off in the end. The landlord came down and shouted that he'd called the police. The police arrived pretty quickly with an ambulance. None of them would get in the ambulance. They also told the police to fuck off. They told them they'd sort it themselves. We just went upstairs to the private party. A few weeks later Dino was raided by the police. They raided my old address but I wasn't there. They told Dino it was in my best interests to contact them. They told Dino he'd been grassed up. They wouldn't say who by. They told him to tell me to hand myself in. Dino went on an ID parade, but they didn't turn up. I went to Steelhouse Lane police station and handed myself in. The old bill were laughing. The one copper knew them all. He was Birmingham City's football intelligence officer. He said 'I can't believe they did this. We know them from the football. I can't believe they've gone and grassed you up!' He added that perhaps they were looking for the compensation. I said to them that they were the ones who had brought it on top and they had merely got what they deserved. Anyway word got round obviously about what they had done. A few weeks later whoever had given the statement withdrew it and charges were dropped.

Chapter Eight: Villa Hardcore. On Top

Aston Villa Vs Wimbledon Premier League 23rd October 1999

No-one was really interested in this fixture. The prospect of playing Wimbledon at home hardly fired the imagination. A group of Hardcore that gathered at The Britannia had no intention of going to the game. It was an afternoon of touring the pubs of Aston having a drink and a laugh. Later on in the afternoon someone suggested going to a place called Shanahan's on Rocky Lane in Aston. About 40 of us made our way up there. The rest of the afternoon was spent there, the place was reasonably full.

Reidy: I had met all the lads in a pub we were using at the time, The Britannia. One of the lads suggested we go to Shanahan's as they had topless barmaids. It was just a done thing in those days. A lot of the lads just turned up on a Saturday and never bothered going to the matches. We just went on the piss round the ground. There must have been up to 40-50 of us in the pub up until about 6 o'clock. After that, lads started drifting off to do whatever they were doing on that night. By around nine o'clock there were thirteen of us left including two Blues fans. Around seven of our girlfriends were with us.

Fowler: Earlier on there were some Blues fans playing pool. Some of the younger lot went over and said 'Put your chains away lads you taking the piss?' I went over and said 'Whoa, whoa! We're not fucking Blues; don't bully 'em. We're not bullies like them!' The geezer must've got on the phone to them, wherever they were. I was outside, waiting for a taxi. There was about eight or nine of us left in the place. We had our birds with us. I walked out to have a look for the taxis. Nostrils was standing there. I walked out and there were Blues. They were coming down the fucking road! One of them was coming down the road with a starter pistol in his hand. He pointed it at me. It looked like a real gun. I ran forward and put him down. Then the rest of them were still coming down the road. Nostrils and me, we stood against them. We got battered.

Reidy: The first thing we knew was when Blues came charging towards the bar. We held our own at the beginning. I remember one of Blues main boys holding what we thought was a gun. We found out after it was a starter pistol. Fowler just stood there in the road and said 'If you're going to use, use it!' He didn't and Fowler put him down Blues seemed to come from everywhere. I was whacked round the head with something. It put me on the floor by a car. I was getting a good kicking. I managed to get away. I turned back to see one of the lads getting a real bad kicking and getting hit with everything. I felt ashamed that I couldn't get back to help him but we were totally outnumbered. After about five minutes the police arrived and the Blues were off. It was Nostrils who had been taking the kicking. Fowler had taken a kicking as well. Nostrils was unconscious. They both went to hospital in an ambulance and I made my own way there. I will admit Blues did give us a kicking that night. They came prepared. They were all tooled up and there were only 11 of us left. They classed that as 'a result.'

Nostrils: At the same time two transit vans pulled up at the end of the road and screeched to a halt. Around 30, mostly black, lads spilled out of the vans. They were all tooled up. Fowler was having it with them already and the other lads were steaming in. We had nowhere to run to so we stood our ground.

Mark B: Blues have their factions like any other club. Certain areas stick together. There's Acocks Green, Chelmsley Wood, Yardley, Kings Heath, Kings Norton and Northfield, all areas of South Birmingham. Acocks Green, Yardley and Chelmsley tend to know each other well and associate closely but there is often conflict between Acocks Green and Chelmsley. Kings Heath, Kings Norton and Northfield do likewise. They're not technically the same firm. Disputes have occurred between the two main factions over the years. The one's who landed at Shanahan's were the Kings Heath, Kings Norton and Northfield lot. Most of them that night were part of a door firm. That's how they got it arranged so quickly. They were all working for one of Blues top men.

Nostrils: They swarmed round me. All I could feel was the digs hitting me. They had bats and iron bars. I remember trying to get something out of the scrap yard which is on that road but I didn't have time. I emptied a whole can of CS Gas at them trying to get them off me but it was useless. They all had bats and luckily for me I was knocked out. It was a brilliant ambush, one you'd be proud of if you'd done it yourself, hats off to them. I will say however with the numbers they had they could've taken us anyway without the weapons. The lads were saying they had been dropping slabs into my head while I was on the floor. I had a lot of cuts and bruises. They broke my fingers. I had two black eyes. All I remember is waking up two days later in hospital. The police were waiting there to question me. I refused to make a statement. It's the risk you take. No matter how bad they'd have done me I would never grass.

Leicester City Vs Aston Villa League Cup Semi-Final
2nd February 2000

Around 20 to 30 of us met at the Old Royal just off Colmore Row in Birmingham city centre. The game was an evening kick-off. A lot of people had struggled to get the afternoon off work. Many were travelling independently. There was a police presence outside. They had clocked and followed some of the lads on their way to the pub. It was decided we'd leave the pub and meet up somewhere else to try and shake the police.

Baz: We headed of through town trying to shake the old bill. We eventually split into two groups and shot off doing a runner around the back of New Street. Eventually we all linked up again in a boozer at the back of town. It was decided that we would get two vans. We were unsure where would we meet the drivers without the plod finding us. The plan was to get on the train as if we were going to Coventry. The police would follow us expecting us to change at Coventry for a train for Leicester. When we got to the next station, Birmingham International at the NEC we would leave the train and run out to the vans that would be waiting in the big lay-by outside the station. The plan worked a treat. After what seemed an age cooped up in the back of a sprinter van with no windows we arrived at a big boozer on the outskirts of Leicester called the Braunstone. There was quite a few Villa in there, but they weren't all lads.

Stan: I went with Carl and Russell. They are two brothers who used to go everywhere with us in those days. We found the lads at this pub before the game. We were all having a drink in there. Someone came in and said, 'Leicester are coming. They're coming up the road now!' As soon as they'd said this, Leicester appeared outside the pub. We ran out of the pub. It went off outside on the car-park and in the road.

We left the pub to confront Leicester. One Leicester lad comes bouncing up towards Steve Baker. He was chanting 'B...S! B...S!' Baker threw a punch and the lad went straight down. 'BS that, you fucking mug!' Baker said and waded into the next one. There were loads of Leicester. We were being forced back. We had expected the rest of the pub to have emptied. It seemed they didn't fancy it. There was around 25 of us facing around 80-100 Leicester. They were slowly forcing us back towards the pub. Some of our lot were trying the pub doors to get back in. They had been locked. It was really on top now. They were surrounding us at the front of the pub. The doors were locked. We couldn't go anywhere. Fowler was laughing at them. 'Come on! I'll have any of you, let's have a straightener!' He was trying to lengthen the odds of the rest of us getting pasted. He's done it a few times when it has come on top. When we've been dramatically outnumbered he has put himself up there. He picks out one of their main lads and offers him a one on one. Invariably they don't accept, but it always gives the rest of us a bit more time.

Baz: They pelted us with glasses and bottles. Two coppers that were on the corner of the road came running across to try to stop it going off. They had their batons drawn and were yelling at me to drop my bottle as they came towards me. Swigsy, an older lad I knew from the Swan and Mitre, ran past me and into the Leicester lot throwing punches. I ran to get in with him. The copper smashed me across the hand with his cosh. Leicester were swarming all over us. We couldn't get out of the corner of the car park. Everywhere I looked there were little groups of two and threes having it toe-to-toe. I threw a couple of bottles at two lads who were pushing forward screaming at me. They steamed me and I put my arm over my head. I was on the back foot. I was trying to fight my way out. A big black litter bin came crashing into me followed by more bottles. Police sirens started filling the air. When they heard the sirens Leicester did the off. One of the lads, Ginge, got lifted by the old bill and was taken away.

The old bill were arriving now in numbers. They managed to separate the two groups. They then set their dogs on us. We still couldn't get back into the pub. The landlord had locked the doors. The Villa inside were using it as an excuse for why they hadn't come outside. We were pissed off about it to say the least. Once the pub doors were re-opened the recriminations took place. 'Where the fucking hell were you lot?' Leicester were still milling about. They got the result. They had the numbers granted but for us that was no excuse. There was no excuse. People were angry. Not angry about getting turned over. They were angry that a pub full of Villa, possibly 200 plus hadn't come out to help us. A Leicester bumpkin of a landlord standing at the door saying 'No lads you can't go out there,' and they didn't. If it was the Hardcore trying to get out he'd have been walked over and the doors would've gone. There were insults flying across the Police cordon, 'We done you Villa!' They were laughing at us. Most of us were muttering to each other, they were having it. It'll be us with the numbers afterwards.

We were all escorted to the ground by the police. Other lads had made their own way over to Leicester. It appeared we had a lot coming over - it was a semi-final after all. Arrangements were made by various people for us to meet up underneath the away section at half time. At half time a large group, slightly larger than we had before the match, met underneath the stand. Fowler decided he wanted to leave there and then and go looking for Leicester. The plan was to plot up in their main pub close to the ground and wait for the game to finish. We would wait for them to come to it then confront them. The police would hopefully be looking solely at the Villa fans that would still be leaving the away end. A group of about 40 of us left the ground and made our way to their main pub. The old bill had clocked us and a couple followed us as we left the ground. We tried to lose them. We thought we had by making a few turns on the way. We ended up at a pub a stones throw from the ground and plotted up there. We settled down for the half hour or so we had to wait for the match to finish.

Baz: The pub was big modern building and was made up of lots of big glass panels so you could see out on to all of the front and the car park.

About ten minutes before the game ended, a group of Leicester approached the pub. There were around 30 of them. They tried to enter the pub and Clinchy who was the first man nearest the door exchanged words with them. 'Who the fucking hell are you?' they asked him. 'Who do you think we are, we're Villa Hardcore,' said Clinchy who was laughing. As he said that he stubbed a cigarette out in the face of the bloke. 'Come on!' the shout went up. We surged towards the door. The bloke whose face had been used as an ashtray fell back. The people behind him were on the back-foot. We surged through the doors onto the car park. 'Let's fucking have it! We're fucking Villa!' Leicester were backing off as we filled the car park. The police weren't long arriving. It seemed they'd followed this Leicester lot from the ground. They waded into us and managed to separate us. 'Come on Leicester! We've taken your fucking boozer!' We were laughing at them now. They'd been on the back foot there and if the old bill hadn't arrived we'd have run them. They knew it and they were trying to have a pop through the police lines. They were chanting, 'B...S! B...S!' Missiles started to fly. The Police could see things were getting worse. The ground was starting to empty. Villa had lost 1-0. The Leicester numbers behind their cordon were being swollen by late comers. The police forced us back in through the front doors and back into the pub. Our mood was upbeat. We considered our little fracas on the front of the pub sufficient to equalise what they had done to us earlier. We were contemplating what to do next. We were wondering if the police were going to wade in and make arrests, they'd caught us virtually red-handed. Steff emerged from the rear of the pub.

'Fucking hell lads! There's a door round the side! It's open and there's no old bill down the side of the pub!' We didn't need telling twice and steamed towards the side door. We emerged from the door onto the car park. The police were still diligently guarding the front doors. Leicester were still milling around outside. There were other fans present, mostly Leicester supporters who were wondering why they are not being allowed into their usual after-match pub. We burst out of the side of the building. 'Come on! We're fucking Villa!' The roar went up. We waded into the Leicester group. Some had clocked us as we came out of the doors. The speed with which we crashed into them however put them on the back-foot. The whole crowd moved as one as they scrambled to get out of the way. A circle formed around us. Some Leicester were keen to confront us and they were dealt with. We now had the momentum and we cleared the car park quicker than the police could have ever have hoped to. Some Leicester were getting it together and having a pop back at us. Our group split into smaller groups as various fights ensued in the darkness. The old bill were running round clueless. They couldn't control it this time.

Baz: The Leicester lads had picked up bottles and even lumps of mud. They began throwing them at us. This time it was more even. After the missiles stopped landing we got stuck into them. Again it was toe to toe fighting and Leicester weren't having it their way this time. They started to back off and the old bill swarmed across the car park.

We'd got the upper hand and Leicester were backing off. The old bill came in between the two groups yet again. They were obviously pissed off that they hadn't thought to cover the side door. They waded in with batons stopping fight after fight on the car park. We owned the fucking pub as far as we were concerned and the car park now. 'Villa! Villa!' We made it known this small piece of Leicester was then, albeit temporarily, the property of Aston Villa's Hardcore. More and more police arrived. We were marshalled into some sort of order and taken back to our vans. An away trip to Leicester was again eventful and our old enemy hadn't let us down.

Tottenham Hotspur Vs Aston Villa Premier League 15th April 2000

While I was interviewing the lads for this book I noticed that a lot of stories of good days out didn't always include violence. Some of the days mentioned were really mentioned for other reasons, things that were said or done which solely included the Hardcore and no-one else. We enjoyed each others company and at times the violence was a side issue. It was what we were there for but having a laugh was just as important as taking on other firms. People wanted certain things mentioned, such as Steff pretending he was a dog and snapping at the ankles of the bloke who used to come round selling the Sports Argus in the Aston Hotel. He did that after every match for a couple of seasons. Steff would be on his hands and knees trying to bite the trouser legs of this old bloke. We would be howling as the poor bloke would be kicking at Steff shouting, 'Get off you mad bugger!' He just couldn't understand why this bloke was acting like a dog, mind you on reflection I still don't know why Steff used to do it. That was what it was about though, us having a laugh. This trip to Tottenham wasn't memorable in the sense of anything major happened, but it was mentioned by everybody I talked to. I didn't attend because I had a Thai-boxing fight that night in Birmingham and had been in training for it for weeks.

Fowler: I'll tell you what happened here. Spurs came to Villa Park the season before and were mouthing off. I had some geezer ring me. I said, 'Who the fuck are you?' He said 'I'm Spurs. Where were you Villa?' I said, 'I tell you what mate, we'll land on you.' We took a firm to London for the next game against Spurs. I think we were at Swiss Cottage in North London. I rang him up and said, 'Where are you, where's your firm?' he seemed surprised. He made a few excuses then led us on a wild goose chase round London.

Reidy: Fowler had organised a coach. It turned out to be the oldest, slowest coach you could possibly get. We got off the coach at St. Johns Wood where we met some more Villa. Spurs had been on the phone telling us to meet at the Worlds End pub in Camden. When one of our lads asked a barmaid how far it was she had told him it was about a ten minute walk. A lot of the lads at that particular time were dropping Ecstasy tablets. They all dropped an E thinking it would take only 10 minutes. Well, it wasn't a 10 minute walk. It was more like a 3/4 of an hour walk. By the time we had arrived at the Worlds End, all the lads who had took pills were going mental. The pills had kicked in. Anybody who used to watch Thunderbirds in the old days with the puppets on a string walking round, it must've looked like that. It must have been a sight to see most of our firm arriving like that! They could hardly walk, let alone get into a fight. We had the run around from Spurs that day. We never got to meet their Firm.

Tucker: The lads were that bored by now with looking and not finding anything

remotely resembling a Spurs firm. They were that fed up that they all started popping these pills. It was madness. You had 40-50 lads staggering down the road through the Saturday crowds. They were going, 'Is this them?' and then pointing out a group of shoppers. We were sitting in pubs going, 'Watch that door!' People were replying, 'What door?' It was madness, absolute madness but funny looking back. After a fruitless day in London we headed back on the coach. Halfway up the motorway the coach caught fire.

Dandy: The coach was suddenly ablaze. Steff pulled out his phone. He rang 999. 'Hello our coach is on fire on the M1. Could you send a fire engine please? Oh yeah and can you send an ice cream van for Fat Stan. That was a fucking classic, we were falling about laughing.

Reidy: The driver was telling us all to get off the coach while he was trying to put the fire out. The coach had overheated. I climbed into the driver's seat and took off with the coach. I nearly knocked the driver over. The driver was running at the side holding onto the side door threatening to call the police. He was telling me to stop and get out of the drivers seat. I expected, stupidly in hindsight, that the rest of the lads would get off the coach with me. Only about a dozen of them got off with me. The driver closed the doors and drove off. He left us stranded on the M1 in the pitch black. We started walking up the hard shoulder of the M1. Three car loads of 'armed response' police arrived. They weren't too happy about us being on the motorway. They asked what had happened. Steff started telling them he knew all about all different types of guns. With the knowledge he had, the coppers were looking at him with amazement. It eased the tension somewhat. They took us to the next service station where the coach had pulled in. The lads were waiting by the side of it. We had to hang around for another three hours while the driver ordered another coach. To this day I still think Fowler bought the coach for £50 and paid some bloke he'd met in a pub £20 to drive us there and back.

Aston Villa Vs Coventry City Premier League 5th May 2001

Coventry have always been a game set of lads. In my opinion they are underrated. They have never had massive numbers but always given us a show home and away. We've never had any strong feelings about them as a football club to be honest, but they hate us with a passion. They always go mad at Villa. We've also had some cracking rows against them. Cov was always a fixture I looked out for. This match was at the end of the season. Coventry were always fighting relegation. In previous years they had managed to escape the drop to the lower league on the last day of the season. This game was important, not for us, we were safe. Coventry, however, they needed a result to stay in the Premier League. They brought a large following to Villa.

Big Tony: We'd had it with Cov a few years earlier in Birmingham City Centre. We were waiting by New Street train station for them to come off the train. We noticed they had come off the train and were underneath us in an underpass. We ran down the stairs to meet them. Skinhead Neil ran in and tried to gas them. He didn't take wind direction into account and ended up gassing us and not Coventry.

Kas: One of the Cov lads was swinging a big camera around his head trying to hit us with it. It flew off the strap and into the road. Victor clocked it. He was trying to stop the traffic to get to this camera and pick it up. As he stood on the pavement the next car that came past drove straight over the camera and smashed it.

We met at The Carpenters Arms in Digbeth. It was Blues territory and the last place the old bill would expect us to meet. It was the last direction they would expect us to come from into the city centre when Cov landed. We got there early doors, around 10am. By noon we must've had 250 lads there. People were drinking outside. It was a nice day and the pub was packed. It wasn't a worry though, the old bill were hardly going to be touring Digbeth looking for us. We stayed there totally undetected. About 1pm we got a call to say Coventry had landed in Birmingham city centre. We walked through the back streets of Digbeth. We came up Hurst Street into the city centre. Not a sign of the old bill. It looked as though we were really going to give Cov and the old bill a surprise. As we walked up Hill Street towards New Street a shout went up and you got the usual,' They're here!' Everyone started running towards New Street. The police appeared then from nowhere. A couple on foot at first, followed by more in vans. No-one took any notice and virtually ran through them. Cov were in The Shakespeare, a pub just off New Street. The old bill were outside The Shaky. They were also coming in numbers behind us. A few bottles were thrown at the pub before the old bill baton charged us away. They charged us to the end of the road and onto New Street. People were throwing missiles back towards the police. Most had been drinking since ten that morning and had by then had more than a few pints. The old bill tried to baton charge us again. We half retreated to The Trocadero on the other side of New

Street. It was a battle with the police now. They wanted us inside the pub or up the road away from the Cov. People started passing chairs and tables out of the Troc and these were used as missiles to throw at the old bill. They backed off to the bottom of the road we were on. I'm sure this was one of the first times we saw them filming at the football. We thought it was a laugh at first, them filming. Little did we know what impact one of them with a digital video recorder would have in the future. We were outside the Troc and Blues suddenly appeared down the bottom of the road on New Street. A few of us ran down and Blues shit it. They scattered up New Street towards Victoria Square. The old bill were down the bottom of the road.

Tucker: When we ran down towards Blues. We clocked them and went over. I tried to drop the nut on one and he moved away. He and his mates then made a sharp exit up New Street towards the Town Hall. They couldn't get away quick enough. They'd have got a slap if they'd have stayed much longer but the Old Bill were clocking us and that put us off.

We stayed up by The Trocadero. We were waiting for Cov to make an appearance out of the Shaky. The idea was that we'd all split up and mingle in with them as the old bill tried to get them to New Street station. We knew Cov would be playing up. They always played up when they visited Brum. We thought we'd take advantage of that, and get in amongst them if possible. Suddenly we heard they were coming out and we made our move down towards New Street. The old bill were waiting and they tried to baton charge us away. We could see the rear of Coventry's escort as it made its way down to the station. We really started going for it, trying to break through the police lines but the old bill were having none of it. It was futile, we couldn't get through. We then decided to make a detour. We would go round the long way and meet Cov as they entered the station. We headed down Hill Street. We went in the back way to New Street Station. The police had sussed and were chasing us by this point. They were trying to cop hold of us. They were also waiting when we get round to the station. They had got us now. It now looked like a police escort all the way to Aston. They took us into the station. They obviously didn't fancy the long walk to the ground. They were going to put us on a train. We were led through past loads of police vans. The van lights were flashing; they had dogs barking at us. The police were smiling as if to say 'Yeah we've got you now.' What did they do? They put us straight onto a train containing Cov's lads. We went through it like a dose of salts. The first people on the train were straight into them.

Mark B: They put us on the train with the Coventry fans. They started singing, 'Shit on the Villa!' Screw looked at me as if to say, 'Shall we?' I nodded. We steamed straight into the nearest lads to us. It was mayhem. Coventry panicked. The old bill piled onto the train. Screw and I were arrested straightaway. They weren't going to charge us at first. They were just going to let us go. A sergeant came running over. He said, 'I want those two charged!' We were taken to the police station.

Jez: They got mixed up, the police did I think. They had forgotten what team we were. As soon as they put us on the train we steamed into Coventry. Cov didn't want to know. It was a bit of a massacre for a while until the old bill realised their mistake. They managed to get in between the two sets of fans. They kept us up one end of the train and the Coventry fans up the other end of the train. They stayed between both sets of fans all the way to Witton station.

We stayed on the train till Witton station. They tried to get us off at Aston but we were having none of it. We were going to Witton and we refused to leave the train. We knew if we got off at Witton we'd follow the Cov and also walk past the Witton Arms where Cov usually drink before the game. They kept the Coventry fans on the train and we surged off at Witton station. There was line after line of old bill searching us all and preventing us walking up Brookvale Road past the Witton Arms. A few missiles were thrown at the police and they baton charged us up Manor Road towards the ground. We still had to walk past the away end but they were starting to nick people by this point. We were all getting split up with each baton charge.

Big Tony: It went off by the away end. The coppers rode their horses into us. One just rode straight at me and hit me. I was knocked clean out. It's the only time I've been knocked out at the football. Kas was going mad while I was lying unconscious and they arrested him.

We walked past the away end, we were in small groups. You could feel the tension. Cov knew we were up for it and so did the old bill. There was a great atmosphere. Cov had brought loads. They scored first and it looked like they were going to escape relegation yet again. Villa however turned it round with Paul Merson and we ended up winning the game 3-2. Coventry City were relegated.

Simmo: Juan Pablo Angel, our Colombian centre-forward, scored one of the goals for Villa. Bruno got onto the pitch and was hugging him during the goal celebrations. I could see him saying something to Angel. When he came back into the stand I asked him what he had said, 'I was asking him if he had any coke,' said Bruno.

At the end of the match we all left at the final whistle. The idea was to get through down to Witton Island past police lines at the away end of the ground and see what the score was once we were down at the island. It usually goes off against Cov straight outside on Witton Lane. They'd got CCTV there by now covering the whole road. Ideally we wanted to get down to Witton Island where it wasn't so well covered by CCTV.

Stan: I remember at the end of the match. Villa flooded out of the ground and the Villa were chanting, 'We are Premier League, we are Premier League!' We walked down towards the Witton End. There were some Cov in the road in front of us coming out of the ground. Bruno just steamed straight into them. He must've hit two or three of them before they realised what was happening. They melted and the police were then stopping anyone going any further. That's when the rioting started with the police. There were running battles with the police for about half an hour. Villa tried repeatedly to get down to Witton to have it with Coventry.

A few of us managed to get through before the police closed Witton Lane. Cov were going mad. They'd just been relegated and were obviously pissed off. The road was full of Old Bill. We were walking down amongst the Coventry fans. We could hear them mouthing off. We could've kicked it off there but there were too many police around us. We got to the island and we were walking alongside the shops opposite the Witton Arms. Cov were there in front of us, they were lads. There was me and Steamy. I looked at him and I nodded in the direction of the Cov. He nodded back at me. We walked into the road and alongside them. I spotted some ex-Villa Youth lads. They were coming up behind us. I could see they were up for it. It was mainly all Cov around us. The group in front of us was about 20 strong. We were walking at the side of them. We turned towards them, 'Come on Cov, let's fucking have it!' The one laughed at me. He thought I was on my own. Steamy chinned him. The Youth lads surged into them from behind and we were into them from the side. I punched the one and he went through an open shop doorway. They had a go back at us. The old bill came flying in. They were belting us with their batons trying to get us away. More police came running up from the station. We mingled in with the crowds again. They managed to get Cov tight up against the fence queuing to get into Witton Station for the train back to New Street. We walked past laughing at them. We were trying to wind them up. We were trying to provoke them. They were mouthing off and they started singing, 'Shit on the Villa.' As a Villa fan if you hear that song it's going to go off. It will if you're a Villa lad worth your salt. They were singing and we were now the ones getting wound up. They were safe on the other side of the old bill. The old bill started to shepherd us away up towards the Witton Arms. A few of us stood on the car park of the pub. Stan was there and he was moaning about Cov hiding behind the old bill. There was a small group of us. We looked down the road and could see there was loads of Cov waiting for the train. A bus into the city centre came up the road. It stopped at the bust stop by the queue of Cov by the station, 'Fucking hell Stan, there's loads of them getting on that bus,' I said. Stan could see them, 'Yeah you're right!' About 20 of them were allowed to leave thc queue by the police and they jumped onto the bus. It was a short walk to the next bus stop. There was no old bill about where we were or by the bus stop. They were all down the train station with Cov. We rushed over the road to the bus stop. The police thought they'd just packed this 20 or so off into town on the bus. Now we were standing at the next bus stop waiting for them to arrive. There was about fifteen of us in all. It would be similar numbers. I was on first. The driver looked at me as if I was going to pay. I walked straight past onto the bus followed by Stan. There was a load of Cov sitting downstairs. They knew who we were, their faces dropped as soon as we got on. They were horrified. Some stood up. They knew what was coming. 'Shit on the Villa eh Cov?' I said as I fired straight into the one who was standing closest to me. He flew back over the seat. People were screaming and Cov were scrambling to get out of the emergency exit at the back of the bus. Stan's got hold of one and he was pummelling him. He was repeatedly saying, 'Shit on the Villa eh mate? Shit on the Villa eh?' A couple tried to stand their ground at the back of the bus. We steamed straight into them. Cov bolted it and we jumped out of the emergency exit after them. The bus was stationary and the driver had jumped out by this point. The police started to arrive and I shouted to Steamy that a couple of Cov had run up Witton Road. We chased after them. We were at the top of Witton Road now where it crosses Trinity Road. The jammy bastards managed to hail a black cab. We were feet away from it just as it sped off. The Cov were waving as they headed off into the distance.

Mark B says: I was taken to court for my part in the disturbances on the train before the match. The police didn't turn up. Three times the magistrates adjourned to give the police more time to produce the evidence but they didn't show up. My solicitor said it was because the incident happened due to a police mistake. It was their blunder which led us to be on the train with Coventry in the first place. They'd walked us there and even held the train up so they could get us on it. It wouldn't have looked good for them for that to come out in court, not good at all.

SOCCER FANS IN CLASHES

Police fought running battles with football fans after the local derby between Aston Villa and Coventry City yesterday.

Officers in riot gear mounted a series of baton charges in the streets around Villa Park to keep hate-filled rival supporters apart. Police came under a hail of missiles, including stones and bottles.

The biggest flashpoint was outside Witton railway station where valiant officers were made to ensure the visiting fans could be shepherded aboard trains into the city centre and on to Coventry.

Thousands of fans who gathered in Witton Road and nearby Aston Lane were driven apart by police squads who struck out at the troublemaker's legs with their staffs to make them move on. The post-match violence came at the end of a tense day in Birmingham in which Villa's dramatic 3-2 win led to the Sky Blues being relegated from the top flight for the first time in 34 years.

Before the game shoppers cowered in fear as hooligans clashed in Birmingham city centre. More than 100 Villa and Coventry fans fought savagely in New Street.

About 50 officers from West Midlands Police - 25 in riot gear - chased the mob along New Street and into Colmore Row.

Everton Vs Aston Villa FA Premier League 20th October 2001

You have to laugh at Everton's book. They state they don't rate Villa. Although for some reason in the book a visit from Aston Villa in the early 80s was 'one of the worst nights on record at Everton, for arrests, for injuries and for pure violence. In 1990, when we were going for the league title we virtually took over their ground. We really took the piss that day and had lads all over Goodison Park. We bashed a few on landing in Liverpool. We took over the Stanley Park pub before the game. They knew where we were but they had nothing worth bothering with out that day, it happens to the best of us but few will admit it.

Fowler: There's so much bullshit in the Everton book it's untrue. The doughnut who wrote it, he wrote utter bullshit about this incident. We were in Liverpool city centre.

We'd gone up for the day. Screwdriver was in court the following Monday and it looked as if he was going to get a stretch. We'd gone up for a final drink. We hadn't gone to the match. We didn't a lot of the time. We found it made it harder for the old bill to get hold of us. We were drinking round Liverpool. The match had finished. We were in a pub near Lime Street station. A few Tranmere came into the pub. They were good lads, and we're not bullies like I've said before. We had a drink with them. They were decent lads. We were having a laugh.

Mark B: We were standing at the bar and this tubby bloke came up to me. He said, 'Are you Villa? 'Yeah mate,' I replied, 'Who are you?' 'I'm Everton mate,' he said, 'Listen I'm doing a book. Would you mind giving me a few lines about Villa and Everton matches?' Screwdriver came over to the bar. We were chatting to this character. He asked me, 'Which ones Fowler?' I pointed to Fowler. He said their top lad was going to a wedding or something otherwise he'd have got him to pop down and have a chat with us. We had another beer. We explained we were just up here for a drink because Screw was getting sent down on the following Monday. He finished his drink and left. Ten minutes later he came back in. He stood by us again. He seemed nervous. I clocked it straightaway. 'Are your lot going to land mate? Is that what it is?' I asked him. 'No, no, of course not mate,' he said. Then he popped out again. He came in for a third time. This time we noticed a few ones and two's coming into the pub. We knew then they were going to land on us. Then the doors flew open and three massive blokes walked into the pub. They walked over to us because one of theirs was standing talking to us. 'Which one's Fowler?' the one at the front asked. I pointed Fowler out to him. As this was said about 25-30 lads came in the door.

Screwdriver: Lads started filing into the pub. The Tranmere who were drinking with us said to us, 'This is Everton's lads! Don't let them in or you will be fucked!'

Fowler: I heard someone saying 'Who's Fowler? Which one's Fowler?' He was asking Mark B. When I heard my name mentioned I turned round and stood up. I was thinking who the fuck is this? Mark pointed him in my direction. They walked over to me. 'Who the fuck, are you?' I asked. 'Sit down, just sit down Fowler!' he said. I couldn't believe it. 'Who the fuck, do you think you are?' I replied. I couldn't believe the cheek of this clown. 'Listen Fowler, I'm gonna do you a favour, we've got 70 lads round the corner and were gonna land on this pub!' 'So fucking what?' I said. 'Who the fuck, do you think you are? I continued. I head-butted him there and then. The rest of his lads started piling into me. The rest of our lads realised what was happening and they piled into them. The cheeky Scouse fuckers made a move for the door. I was shouting, 'Get him! Get that fucker!' I was pointing to the one who had been mouthing off. They grabbed the last one leaving the pub. He was annihilated. They glassed the life out of him. The ones who had run outside did fuck all.

Screwdriver: We just annihilated them. We threw everything at them and they did one out of the pub. We chased them and there was fighting outside the pub but most of them had run away. The police broke it up outside the pub and I was arrested.

Fowler: What I cannot understand is why did they do that? Why come in a pub and warn people you're going to land, especially if you're not in any position to. There was about fifteen of us out we had planned it late so only a few of us had travelled. So 70, if they had that many they could've walked through the pub. I just can't understand it? I think the geezer who was caught received 140 stitches. They thought they could walk in like that? As if we were mates with them? 'Oh look lads we have 70 down the road, I'm gonna do you a favour?' Why? Why would they do that? Truth of the matter is they'd got fuck all and thought they could bully us with threats. They underestimated us. If that was us, I'd have gone in with two of us, anymore than that is taking the piss. I'd have gone, 'Look lads, there's only two of us. Don't kick off. We've got 60 round the corner. Come down and have it with us,' as simple as that. They thought they could come in taking the piss. They thought wrong. You don't come into a pub to a firm who have been drinking all day, mouthing off. Who the fuck did they think they were?

Mark B: They thought they were going to do a job on us and make us look stupid in the process. There were about fifteen of us and a couple of Tranmere who we had been talking to. They joined in on our side. They had at the very least 30 lads there. They got done. If Fowler hadn't kicked it off when he did, we'd have been murdered. They weren't expecting the ferocity of our attack. They underestimated us badly. The one who was glassed? He was the one who came in mouthing off. He was dragged back by his ankles and glassed to fuck. What did they expect? When we emptied out of the pub and chased them, most of the Everton ran off. They didn't even look back. The bloke who had been glassed was still game. The old bill when they started arriving had to gas him to stop him from having another pop at us. I have a lot of respect for that bloke. He and the other two must be the three biggest blokes I've ever seen at football. They were fucking massive. Perhaps that's why they came in with so much confidence. I don't care what anyone says, the geezer who got glassed, he just stood on. He just wouldn't stop having it with us. He has got to be the gamest geezers I have ever seen at the football

Fowler: They've moaned about this. I've had threats etc. That's the thing about

Scousers, they catch you up there and cut you to fuck and no-one bats an eyelid. One of them gets a few little cuts and they don't like it do they? The old bill came steaming through the door and they gassed us to fuck. Screwdriver was nicked. The reason we're up there is for his drink because he was already in court on the Monday!

Screwdriver: I was in prison in Shrewsbury. I had it cushy there. They suddenly came in one day and said, 'Right get your stuff together you're going to Walton!' I was being transferred up there for court for the Everton incident. What can you say about the place? It is the lowest of the low. It was full of bag-heads. 23 hour a day bang up in your cell. Proper fucking strip searches, it was a nightmare. No television and my cell was below ground. It was dark, dank and horrible. So I was up for the Everton incident where a Scouser got 140 plus stitches. I thought it would be wise to keep that to myself. I was given a job working in the shop. Out of the blue one of the Scousers I was working with asked me what I was in for. 'Credit cards mate,' I replied without thinking. 'Fuck off,' he said, 'you're not in for credit cards!' 'This is Liverpool mate. You'd be stupid to come up here and try and pass moody credit cards. What are you really in for?' I kept to my story but they were onto me. It wouldn't take long for them to find out. Suddenly I was re-called to Shrewsbury and did the rest of my sentence there. I don't know what would have happened if I hadn't have been called back when I was.

Fowler: If you read the Everton book it's a joke, they try and make it into something it wasn't. Scally, what a fucking joke, have you seen the state of the fat tramp? He tried to get my number I heard to apologise for what he'd written in his book. He apparently said he was sorry, his mate had got stitches and he was angry when he wrote it. The fat tramp, even his lads think he's a div. I told the lad who he'd asked for my number to tell him to fuck off.

Aston Villa Vs Manchester United FA Cup 3rd Round
6th January 2002

We had good quality turnout for this game. We decided to meet in the city-centre. United have this habit of landing at the first available pub off the train at New Street or the nearest pub to the train station in Witton. They then get wrapped up by the police and start getting lairy. They have done it for years. They mob up then and as numbers grow they'll get an escort to the ground. In my experience United have never turned up somewhere out of the way and called it on. They've got great numbers and good lads you can't knock them for that especially at home but turning up off-side isn't something they do. We thought we'd beat them to it that year and were about in town early that afternoon. They hadn't made an appearance by about 5pm so we walked towards New Street Station. We knew what time the train from Manchester was coming in so we decided to march down to the platform to meet it. We tried to time it well and used the back entrance to New Street station. As we got on the main station concourse a few United appeared in front of us. The train must've been early. Some of our lads ran towards them and some of them received a slap. We flooded down onto the platform. There were hardly any lads on the train. We decided we'd catch the next train down to Witton and see if we could have it with them as they stood outside the Witton Arms. There were a few United on the train down to Witton but they were normal fans and left well alone. As we got off the train at Witton we could see it was police overkill. They were everywhere but so were United. They had lads floating about and they were surprised as our mob cut through them. A few got a slap but it was too risky for most with the amount of police around. I walked up the road with Dandy. A couple of United were in front of us. We were on the opposite side of the road to the Witton Arms. There were two police standing immediately behind the Mancs. As we approached the lads Dandy just hit one of them. The blow made such a noise that one of the police turned round. It was Hamilton. 'What happened there?' He asked the United fan. 'Nothing mate nothing at all,' the lad replied. Fair play to him I thought, he was a lad obviously and he behaved like a proper one even after being on the receiving end.

The match was a game of two-halves. We were winning comfortably but United came back to win 3-2. They had been given the whole of the Witton Lane seats due to them being given more tickets as it was a cup-tie. As they scored their third goal a few of their fans came onto the pitch. We were fuming, losing the game after being ahead was bad enough but seeing some of them celebrating on the pitch pushed a few of us over the edge. We flooded out of the Holte End and down Witton Lane. Some of them were coming out of the seats singing and shouting. That soon stopped as we gave out a few reminders of where they were. Trouble seemed to be breaking out everywhere as the two sets of fans clashed in pockets. We were joined by more and more lads as we progressed down the road. The police were virtually dividing the road in half to keep us away from the United. As we arrived at Witton Island we could see a mob across the road outside a supermarket and off-licence which is there. They were reds and we fired into them. I couldn't say how many of us there was as I wasn't paying much attention. The United mob split into two as they scattered as we charged. A few of them stood but we steamrollered over them.

Daz: I remember it well down by Witton Island. The faces of the Man U lads faces as we appeared and charged at them was a picture. They thought they had taken the piss on the pitch and then at the island they thought we were nowhere to be seen. Then we landed. One of the best battles I've seen at Villa Park.

Riot police were soon in attendance and we were forced up Aston Lane. There seemed to be United everywhere and we were clattering their lads wherever we found them. We were furious. We knew some United had run up Aston Lane and we were determined to catch them. We were fuming not so much at the result but the fact that they had the cheek to celebrate on the pitch. We hurried up Aston Lane. There weren't many of us it didn't seem but we were all split up in the large crowd which was heading home after the match. Halfway up Aston Lane we noticed something going on. We ran towards the melee and in front of me I saw a group of lads swinging what looked to be lengths of wood. They were hitting normal people indiscriminately and someone shouted they were United. I remember shouting to the Villa who were with me 'Come on! Are we Villa or what?' Ginge and I ran over towards them. We burst out of the crowd into the gap which had opened in front of them as people dodged their blows. We ran straight into them. I'd barged into the one before he had time to take a swing at me. It was no use me punching him and keeping my distance he'd have just started belting me with the stick. He hit the floor and the rest of the lads followed me. I was wrestling around with this bloke until someone pulled me up and others laid into him and his mates. More United were standing by a minibus and they joined their friends on the floor or ran up the road towards the Crown and Cushion. Scuffles were breaking out as more United fans were discovered. The police were soon on the scene and baton charged us as we fought.

Daz: Big Irish Jim ran onto a mini bus through a hail of full bottles of ale. He knocked a couple of them spark-out before having to do one because he couldn't see what he was doing due to a 3 inch gash on his forehead. Spenna and I knocked on an Asian bloke's door for some toilet roll to stem the bleeding. The feller who answered the door just slammed it! You couldn't blame him it was virtually a riot on Aston Lane. The old bill then legged us up the road towards Perry Barr.

We were forced up Aston Lane and the United stayed by the now wrecked minibus. Police were repeatedly baton charging us up the road and some Villa were turning and throwing missiles at them. As soon as we got to the Crown and Cushion at Perry Barr Island they stopped chasing us. We went into the Crown for a drink but some lads waited outside to see if any United were about. A lot of United cars and coaches passed the Crown on the way to Junction 7 of the M6. A lot were trashed as they went past by a large mob of Villa outside the pub. The trouble made the local papers.

Following the game Adam Smith of The Great Barr Observer wrote:

VIOLENCE FLARES AS FANS FIGHT ON THE STREETS

Gangs of stick wielding football hooligans fought pitched-battles through the streets of Perry Barr when football violence spiralled out of control following an Aston Villa match.

Police in riot gear were forced to keep fighting fans apart as innocent bystanders and motorists were caught up in the violence. The fighting erupted at 9pm for half an hour after the end of Sunday nights FA Cup match between Aston Villa and Manchester United.

Rival sections of fans charged at each other at Witton Island, then police escorted Villa fans along Aston Lane but violence flared up again around Perry Barr island. The opposing fans grabbed sticks, bottles and bricks to attack each other and several eyewitnesses described a gang with sticks in a white van targeting Villa fans. The Crown and Cushion pub closed its doors early after staff feared the pub would be targeted by hooligans. Assistant Manager Nigel Horsewell said: 'We decided to close the pub when we were getting text messages and calls from regulars outside the ground describing how bad the fighting was. It just wasn't worth it. The pub lost a lot of money, 7pm was a stupid time to kick-off everyone was drunk and we had to employ bouncers not to let away fans in which is something we never do for Villa games.' Aston Lane resident Mary Davis was shocked at what she saw on Sunday night. Mrs Davis said: 'I opened my door and police in riot gear were running up the street towards the Crown and Cushion telling everyone to get indoors. I couldn't believe my eyes, you don't expect to see that sort of thing on a Sunday night and ten minutes later they all came back again on a number 11 bus.' Simon James who lives on North Road also witnessed the fighting. 'It was complete mayhem.

I've never seen so many people fighting in my life. The police told us to go somewhere safe.'

There were 7,000 away fans almost double the amount permitted in a league game and the late kick-off was due to the match being televised.

Chapter Nine: Villa Hardcore:
The Battle of Rocky Lane

Birmingham City Vs Aston Villa Premier League
16th September 2002

We were playing Birmingham City at St Andrews. The first time the clubs had played a competitive match since 1993. St Andrews has never been my favourite ground. It is real bandit country around there for away supporters. For Villa fans you can multiply that by ten. The game was an evening kick-off but a lot of people had taken the day or afternoon off work to make an early start. We were undecided where to meet. Fowler had eventually chosen the O'Reillys on Lichfield Road as the initial meeting point.

We hadn't played Blues for ages. We did play them in a friendly match in 1997. I think it might have been John Frain's testimonial. We met in the Square Peg in the afternoon. The plan was to go to St Andrews but we had no intention of paying in and watching the game. I'd say there were about 50 of us. We left the Peg and marched towards the ground. The police rounded us up in Digbeth and gave us an escort to the ground. A few Blues started tailing the escort and they were mouthing off beside us. We went for them but we were charged back by the police and a few of our lot nicked. We got to the ground and didn't pay in. We went back to the Square Peg and waited in there until the match finished. After the game a few Villa who went to the game showed up. At about 10 o'clock we noticed a few Blues were scouting about. A couple of Villa went out and chased them. Ten or so minutes later their main mob came from the one end of the road where the Cabin pub was. They also had a small mob coming up Corporation St. We went straight for the mob from the Cabin. They were throwing bottles at us. We launched bottles and glasses, the lot, straight into them. They fronted us for a few seconds then turned and ran. The few that came from the other direction tried to Judas us from the back. I remember one of them trying to give Pete Mc a dig but he just put the bloke straight on his arse. They turned and ran as well. It was mostly their older lot there that night - all their main faces were there so it wasn't a case of them being young mugs. They were disappointing. When they ran towards us they froze a few feet away. Then they turned and legged it. Just as this was happening the old bill turned up. They baton charged us and were using CS gas. They backed us up the steps of the Peg. There was a mad crush in the stampede to get into the pub. My back had a few truncheon marks the day after. The police told the landlord to shut the pub. They took us out and escorted us up to Snow Hill station where they gassed us and baton charged us again. We ended up in the Bull's Head pub by the Ben Johnson. Dandy had picked up a phone that one of them had dropped when they ran from us. He rang one of the numbers in it. A lad answered. Dandy pretended to be Blues and said 'Why did we run from Villa mate?' The lad on the other end of the phone said, 'I know, I can't believe we ran from Villa!' Dandy just laughed and said, 'We are Villa you mug, have you stopped running yet?'

Fowler: We had a meeting before this match. A couple of us went over to meet the older lot in a club near the city centre. Basically we said that we'd both mob up independently then meet up at some point before the match. I get criticised for choosing O'Reillys. People say it's near a police station. It isn't near a police station at all. There is a police building over the road but it is for traffic police and their cars etc not for normal police. It was the last place they expected us to meet. We couldn't go to town because of police and CCTV. It was the nearest place we could get to the city-centre without being spotted. We had around 250 lads there. Again it's the same scenario with big mobs; you can't rely on them all to stand their ground. Blues rang and asked where we were. They told me they were making their way down to Shanahan's a pub just down the road. We sent spotters down there and they weren't there.

On the day of the match we found that the police had told a lot of pubs in Aston not to open, O'Reillys was open as normal. They didn't expect us to meet there because of its location. Over the last few years a lot of the older generation 'lads' had started to appear on the scene again. The Steamers and the C-Crew as they were known had always still gone to games but some had become active again. They were meeting at a club on the other side of the city in Moseley. I'd spoken to one of their lads I knew well. He had told me they intended to hit Blues from the other side of the ground that we were aiming to approach from. I met up with Dandy and a few others in Perry Barr. We headed down towards Aston in a taxi. We were all making phone calls along the way to see if anything was happening yet. We soon found out the majority of pubs in Aston and Witton were closed. We were left with fewer options. We finally heard O'Reilly's at Aston Cross was open. We headed there. When we got there around 3pm it was just starting to fill up. There were quite a few faces there. It was mostly Hardcore but some older lads who hadn't got over to their meet yet and a few of the usual hangers-on.

Baz: The press had gone into overdrive in the week before the game. They had generally done their best to stir things up. As a result of the media coverage the police decided that they would close all the pubs in town so they could keep fans from consuming too much alcohol.

I caught the train to Birmingham city centre. I bumped in to one of the lads and we caught the train to Aston station. We then walked up to O'Reilly's.

The pub filled up as the afternoon dragged on. More and more lads landed. Some were staying and travelling to the game - others were on their way elsewhere and had just popped in for a quick look. In all we must've had 200 lads in there by 6 o'clock. This didn't look good for Blues. We had another firm meeting over in Moseley. We knew they'd struggle to cope with what we had out. We didn't know however they were struggling for numbers and couldn't even raise one decent sized firm let alone two.

Baz: The pub began to fill more and more and soon they started running out of beer. The firm we had inside the pub was looking good. They wouldn't know what had hit them. When I got to the pub there were no coppers to be seen.

We were keeping a look-out for the old bill. There were surprisingly few about. We'd had a couple of vans slow down as they passed but we'd made sure everyone without exception was inside and not outside the pub. We didn't want to bring any unnecessary attention to us or our location. We were receiving phone calls. People were on the phone to lads on the other side of the City. 'They're pulling 150 plus over there. Blues won't know what's hit them tonight,' was the sort of stuff they relayed to the rest of us. Tucker was getting calls that Blues were trying to get down to Nechells to meet us. They were quoting the usual inflated numbers to him. 'They've got 200 plus out!' That would remain to be seen. If they had got it together and met ONE of our firms today they'd have their hands full. We were getting bored hanging around now. The tension was starting to build. We knew they hated us with a passion, but we had grown to hate them just as much. We were just as game as they were and we intended to show them once and for all tonight. Tucker received another phone call, 'Hey lads, they reckon they're only down the road!' 'No-one move yet' said Fowler, 'we'll send someone down to see if they're about. It was decided I would go down to have a look.

Dandy: Little Ginge and myself decided to go down with Luddy and have a look. They reckoned they were in Shanahan's a small pub just down from O'Reilly's. It was

about half a mile away. We walked down the road. We were being filmed at this point but we didn't know it at the time. West Midlands Police had followed Blues all the way from the city centre. They had met in a place called PJ's. We didn't know about the old bill. We were totally oblivious.

We had been set up. It would appear Blues were unaware the old bill were watching them. They had brought the police with them. Later video footage shown during the prosecutions which followed showed them meeting at PJ's in the city centre. (West Midlands Police were sitting outside in a car with a video camera) They then made their way down to Nechells to try and ambush us on our way towards the ground. In their book they state that they had 200 out and they met in Balsall Heath. They then state that they made their way down a pub called Moriarty's. All of a sudden they reckon they've only got 25 at Rocky Lane. Where did the other 175 disappear to? The truth of the matter is, the lads they had at Rocky Lane met at PJ's. The police were filming them there. The police followed them down to Rocky Lane. They didn't have any more out than what they had at Rocky Lane. They couldn't pull more than that, they are a washed up firm. It's there in black and white on the statements. It's also there on the film. Balsall Heath was bollocks. They won't admit it, but they never explain where that other 175 went to. They had 50 at Rocky Lane. Every statement made by officers on the scene state it was 50 Birmingham City fans fighting similar numbers of Villa fans. Our firm did number in the hundreds, but it was spread over a distance of 400-600 yards. The numbers facing each other at the front were similar in size.

They were at Shanahan's now. The three of us made our way down Rocky Lane. We were completely oblivious to the police videoing us in the distance. I was fully wrapped up as was Dandy. We'd purchased these ski mask things which you pulled over your head and round your neck and it doubled as a face mask. CCTV was being used so commonly we'd learnt it was best to keep covered up. We walked down the road. We didn't think we would find anything. We thought it would be another wild goose chase. They were probably sitting in Digbeth and thought they'd give us the run around a bit. 'If they're down there we'll be on our toes you know,' said Ginge. 'They'll have people out spotting,' I didn't fancy that. I was still limping from a hip replacement that I had to have a few months earlier. Stupidly the pull to get involved again had been too much. I was now limping down the road towards goodness knew what. A car slowed down alongside us. It was Roger an old C-Crew face. 'Blues are down there you know, don't know how many of them but they're there. They're drinking in Shanahan's.' We saw Carl one of our older lads then. He also drove past. A few lads had just left work and had decided to scout round the areas where either firm was to be expected. They'd gone to have a look what was happening. Carl slowed down, 'They're down there! There's quite a few of them. It looks like they're just leaving to come up here!' he shouted over. No police around. Blues down the road. It appeared it was game on.

Baz: The pub was now heaving. I would say we had a good 150 lads inside. I went out side for a breather. In the Zulu book one of theirs said that he drove past and saw Fowler with one hundred and fifty outside. He couldn't have. We weren't waiting outside we made a point of making sure no-one was outside the pub. Speaking from my own experience that day I did not have a clue that Blues were in Shanahan's. I think that only a handful of people like Luddy, Tucker and Fowler did know. It was kept quiet as best it could be. People were getting restless and jumpy.

We were just watching. Down the road close to Shanahan's I could see a group starting to leave the pub. After what we'd been told and what I could see I guessed it was Blues. I got on the phone. I rang Fowler. 'They're here! They are definitely here!' I shouted down the phone. 'Are you sure?' he asked. I don't want to leave these drinks if they're not! It's three deep at the bar!' Just as he said this I saw the group were coming towards me. It was Blues.

Baz: Suddenly the pub began to empty from the corner door. It was gonna go now. I was fucking trapped over by the bar. I pushed over to the corner and out onto pavement outside. I looked to my left and saw everyone starting to jog down the road. There was loads of shouting and shouts of 'They're here! They're fucking here!'

Fowler: When I got the phone call from Luddy, I turned to Pete and said, 'They're here. They're down the road.' Pete's one of our older lads, he's been going down for years. He turned to me and said, 'I've been fighting these cunts for years. They've always liked to bully us. We've always been younger than them and they've taken advantage of that. We're not kids anymore. For the first time in years these cunts are going to be fighting men.' We left the boozer and raced down the road.

They were coming and there were three of us standing there. We were all trying to convince people by phone they were actually there and it wasn't a false alarm. 'Nah Fowl, they're here, I can see them myself. Get the boys down here!' I shouted. We looked for missiles. We could see the fluorescent jackets of the police now. Blues were on the right hand side of the road as we looked. The fluorescent jackets of the police appeared from the left. We were masked up so we hurled a few missiles at the approaching Blues and backed off. We were not even pretending we were going to stand. They saw us and they roared, 'Zulu! Zulu!' One of them was swinging something around above his head. It looked like an exhaust assembly. We then heard the roar from behind us as O'Reilly's emptied. There was scores of Villa fans running down towards us. We were standing in the middle.

Fowler: I made my way down the road. I suddenly saw them in front of me. I ran towards them. I thought I'm having some of this! On the video the police made you see them emptying out of the pub, then the copper dropped his camera and runs up to where the fighting had begun. So they didn't manage to film it all. I put one of them straight on his arse. Fair play to them Blues stood. Bottles and glasses were flying. There were about 60 of them there in total. Afterwards they said to me, 'Fucking hell there was only 60 of us and hundreds of you!' I always say to them, 'So what? It was your local derby!' They're always going on about how good they are how many they can pull, and they only had 60 lads out? They were telling us they were going to kill us and they could only pull out that number of lads? They say they're Birmingham's number one and they can only pull 60 lads for a local derby game? Its no use them coming crying to me afterwards.

Baz: I sprinted to try and get to the front. I could hear the Zulu's chanting. Glass was smashing all over the road. I was absolutely on fire with adrenalin. I noticed a couple of police stood at the side of the road. Blues had made a bit of a line but it was more across to my right hand side. They were bunched up and holding on to each other. They were well tooled up. Someone came at me with an exhaust manifold. I threw a punch and got whacked with the exhaust. Behind us there seemed to come a second wave and a bigger roar as more Villa lads poured forward. The Blues on my side of the road turned and got on their toes. You could hear someone screaming 'Stand! Stand!' They stopped and formed a better line. We went forward again. There was an Indian guy with Blues. He came at me with an engine block. I backed away and from my right someone smacked him. There were wheel trims, bottles, bits of metal. Everything you could imagine was being used and thrown by Blues. They tend to deny this in their book. They say that just one lad had a piece of car engine. I stood now at the front There were lots of exchanges of punches going on. Fowler was exchanging blows with Ginger Maurice. A black geezer started lunging at me with a bottle. He walked backwards, shouting the Blues on. He began pulling bottles from his jacket pocket and chucking them into us. Another black bloke came flying at me. As he did I threw a punch at the side of his head and he went past me and into the lads behind me. The fighting and noise seemed to go on for ages.

We started to shout to our lot that the old bill were there. It fell on deaf ears as they raced past us. People were full of beer and adrenalin. The two firms met in the middle of Rocky Lane. Half the lads I think became aware of the cameras. Both firms clashed then there was a stand-off in the middle of the road. The road narrowed where the two mobs met. We outnumbered them. We couldn't turn that to our advantage because of how the road narrowed. To add to that there was a steel railing on one side protecting the pavement from the road. This narrowed it down even further. They couldn't have picked a better spot if they had planned it. The police were there filming and a lot of our lads clocked that. The ones at the front simply stood their ground. More Villa were coming down the road but they couldn't get to the front. They could see the police and decided it was worthless bothering. They started throwing bottles but they were mainly landing behind the Blues as their numbers were so small. Punches were exchanged and Blues were on their toes twice. The Police soon arrived and people started to scatter.

Fowler: No matter what anyone says about Rocky Lane there's only one person who kept it together for them. It was Ginger Morris. If it wasn't for him they would've been gone, on their toes. They ran a couple of times. He was dragging them back, calling them back to have a go. If the police hadn't have been there Blues would've been leathered. It's as simple as that. When the police arrived in numbers they arrived behind us. They were driving their vans into the Villa, scattering us.

You can't knock Birmingham that day, they did well with less than half the numbers we had. They'd also brought the old bill with them. If the old bill hadn't have been there they'd have been obliterated. The police now landed in numbers. They herded us back towards O'Reilly's at Aston Cross. They herded Blues in the opposite direction. They forced us into a group outside O'Reilly's and filmed us all. Some arrests were made there and then.

Fowler: I was arrested straight away. The old bill were shouting, 'Get Fowler! Get teven Fowler!' They nicked Steff, Pete, H and me. They also nicked a few others. They ept us over night and let us go the next afternoon. They bailed me and I was told to o back sometime in November. A few weeks before I was due to go back they had my

door in at 5am in the morning. It was all riot squad, clad in full robo-cop gear. When I came outside there was an inspector standing outside. He was running the show. The old bill were going, 'We've got him boss, we've got him!' This clown went, 'Nice one!' and jumped in his car and sped off. They charged me with violent disorder.

Baz: I hadn't clocked that the police were filming it as I was more focused on the Blues and what they were throwing and doing. I was stood at the front and had it with Blues. At no time did we attempt to retreat. The first time I watched the video at Stechford Police Station I was amazed at how much of it they had filmed. I heard the inevitable sirens as the old bills back up eventually arrived. A lot of the lads from both firms saw this as their last chance to go for it and there were a lot of punches being thrown. I was hit with a big orange crate and decided that that was my cue to get back up the road and try to avoid arrest. As I jogged back up the road in the middle of it was an armoured van the type that they use for delivering money to banks. In the front were two blokes who were laughing. The old bill tried to say that the men in the van were in fear of their lives. They also said that the officers filming were also terrified. If you look at the video you can clearly see P.C. Kelly with his arms folded taking it all in. They had it on a plate and they knew it. I got back to the pub. Along with everyone else I was rounded up outside. Some of the lads had gone into the car-park to try and get away. They were caught and were now being dragged about by the old bill. One of the coppers was pointing people out and they were being arrested. They came towards my direction and grabbed Chester Phil by the neck. I pushed forward and grabbed Phil's arm and tried to talk the copper out of it. As I did this I was grabbed by the arm and turned to see P.C. Adrian Kelly. He said to me 'You were there as well Barry, I saw you fighting.' I was arrested on a public order charge and put in a van. I was then taken to Steelhouse Lane Police Station.

Tucker: I think I was the first one arrested to be honest. I was rolling across the floor with one of the Blues lads. We finally heard the sirens. As I stood up, PC Gant, Blues police spotter ran over and grabbed me. 'You're nicked!' he said. 'I haven't done anything!' I replied. 'I've just seen you! I've just watched you fighting!' He said as he took me over and put me in a van. At the station a copper came up to me and said, 'Are you Tucker? What happened? You've got no arresting officer.' I told him I'd been scared when the trouble broke out and had just jumped in the police van. I was hoping they'd believe it and just let me go. He said to me, 'Have you got a ticket for the game?' 'No I haven't,' I replied. 'Well get one!' he said. 'Why's that?' I asked him, 'Trust me,' he said. Chester Phil slipped me his ticket. The copper took me up to the desk. He said to the custody sergeant, 'This lad says he was scared and he jumped in the wagon.' 'What do you mean?' replied the custody sergeant. 'He's got no arresting officer

replied my man. My arresting officer wasn't there because it was Gant the Blues spotter. He was obviously needed more at the game rather than worrying about charging me. They couldn't charge me without my arresting officer. 'All I know is he says he jumped in the van. We can't charge him so let's bail him. We know who he is and he can come back.' So the Custody Sergeant agreed. I had a ticket and I went and saw the game. Fair play to that copper. I'm sure I spotted a Villa tattoo on his arm.

They then formed us into an escort and took us through Nechells towards Bordesley and St Andrews. That went without a hitch for them. They were deliberately taking their time. They wanted to clear the way and for us to arrive late when most of the crowd had already gone into the ground. We hadn't played them for a while, but if all they could pull was 50 odd we knew that was a major comedown for them. At the other side of the City, the Steamers and the C-Crew had joined forces and were marching towards the ground from the other side of the city. Some Blues had bumped into them as they approached the ground. Blues had made a mistake by coming down to Aston. They'd done well but it left them with nothing to cope with what was now coming down the Coventry Road. It went off an island. As we were nearing the ground from the other direction, we could hear it happening on the radio's of the police who were escorting us. It was dead as we arrived at the stadium late. We went inside. The atmosphere was electric as is usual for these encounters. Villa didn't turn up. Birmingham beat us by three goals to nil. There were various flashpoints during the game. Some Blues got on the pitch. We tried to get on the pitch. The stewards and police forced us back. People were boiling as the game ended. We left the stadium. We grouped together as best we could. It was confused. There was both Hardcore and older lot in our police escort as we walked down Garrison Lane. The police always divide the road into two and the idea is that we walked down one side and they walked down the other side. At the bottom they turned us towards Aston and turned them towards Digbeth. Some of them had a pop. They tried to break through the cordon but by now the police had it all under control.

Tucker: I went to the game. Afterwards, when we'd been stuffed 3-0 I was walking down the road with Simmo and Irish Jim. This big burly copper came over and said, 'You were nicked earlier. What are you doing here?' He kept me there on my own. The others were made to walk on. Villa finished filing past and it was all Blues then. Some of them sussed me and were saying stuff like, 'You're having it!' The copper then smiled and said, 'Right you can go now,' I walked down the road and took a right turn. was bricking it. I daren't look back in case any who had walked past and sussed me

POLICE STILLS FROM ROCKY LANE

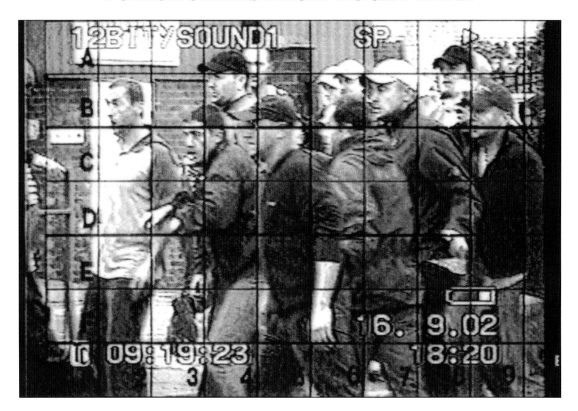

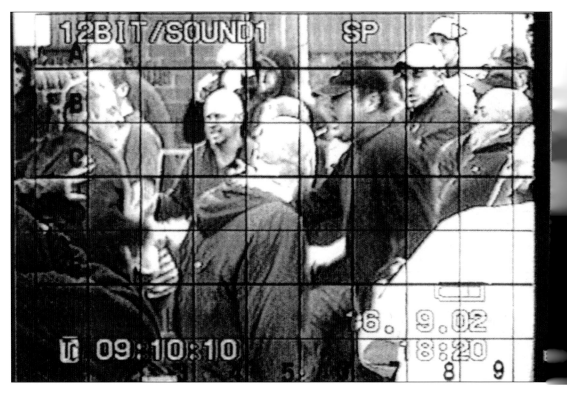

POLICE STILLS FROM ROCKY LANE

POLICE STILLS FROM ROCKY LANE

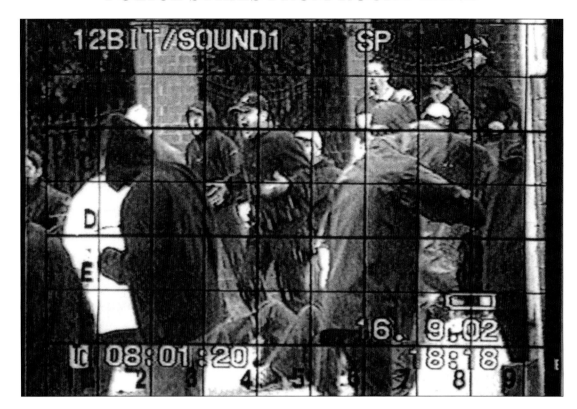

Night of shame for the crowd

● FROM PAGE ONE

Meanwhile, the Football Association today confirmed it would investigate the scenes at St Andrews.

But police hit out at a minority of rival hooligans who clashed with each other and police in the build-up to the Second City derby game for "disgracing their clubs and their city".

Rivals groups of soccer louts were found armed with CS gas canisters, home-made knives and billiard balls in socks.

The worst violence came when a group of around 200 hooligans were involved in street brawl in Rocky Lane, Nechells, an hour before kick-off. There was also sporadic fighting near to the McDonalds restaurant on Coventry Road which required a "robust" police response.

Bottles and rocks rained down on police officers as they confronted crowds. One woman officer was hit in the face by a missile. Coins were also thrown at rival fans.

A total of 41 people were arrested for public order offences, the majority inside the ground. Four people were also ejected from the ground.

● DO you know the mystery man? Ring the Evening Mail newsdesk on 0121 234 5564.

Hooligan leader was notorious throughout world of football

Among the Aston Villa fans jailed for fighting before the 2002 derby game with Birmingham City at St Andrew's was one well-known hooligan.

Steven Fowler was refused entry to both Japan and Belgium when the countries held football tournaments in 2002 and 2000.

He was also thrown out of France during the 1998 World Cup as part of a new get-tough policy that targeted known hooligans who might not have caused any specific trouble at tournaments.

He was arrested in Toulouse shortly after being recognised by a hooligan "spotter". At the time, the National Criminal Intelligence Service said he was a hard-core category C hooligan leader. Fowler was also known to Belgium, German and Dutch authorities before the Holland/Belgium European Championships in 2002 after his name was included on a 1,000-name list of offenders sent out by NCIS.

He was turned away from passport control at Ostend after taking a ferry from Dover.

The same NCIS crackdown, which involves British police sharing intelligence with their foreign counterparts, led to Fowler being refused entry into Japan in 2002.

However, it emerged later that he had not been made the subject of a football banning order, which would have prevented him from leaving the UK.

Steven Fowler

Blues v Villa police raids

■ SWOOPS... police kick open a door today

By Mark Cowan

SOCCER fans suspected of clashing with police following the Second City derby were arrested in a series of dawn swoops today – after being named by *Birmingham Mail* readers.

Police targeted them as part of an investigation into violence which flared outside St Andrew's after Aston Villa's 2-1 victory over Birmingham City last month.

Two weeks ago, the Mail printed images of 27 faces which police took from CCTV footage in or near to a 200-strong crowd, some of whom fought with police.

Detective Sergeant Neil Groutage, from Stechford Police, who is leading the investigation, said: "As a result of the excellent response from Birmingham Mail readers, we have identified the vast majority of those who we sought in connection with the disorder."

A number of the men also voluntarily handed themselves in to police after seeing their faces.

Today's operation was led by detectives from Stechford and backed up by 130 police officers from across the city.

Within the first two hours of the operation, 16 people were in

TURN TO PAGE 2

A 'Your Shout' special on the derby battle no one will forget

I FEARED FOR MY LIFE

- AFTER the media fence over the crowd trouble I hope that all the Press are going to come out in defence of Birmingham City fans.

I was in the away section at Villa Park and despite severe turnstiles, blaming the Villa fans in the Doug Ellis Stand, the Blues fans did not react and stayed calm.

I think the accusation slating we took following the first match – and rightly so – we should have at least some praise for Wednesday night.

CHRIS KELY,
Solihull.

Instead what I got actually made me fear for my life before kick-off, hundreds of so-called Villa supporters charged at Blues fans and hurled bricks and bottles.

I must commend the bravery of the police who risked their own safety to protect us. Am I looking forward to another Midland derby? NO thanks.

RUSSIL TOWNSEND,
Castle Bromwich.

I would put all the blame on Villa for the trouble on Monday. The Blues fans who got into the home areas after the tackle, it won't be for their footballing skills, it will be for their bully-boy tactics.

MICHEL RAY
Nuneaton.

MANY thanks to the police for the embarrassing night in front of the watching millions.

What is it with the cameras and these so called fans laughing stock? I dread to think what will happen when Southampton come to Villa. He also spent last summer on

Dublin was sent off in the 51st minute after butting Savage. The Villa star has since apologised, saying he was ashamed of his actions.

The violence at the ugly scenes at last September's encounter at St Andrew's.

On Thursday grinning Aston Villa fan Daniel McKeon, who ran onto the pitch to confront Savage, was banned from attending any football match for three years.

McKeon, 21, of Redditch, later said he "felt amazing" when he sprinted onto the pitch describing it as "a real moment of glory".

The Sunday Mercury has now learned that Blues fans are threatening to target him in a revenge attack for "embarrassing" Savage.

Police blitz after Villa-Blues violence

FLASHPOINT... police line up in front of fans at the Villa Park derby and (inset) Dublin headbutts Savage

DOZENS MORE FACING ARREST

POLICE are planning to swoop and arrest DOZENS of football thugs involved in trouble at the Birmingham soccer derby.

Twenty people have already appeared before the courts following the violent scenes which marred the Villa Park match on Monday night.

Forty people were arrested before and after the game, which saw Aston Villa striker Dion Dublin sent off for headbutting Blues midfielder Robbie Savage.

But now West Midlands Police have confirmed more arrests will follow.

A spokesman said: "Officers are examining all the evidence from witnesses as well as CCTV footage. We are expecting to make more arrests."

A police source added: "There could be dozens of raids at homes across the city in the next couple of weeks. A lot of intelligence has been gathered over the last 48 hours.

"Police won't be aware there was the possibility for trouble on the night. Spotters and intelligence officers were out in force.

"What we have seen so far in terms of arrests is only the tip of the iceberg. Police want to bring many more thugs to book."

There was trouble on and off the field during Monday's game, which Blues won 2-0.

appeared on a Birmingham City fans website along with the chilling message: "Know the road where he lives well. I am sure that he'll have to produce an important recognition.

revealed he has received death threats on his personal website.

Fan's death has not curbed louts

RAIDS NET A RESULT

Derby day 17 charged

BY MARK COWAN

THE 17 suspected soccer yobs detained in dawn swoops have all been charged for fighting before the Birmingham City v Villa derby clash.

The men, from across the West Midlands, were arrested yesterday in a series of raids co-ordinated by police in Stechford.

Accused

And in separate development, two men whose faces were among seven published in the Evening Mail have called police to hand themselves in.

All 17 – supporters of Birmingham City and Aston Villa – were accused of taking part in a mass street brawl just hours before the first city derby game for 16 years.

A 200-strong mob had gathered in Rocky Lane, Nechells

and between 30 and 40 were involved in fighting in what was thought to be a pre-arranged meeting.

Rival fans were found armed with CS gas canisters, batons, knives and parts from a car engine in some of the worst football violence in Birmingham in recent years.

Det Insp Simon Vowles, from Stechford CID, said the men had been charged with violent disorder and released on conditional bail to appear before magistrates in two weeks.

He said police anticipated nine more arrests over the weekend and another half a dozen in the coming weeks.

Det Chief Insp Clive Burgess, who co-ordinated the operation, added: "It was all a big success and I am delighted with the results.

mark.cowan@mrn.co.uk

VILLA GANGS 'HIRED NAZIS'

VILLA hooligans are recruiting members of a hard-core neo-Nazi gang to fight for them, it has been claimed.

Birmingham City's notorious Zulu firm say that Combat 18 members were hired for derby day brawls and an England international last year.

Running battles between Blues and Villa fans took place in Rocky Lane during the local clash last September, leading to the worst soccer violence seen in Birmingham for years.

Last night one self-confessed Blues thug said: "There was a three-mile pub closure around Villa Park and we knew Villa had recruited Combat 18 lads.

"The police used different tactics for Rocky Lane. They filmed the fighting and we were not as quick to step in. We think the police wanted to draw the big players out and get us at the same time.

"My impression is that a minority of Villa hooligans did link up with right-wing groups from Chelsea at the Villa Park England friendly against Portugal in September 2002."

A spokesman for Aston Villa said: "We, like all clubs in the Premier League, take any hooligan-type behaviour very seriously and work very closely with the police to ensure the safety of all our fans.

DEADLY RIVALRY... Crowd disturbances in Witton Lane before the start of the Villa v Blues match last March

---

DERBY DAY SWOOP ON SOCCER THUGS

BY CAROLINE WHEELER

POLICE are set to swoop on the homes of known soccer hooligans on the day of the Blues v Aston Villa derby game next month.

The thugs could face arrest hours before kick-off and b released only once the final whistle has been blown on October 19, a police source has revealed.

Cops plan to use new powers to make pre-emptive raids following a trouble-fuelled season last year, during which 575 Midland soccer fans were arrested.

Revenge

Last week the Sunday Mercury revealed how Villa thugs were plotting revenge against Birmingham City rivals who invaded the Villa Park pitch last year during a friendly football game.

One Villa fan boasted on an illicit internet site: "It's all going to go off this season.

"My money is on us showing you up on the pitch this season as well as off it again."

Now West Midlands Police are ready to take a more pro-active stance to football violence by using new powers to curb potential derby-day trouble.

"Officers are considering picking off known trouble-makers on the morning of the derby in order to avoid trouble," said a police source.

"They will be arrested at home and detained until the match has finished.

"Officers will use common law powers, which entitles them to arrest anyone who is likely to cause a breach of the peace, rather than more regular football legislation.

"It is believed the powers will be used for the first time before the Blues v Villa derby on October 19."

West Midlands Police has also insisted on earlier kick-offs for derby matches in a bid to avoid clashes among rival fans.

Last week Inspector Sue

Parker said: "West Midlands Police intends to continue to clamp down on the minority of football fans who spoil the enjoyment of the game for the majority of peaceful fans.

"We take a proactive intelligence-led approach to target all hooligans.

"Kick-off times for all local derbies have been brought

forward and will now be earlier than last season."

● The 2002/2003 season saw 4,793 arrests in England and Wales, compared with 4,035 the previous year.

Supporters of Midland clubs were among the worst culprits. Birmingham City fans clocked up 138 arrests. Villa 101 arrests, Wolves 96, Leicester 80, Stoke 69, West Brom 63 and Coventry 28.

Vass: Trouble scared me

ENGLAND and Aston Villa striker Darius Vassell has admitted he became worried as trouble erupted during last year's heated derby match with Birmingham City.

"We all have families and you've got to think about your

own safety," he said. "In games like that there's not much that can be done to stop fans getting on the pitch.

"Sometimes they hate us with such a vengeance that you never know what they're going to do.

Thugs ruin big match

Police move in to keep order during the match at Villa Park last night. Right, goalkeeper Peter Enckelman helps halt one fan who confroted Robbie Savage

Pictures, TIM EASTHOPE

Post Reporting Team
Neil Connor, Sarah Probert,
John Revill, Richard Warburton

More than 40 fans were arrested and there were several injuries, including police officers, as violence scarred last night's football derby between Aston Villa and Birmingham City.

Running battles broke out between hooligans and police in riot gear before and after the game at Villa Park.

Bottles and bricks were thrown at police as hundreds of officers tried to prevent clashes between rival supporters outside the stadium.

An army of stewards battled to keep control in the ground as Villa went down 2-0 and had two players sent off in the highly-charged match, which also saw fans running on to the pitch.

One tried to confront several Blues' players before he was marched off by stewards. The episode – reminiscent of the first game between the teams at St Andrew's earlier this season – left Blues' striker Geoff Horsfield admitting he had feared for his safety. Seats were ripped up – one was thrown by Blues' fans into the goalmouth in front of the North Stand – and there were reports of coin throwing in the Doug Ellis and North Stands during the course of the second half, while kiosks in the Holte End were attacked during the half-time interval.

Small skirmishes also broke out around the ground as Villa fans attacked their Blues counterparts who had managed to get tickets among home supporters.

There were even reports of scuffles in hospitality boxes.

About 300 police and 400 stewards were on duty and afterwards senior West Midlands Police officers condemned the hooligans.

Insp Bob Peebles said the behaviour of some supporters was "atrocious" and had put many people in danger.

"The first half of the game was lively but relatively well behaved. During the second half there were events in the game, sendings off and goals, which led to a small pitch invasion and a rise in tension in the ground.

"After the match there were a number of disorder incidents and a number of people were arrested.

"The behaviour of some the supporters has been atrocious and put many people in danger. A police inquiry will continue and seek to identify those not yet arrested."

The clashes outside the stadium after the match broke out as Villa supporters left the Holte End – their 'home' stand – and tried to confront Blues' fans in Witton Lane.

Dozens of police in riot gear forced the Villa fans from the Witton Lane island to Lichfield Road and into Queen's Road, where officers found themselves under fire from bottles and bricks.

Even before the match kicked off, police had to cope with trouble around the ground at three flashpoints.

Rival fans clashed in Witton Square and Aston Park before being separated while a mob of about 300 pelted police with bottles in Witton Lane. Chief Supt Douglas Paxton, ground commander, said: "There was organised disorder in at least three locations on a scale which required us to be very flexible. The disturbance in Witton Lane took just about everything we had to maintain public order and keep the crowd moving."

By half time, there were 15 people held in cells at the ground after being arrested for offences including violent disorder and alcohol offences, and by the end of the match that figure had risen to 40, including several who made pitch incursions. More arrests were made outside the ground and others are expected to follow.

Chief Supt Paxton said: "It's the usual story – the vast majority of fans come along to enjoy the match. It was disappointing though on this occasion there were some hundreds of fans prepared and coordinated enough to confront the police.

"There will be a post match investigation with CCTV footage and other information gathered by officers being examined.

"People may have left the game thinking they've got away with it but they can expect a knock in the early morning in the next few weeks."

Report, Page 2
Sport, Pages 30,31,32

Sixteen held after violent street brawl

BY MARK COWAN

SCORES of football hooligans armed with bottles and pool balls clashed in a violent street brawl after the Second City derby.

Detectives said up to 200 yobs were involved in the confrontation near the Gerard Mann Mercedes dealership in Lichfield Road, Aston, last night. Sixteen people were arrested as the fighting spilled out across the road.

The sickening violence happened around five hours after the match.

Detectives were today due to begin sifting through CCTV footage from cameras in Lichfield Road to identify those involved in the trouble at 7pm.

Thugs rampaged through the street in a violent battle, hurling pool balls and bottles at each other before police swooped.

Det Insp Nick Murphy, from Queen's Road CID, said further arrests could follow.

He said: "Sixteen people were arrested following disorder and are currently in custody."

Spotlight

Mr Murphy also appealed to members of the public innocently caught up in the brawl to get in touch.

"This was a large-scale incident where people were fighting in the street," he said. "There may have been people driving past who have seen the incident and I would urge them to come forward.

The brawl has again thrown the spotlight on the mindless thugs bringing shame to genuine fans of the city's two top flight teams.

In a separate development, two men were arrested in the West Midlands today during an operation surrounding violent clashes which followed the England v Wales World Cup qualifier last October.

One man was arrested in Walsall and another in Walsall Wood in a series of dawn raids that saw 26 arrests across the country. A third man from Wednesbury was due to hand himself into police later today.

had waited to see what had happened and were now following me. I walked down a road. There was loads of Blues. One of them clocked me and said, 'Oi! Mate! Are you Villa?' I quickly replied, 'No mate of course not, I'm from Chelmsley.' I tried to walk on. He shouted after me, 'Well how come you've got a fucking Villa badge on then?' What a doughnut, I'd left my Villa badge on. It was only small but big enough to be clocked. A few others turned round and I turned round and I legged it. They chased me all up the road I had just walked down. I blended in with the crowds and managed to get away.

Baz: We were in the cells. It was a nightmare having to listen to the game there and the police were banging on the door every time Blues scored. I eventually nodded off as the light in my cell didn't work at all. I was woken at about three in the morning. I shot up and began to whistle as I went out the cell door. I bent down and went to grab my shoes when the screw said 'you can fucking leave them there. You're not getting out you're being charged.' My heart sank. I was taken down to the desk where I was charged with violent disorder.

A month later the Evening Mail published pictures of people wanted in connection with the incident and the Mail's Mark Cowan wrote:

NO PLACE TO HIDE

Police in hunt for match yobs

POLICE today appealed to Evening Mail readers to help identify suspected soccer yobs. They were among a group of around 200 so-called fans of Birmingham City and Aston Villa who were involved in a street brawl in Nechells before the Second City derby. One of them is holding what is believed to be an extendable baton. The men are wanted for questioning about the clashes which marred the first top-flight fixture between the two clubs for 16 years.

Fighting broke out in Rocky Lane, near O'Reilly's pub, in what police believe was a pre-arranged meeting. At the height of the fighting, it is estimated between 30 and 40 people were involved. Order was quickly restored when scores of police officers were called to the scene. Det Chief Insp Clive Burgess said: 'These people were certainly present at the scene and we would like to speak to them about what happened. As yet we do not know who they are but we are keen to trace them and I am hoping people will be able to recognise them from these photographs. We would like them to come forward and assist us with our inquiries and if they recognise themselves I would ask them to get in touch.'

Anyone recognising any of the people in the photographs can call Stechford Police or via the anonymous Crimestoppers hotline.

From the Birmingham Evening Mail 10th October 2002:

DAWN RAID ON SOCCER THUGS SUSPECTS
By Mark Cowan

Suspected soccer yobs who clashed in violent street battles before Birmingham's Second City Derby clash were arrested in a series of dawn swoops today. Police targeted 30 fans who they believe orchestrated or took part in pre-match brawls in a swoop on addresses across the West Midlands. In the first hour 13 men - supporters of both Birmingham City and Aston Villa - were in custody and other arrests were due to follow. The running battle in Rocky Lane on September 16 involved around 200 hooligans from both sides and was the worst soccer violence to erupt in Birmingham for years. Rival fans were armed with CS gas canisters, batons, knives and makeshift weapons made of billiard balls in socks.

Today's operation was the culmination of a three-week-long probe into the violence that marred the first top-flight derby game between Villa and Blues for 16 years. Officers from Stechford, who co-ordinated today's operation, were joined by police from across the city with back-up from the Operational Support Unit. A number of officers were dressed in full protective body armour and carried riot shields.

Det Chief Insp Clive Burgess, who co-ordinated the operation, said: "This was the arrest phase of the operation set up following serious disorder in Rocky Lane. 'Supporters from both teams were engaged in fighting using weapons such as batons, CS gas and a car engine. We have identified 31 people responsible who were involved in that disorder. Today's operation was about arresting those offenders and removing identified football hooligan elements from the local community to make the streets safer and also to protect those attending football matches.'

Apart from the fighting in Nechells, trouble also flared near the McDonald's restaurant on Coventry Road.

Tucker: They raided us three days before we were due to hand ourselves in. It had to be for the benefit of the press. We were all due to go back anyway. They knew who we all were, where we all lived. It was purely a public relations thing.

I took it to trial, Crown Court. I got a hung jury. They came to me and said they were going to go for a re-trial, but they'd drop the violent disorder to an affray. They then proceeded to tell me I'd get community service for it. My solicitor wasn't there that day for some reason. I took their offer and went guilty. I got three months. When I next saw my solicitor he was going, 'Why did you go guilty? You had a hung jury, 70% of hung jury cases get a not guilty the second time. If it wasn't football they wouldn't have gone for the retrial.' I also received a five year banning order.

Baz: On my first morning on reception in Winson Green Prison I was told that there were to Blues lads in the cell opposite on our landing. I was then let out of the cell and had to walk down to the end of the wing. As I walked down the landing the two Blues lads were let out at the same time. I looked over and saw Ginger Morris and Darren Morgan. They looked over and said hello. We all walked down towards the screw who said, 'There isn't going to be any trouble is there?' We looked at each other and laughed. I had a chat with them about sentences as they were gutted we had got less time than them.

Tucker: When I first walked out my cell in Winson Green Prison, HMP Birmingham I noticed to my left was Ginger Morris and another Blues lad. On my right was Fuller, who was also Blues. Straight away they said to me, 'Look its football, it doesn't apply in here.' Fair play to them, we got on okay. I had a paper sent in. When I'd finished with it I'd shove it under their cell door. They'd share their stuff with me. Morris was bang on inside, he's a good lad.

In the Birmingham Evening Mail on Thursday 1st April 2004 Mark Cowan wrote:

VILLA YOBS CAGED

Thugs held after derby match violence

THESE football hooligans who heaped shame on Birmingham were today branded 'a disgrace to their clubs'. Organised thugs from both Villa and blues clashed in a sickening orgy of 'extreme-violence' as the clubs prepared for the first top-flight fixture in 16 years. But 11 of the Villa yobs who dragged Midlands soccer through the gutter were today pondering their part in the pitched battle from behind locked doors.

The jailed men were among 24 hauled before the courts for their part in what has now been dubbed 'The Battle of Rocky Lane'. They were caught on video film brandishing home-made knives, CS gas canisters, batons and billiard balls in socks, by five police spotters on the scene as the violence erupted. The yobs were jailed just two days after seven so called Birmingham City thugs were dealt with in the same way by the same judge. The remaining six were handed community service orders. Crucially with the European Championships in Portugal just months away they have now been banned from football games at home, and abroad for up to ten years. One of them Steven Fowler was recognised as a hard-core category C hooligan leader who has been refused entry into Japan and Belgium and was also kicked out of France in 1998. The September night in 2002 was meant to be a night of soccer celebration - but the main hooligan firms attached to both Villa and Blues used the game as an excuse to arrange their own fixture. Their ranks were swelled by drunken yobs and former soccer thugs who had come out for one last chance to rekindle bitter rivalries with those from across the city. Up to 200 men, fuelled by alcohol, a warped sense of team support were involved. The Blues thugs were drinking in a pub on Rocky Lane miles away from St Andrews but crucially less than half a mile from where Villa fans were drinking. Shortly after 6pm the two gangs emerged. An eight minute pitched battle exploded with around 40 yobs wading into each other, before retreating then going back for more. A month after the game police mounted a series of dawn raids to round up those caught on police video of the fight in Rocky Lane. A number also handed themselves in after their pictures appeared in the Evening Mail.

Chapter Ten: Villa Hardcore. Doing It

Aston Villa Vs West Bromwich Albion Premier League
12th December 2002

Geographically, West Bromwich Albion are Villa's closest rivals. The Albion/Wolves rivalry has only become more intense over the last decade or so. That's a Black Country thing. We always laugh it's the Denim Derby. Status Quo (Albion) versus Slade (Wolves) due to their fans penchant for denim jackets and long hair. Albion have got lads, but they haven't got anywhere near the numbers we have. We have always without exception had the numbers against West Brom. In the 80s a lot of Albion's lads started to go with Blues. They've always had a strong connection since then. In the 80s we would turn up at Albion and they'd have Blues with them. When Albion opened their new stand in the mid 80s we went into the new stand, a small mob of us. Albion had a mob of Blues with them in the Smethwick end. We called them Rent-a-firm for quite a while afterwards. Up until Sunderland no Villa firm has had ties with any other firm. It would be like us asking Sunderland to come down for a local derby match because we can't handle our neighbours - embarrassing. As the Villa Youth we took a small firm in the mid-80s to Albion. I think it was Brendan Batson's testimonial. We were only kids and as we almost reached the away end a mob came round the corner. They were all black and they attacked us and chased us down the Soho Road. I was caught and given a good hiding. One of them pulled a machete out at one point before the old bill arrived. These weren't Albion, they were Blues, all of them Zulu's. At Villa we certainly wouldn't stand for another firm knocking about on match-day no matter how much we or they despised our opponents. O'Reilly's in Aston was again chosen as a meeting point for this fixture. They had threatened to come from Birmingham city centre down the Lichfield Road. That's why O'Reilly's was chosen. If they came from town we could get to both main drags from the city centre - Lichfield Road and Newtown Row - within a few minutes. The pub was full of Villa. Everyone was in good spirits, and more importantly there were no old bill about. A few calls went backwards and forwards with Albion. Personally I've always kept out of that sort of thing. I don't want to talk to them, let someone else do that. I'm like that with all teams, just no interest in talking to them. It materialised that they were drinking in Handsworth, which is the nearest Birmingham area to West Bromwich. They eventually landed at Perry Barr the opposite side of ground to where they knew we were. We left the pub about 2.45 and made our way to the ground. We were on Witton Lane. It's the road which runs at the side of the Doug Ellis stand. We could see Albion's firm was being escorted up the road. They had about 80 or so lads. Albion seemed relatively happy being marched to the away end.

We later found out that they had attacked the Little Crown pub in Perry Barr en route to Villa Park. They had trashed the pub. It only had about 20 odd Villa in there that could be considered game. They chose that pub because it was quiet but it used to have a name in the 80s. It was a bit of a result for them. They've never done anything other than that at Villa Park.

Snake: After the match Albion claimed to be in the Square Peg in Birmingham city centre. They were bragging that they had taken 'our pub.' It had become synonymous with the Villa Hardcore. A lot of our lads were banned following the Rocky Lane incident so we were struggling for numbers.

We were sitting in the Aston Hotel. We'd gone there after the game after we'd walked down to Witton looking if Albion had anything about. We heard they were in the Peg so we decided to get up there and have a look. Some people in the Aston Hotel were obviously up for it but some weren't so keen. They were saying it would just be another wild goose chase. Albion had been threatening to show all day and turn us over in our own back yard but they'd eventually picked on a half empty pub with no real lads in it. A fleet of taxis was arranged to take us up to Birmingham city centre. Dandy and I managed to hail a black cab. We got out the cab on Corporation Street by a pub called the Bar Med. We met another few Villa there. Jonesy had come up from the Ads in a taxi as well. Only a few of us appeared to have arrived. We walked toward the Square Peg. We were about 20 handed. We walked in at the one end of the pub. Just before we went in I told everyone to keep it quiet. I wanted to have a look at what they'd got first. I was worried with the numbers we had we were going to get smashed back out as quickly as we went in. That would've been another result for them in their eyes. It's a long narrow pub. It has no music, it's a Wetherspoons pub. It's more like a train station than a pub. It's long and narrow and mainly just a meeting place before people move on elsewhere. We walked toward it. We walked in. Albion were in there. They were 60-70 handed. We tried to clock how many of them were in there. They hadn't sussed us at all. The pub was busy; it usually was at this time of night on a Saturday. We went to the end of the long bar and ordered a drink. Dandy was going mad, 'Those cheeky fuckers, they've swerved us all day and are going to try and claim a result for coming in here.' I told him to wait and told him I thought more Villa would turn up.

Snake: One of the Albion lot came over asking 'Am yow lot Villa?' The lad he asked replied 'We certainly are.' The guy was obviously stunned by the eagerness of the reply. He didn't realise how many of us there was. Admittedly, we didn't have enough to take them on in an open street. In the pub though, things were different. The narrowness of the place doesn't allow you to spread out. He said we could either, 'stay and have it' or we could 'fuck off and come back with a proper firm'. No-one moved. What we didn't know is there was a smaller group of mostly South Brum Hardcore on their way. They were led by Victor. They had heard about Albion and now decided to have a pop themselves.

Spenna: We were drinking in the Trocadero, just down the road from the Square Peg. Most of us were South Birmingham Hardcore. There were about 15 of us, Daz, Wattsy, Steve White-jeans, Little C and me and a few other lads from South Brum. Victor, one of our older lads from Aston, came in the pub. 'Lads, Albion are up the Square Peg! There are 50 of them, all old Smethwick lads,' he said. I remember saying to Victor that there wasn't many of us but we were willing to have a pop at them. We left the pub with Victor, Kas and a couple of their lads and headed for the Square Peg. It took some goading of each other to attack the pub. We could see them in there and it looked like there was loads of them. It was all, 'Come on, who are we? Are we Villa or what?' We steamed into the place.

Wattsy: When we got to the Peg we were hesitant. We had to psyche ourselves up. It looked like there were loads of them in there. Once we had decided though, there was no messing around. We could see them in there and we ran straight in throwing bottles at them. To be fair they were well up for it. I got hit over the head with a chair. As we ran in the one end of the pub, some other Villa, unbeknown to us were running at them from the other end. They outnumbered us at this end heavily and they forced us out of the pub. Then they started to realise that they were being attacked from the other end of the pub so we were able to take advantage and steam into them again. We totally split them up and they started to scatter in all directions.

Spenna: Victor was straight in there. He ran through the doors throwing bottles that he'd carried up from the Trocadero. We steamed through the doors following him. About 8 of us actually managed to get through the doors before they realised what was happening. They steamed back at us. We got hit with bottles, tables and chairs. They started to force us back; we wouldn't budge for a while. We stood at the doors; I was the last one out.

All of a sudden it was going mad at the other end of the pub. Bottles started to fly into the Albion from our group. Someone launched a table into the Albion and we were straight into them. There was a roar which is coming from the entrance on the corner of Bull Street, the other end of the pub to us. A small mob of Villa had landed. They'd got steamed by West Brom as they entered the doors of the pub. Dandy grabbed a chair and we steamed up the pub. Normal pub goers were scattering. Albion were surprised at this attack from behind.

Jonesy: I ran into the group of Albion at our end of the pub. I got hit over the head with a stool. I didn't feel it until afterwards. I was covered in blood. I just wanted to get into them. They'd tried to take the piss by drinking in the Peg. We weren't going to stand for it. A lot of our lads were under bail restrictions for Rocky Lane so it was up to the rest of us to get stuck into them. We backed them out of the doors at the end of the pub eventually. I was in the middle of them as they went through the doors. More fighting occurred outside. I had been split up from the rest of the Villa who were still trying to get out of the pub. Someone hit me. It was right Judas punch from the side. I was then jumped on by about four or five of them. This was outside the pub and I took a bit of a kicking on the floor. I managed to get to my feet and then realised the police were now on the scene. I decided to get away from the area.

Albion had forced the small mob of Villa from the Troc out of the corner doors. We found it easy to push Albion towards the doors. The ones we were steaming thought they'd be safe at the back from the other attack. They were not that keen and were being skittled everywhere. It was going mad for some time. Bottles, glasses, tables, and chairs were flying around. Albion surged back towards us with a big black lad at the front. He was pelted with glasses and he had to retreat. We pushed Albion out the doors. The police were arriving by now. It was dark and both sides were milling around outside. It was going off as people realised who was who.

Spenna: When the police arrived a lot of Albion made a move toward Pigeon Park just up the road. Our small mob met them again. There were only about eight of us and about twenty odd Albion. Again Victor was straight into them. He got put down and they gave him a bit of a kicking as the rest of us fired into them. There was too many of them though and they backed us off. We pulled a few paving stones up from some roadworks and tried to launch them at them. There was just too many of them by this point. We were trying to get them up the road and spread them out a bit but they weren't having it. More police were arriving so we did one

Aston Villa Vs Tottenham Hotspur Premier League
18th January 2003

Snake: Everyone had met at the Trocadero. A call came through that someone had seen a mob of Spurs going into the Yard of Ale. They had about 50 and were looking for it. We had similar numbers. Someone suggested leaving in two's and three's and making our way over there. We left and made our way down. We arrived down there and people gradually started to appear. The Yids now clocked us and emptied the pub. This was a big fucker at the front of them. He was shouting and he was swiftly pole-axed by a punch. We surged at Spurs. We were raining glasses at them that we'd brought from the Trocadero. Someone grabbed a shovel off a road sweeper. A few of us nicked umbrellas off the market. They were launched into them, javelin style. Spurs were being forced back by our attack. Nostrils picked up a 'special offer' board from outside the Pizza Hut. He launched it into Spurs. Someone shouted, 'It looks like the Pizzas are off mate,' everybody was laughing.

Screw: I'd just done 18 months for bottling someone against Manchester United. I'd just popped up to town to see what was happening. It was a stiff sentence but I was made an example of because the old bill, PC Kelly in particular. They were out to stop us from continuing the mayhem we'd been causing for the past few years. He'd asked for the jury to be changed twice before my trial as he didn't like the look of certain jurors. The writing was on the wall when they produced a file the size of the Bible out and I got 18 months. So I popped up town not intending to go to the match because I was banned. I met a couple of the lads who told me Villa had gone down to the Yard of Ale because Spurs were in there. They were facing each other by the time I got there. Spurs were standing in front of doors of the pub and Villa were just about to go into them. I walked straight up to the Yid at the front and sparked him. He was a big cunt with ginger hair in a pony tail. As I did that, Villa ran into Spurs. I just walked off. As I walked away, Nostrils came flying past me and accidentally hit me over the head with a chair. I simply walked over the road and watched it from there. Spurs didn't even try to stand their ground. They just ran back inside pub and tried to close the doors. They'd got hold of Clinchy. He was at the front trying to gas the life out of them and they were trying to drag him inside. The Villa were fighting to try and get Clinchy free. As soon as they did, Spurs bolted the doors and the police started to arrive. We all melted into the Saturday shoppers and disappeared.

Aston Villa Vs Birmingham City Premier League 3rd March 2003

We'd met early that afternoon at The Barrel in Newtown. The match was a Monday evening fixture. After Rocky Lane, we'd lost quite a few lads. At 1pm it wasn't looking good. By 2pm it was looking even worse. The old bill had landed. They had made arrests regarding an incident at Oxford a few months previous. They forced the landlord to shut the pub. Eventually we made our way down to the Adventurers nearer the ground. There was a chance Blues would come by train to Aston, so we wanted to be on the main drag to the ground to wait and see what turned up.

Dandy: The Adventurers had a big fence round it's beer garden so no-one could see in but we had a couple of lads looking over the fence to see what was happening outside. Everyone was getting lairy. Everyone was up for it and most had spent the afternoon drinking. The old bill had been outside all afternoon and since it had been filling up. They'd formed a ring around the place. It looked as if they thought Blues might be coming that way. People started throwing glasses out at the old bill. More missiles followed but they didn't act. Eventually as kick-off neared the shout went up that we were leaving for the game. We walked down towards Villa Park. There were hundreds of us. It was a mixture, the older lot, what was left of us the Hardcore, the Bagot lot and old Villa Youth. 'Carry on down past the Holte let's take them at Witton!' someone shouted. Everyone was up for it. We were going mad. We were going to fire straight into them as they queued up to get into the ground.

Jez: We walked down from the Adventurers. It must be the biggest firm I have seen at Villa. It was mayhem when we got down to the ground. We tried to walk past the Holte End towards the away end. The old bill tried to stop us and it proper went off. The old bill were baton charging us. We were throwing missiles at them, it was absolute mayhem. The old bill really had their work cut out cause there was a mob of Villa attacking at the other side from Witton Island. Blues were backed right off, they simply weren't interested. The only fighting Blues were doing was fighting each other to get away from us and into the ground.

Everyone moved down Witton Lane in an enormous mob. Blues had landed but they'd landed on Aston Park and made their way down to Witton Island from there via Nelson Road. We got close enough to see them queuing to get in. There was a wall of old bill between us and them. A few of ours started to throw missiles. Blues were cowering behind the police lines. A roar went up and we made a charge. The old bill took it for a short while then baton charged us back. Ours at the front scattered and then a fresh barrage of missiles met the oncoming police. This went on for a while but the police were resolute. People started to fade away. They started to go into the game.

It was a brilliant atmosphere as usual. It was moodier though than I have ever known it in Villa Park. They'd threatened they were going to be in our seats. We knew they wouldn't but we were looking out for them all game. We were in the Doug Ellis Stand next to them. It was cold so everyone took advantage of that fact and most of us in that stand were hooded with scarves across faces. They were having it tonight. The match went by in a flash. I remember them scoring and some of them jumping up in our section. They were in ones and two's. They were set upon by our normal support. They were then being dragged out by stewards and police. Even our scarfers were up for it that night. As the end of the match drew nearer, people were flooding into our section of the ground. They had opened the gates and people were coming from all sides of the ground to get in the Doug Ellis Stand to confront Blues.

Dandy: I was sitting in the Holte End. We weren't bothered about the result by then. We didn't look like scoring. Luddy rang and said the gates were open and we should come in the Doug Ellis Stand. He said it looked like it was going to go off. I made my way down. There were loads of lads walking down Witton Lane and into the Doug Ellis. It was like a who's who of Aston Villa hooliganism under that stand. As I walked up the atmosphere was tense to say the least.

Dion Dublin head-butted Robbie Savage and was sent off. The crowd went mad. It was like a goal celebration when Savage hit the deck. Then like a goal against when Dublin was sent off. Everyone in our stand reared up. We stood up and made a slow move towards the Blues fans in their section of the stand. Everyone was shouting, swearing, missiles were thrown by each side, mainly Villa though. People were desperate to get to them. The match continued. We still didn't look like scoring. They scored again and then they were giving i the 'Keep right on till the end of the road' song. This enraged the Villa suppor on the other side of the cordon. Some Villa were now on the track at the side of the pitch. I saw Big Tony who was standing on the advertising hoardings. He was feet away from Blues. He was calling it on. He was gesturing them to have a pop at him. He was telling them to stop hiding behind the police an stewards. They were having none of it. Jonesy was in the thick of it was well I could see loads of faces I recognised. A line three or four deep of yellow coat

(Police) and orange jackets (stewards) separated the two sets of fans. Some in the section behind the goal start to rare up. It must've been some of their lads. The old bill rushed in. Still the missiles were raining down on Blues. The old bill moved in. They were filming. They were running into crowd and uncovering peoples faces so they could be filmed and not remain anonymous. It nearly went again but police in riot gear were now in place. They were in between us and Blues and in between us and the pitch. Minutes before the end, everyone left the ground en-masse. We were losing 2-0. There was no chance of anything happening in the ground now. The moment had now gone for any spontaneous violence in the stadium. We flooded onto Witton Lane. We could see a massive line of old bill barring our way to the exits where Birmingham City supporters were meant to come out of. Everyone was incensed by the result and surged towards the police lines. They had got full robo-cop gear on and they didn't shift. The match was over by now and Villa fans flooded out into Witton Lane. Some joined the throng of Villa confronting the police. They were mostly all masked and they were baying for blood in front of unmoving police lines. The missiles rained down. Bricks, bottles, you name it, it was launched at the police. No-one was coming out of the Blues section of the ground. It's been said since they wouldn't come out. They knew what was waiting for them. Eventually Blues started to trickle out of the ground. Shouts and calls and songs about doing the double over us, pushed some over the edge. A few ran at the police to get through to Blues. Seeing it was pointless a few of us made a move back up Witton Lane. As we were nearing the top of the road we could see the old bill have just started to charge the Villa fans. They were turning and fighting with the police. We headed down Holte Road. We went through the small estate at the bottom and onto Brookvale Road. The place was just full of old bill. Blues apparently have turned left at Witton Island and headed straight into town. They'd taken the quick exit away from Villa Park. We were now undisputed top dogs in Birmingham.

From the Birmingham Post March 4th 2003:

More than 40 fans were arrested and there were several injuries, including police officers, as violence scarred last night's football derby match between Aston Villa and Birmingham City.

Running battles broke out between hooligans and police in riot gear before and after the game at Villa Park.

Bottles and bricks were thrown at police as hundreds of officers tried to prevent trouble between rival supporters outside the stadium. An army of stewards battled to keep control in the ground as Villa went down 2-0 and had two players sent off in the highly charged match, which also saw fans running onto the pitch.

One tried to confront several Blues players before he was marched off by stewards. The episode reminiscent of the first game between the two teams at St Andrews earlier this season - left Blues striker Geoff Horsfield admitting he had feared for his own safety. Seats were ripped up and there were reports of coin throwing in the Doug Ellis and North stands during the course of the second half.

Small skirmishes also broke out around the ground as Villa fans attacked their Blues counterparts who had managed to get tickets among the home supporters. There were also reports of scuffles in hospitality boxes. About 300 police and around 400 stewards were on duty and afterwards senior West Midlands Police Officers condemned the hooligans. Inspector Bob Peebles said the behaviour of some supporters was 'atrocious' and had put many people in danger. 'The first half of the game was lively but relatively well behaved. During the second half there were events in the game, sendings off and goals which led to a small pitch invasion and a rise in tension in the ground. After the match there were a number of disorder incidents and a number of people were arrested.'

The clashes outside the stadium broke out after the match as Villa supporters left the Holte End - their 'home' stand and tried to confront the Blues fans in Witton Lane.

Dozens of police in riot gear forced the Villa fans from Witton Lane into Queens Road where officers found themselves under fire from bottles and bricks.

Even before the match kicked off, police had to cope with trouble around the ground at three flashpoints. Rival fans clashed in Witton Square and Aston Park before being separated while a mob of about 300 pelted police with bottles in Witton Lane. Chief Supt Douglas Paxton ground commander said. 'There was organised disorder in at least three locations on a scale which required us to be very flexible. The disturbance in Witton Lane took just about everything we had to maintain public order and keep the crowd moving.'

By half-time there were 13 people in the cells at the ground after being arrested for offences including violent disorder and alcohol offences. By the end of the match that figure had risen to 40, including several who made pitch incursions. More arrests were made outside the ground and more are expected to follow. Chief Supt Paxton said, 'It's the usual story - the vast majority of fans come along to enjoy the match. It was disappointing though on this occasion there were some hundreds of fans prepared and co-ordinated enough to confront the police. There will be a post match investigation with CCTV footage and other information gathered by officers being examined. People may think they've got away with it but they can expect a knock in the early morning in the next few weeks.'

Birmingham Evening Mail Wednesday March 5th 2003:

VILLA: WE'LL BAN THUGS FOR LIFE,
Tough stance after derby game flare-ups

Aston Villa today pledged to ban for life all supporters who invaded the Villa Park pitch during Monday's stormy derby clash with Birmingham City. The disturbances happened during Villa's 2-0 defeat of their rivals and one fan confronted Robbie Savage and Villa goalkeeper Peter Enckelman before being escorted from the field.

A statement from Villa said: 'Aston Villa will ban for life any supporters who ran onto the playing area during the Premiership fixture with Birmingham City at Villa Park. Any supporters arrested for encroachment on to the field of play will receive automatic bans while the club will also work with West Midlands Police to identify other supporters involved in crowd disturbances in and around the stadium.

Phil Shaw in The Independent Wednesday 5th March 2003:

ASHAMED DUBLIN SAYS SORRY FOR SAVAGE BUTT

As contrite and calm as he was out of control when assaulting Birmingham City's Robbie Savage hours earlier, Dion Dublin sat alongside Graham Taylor yesterday as the Aston Villa manager condemned those who 'let down' the club in a derby also marred by violence off the pitch. Taylor, who had declined to comment in the immediate aftermath of Birmingham's 2-0 victory, was clearly still upset by the hostile atmosphere surrounding the clubs' first League meeting at Villa Park in 16 years, as well as by the recklessness of Dublin and his team-mate Joey Gudjonsson, who were both sent off. 'We let 40,000 people down with our lack of discipline,' he said. 'And we've let ourselves down as a club. We have gone all over the nation [on television] and yet the Birmingham coach couldn't leave until after 11pm. Innocent people were held up because of the things going on in the streets. I'm all for rivalry, but a line has to be drawn somewhere. The game was not an advert for the type of football or atmosphere I believe is right. The way it was played is not what I stand for. People have to be strong enough to say: 'Hold on, that can't be what it's about.'

Chief Inspector Stephen Glover of the West Midlands Police said events on the pitch had "a bearing" on what happened off it. Two officers were injured by "missiles" while 40 arrests were made following a pitch invasion and fighting. The FA, which fined Birmingham £25,000 after hooliganism scarred September's 3-0 win over Villa, is to hold an inquiry. Villa said they will ban for life any fan found to have invaded the pitch. A club statement read: 'Any supporters arrested for encroachment on to the field of play will receive automatic bans while the club will also be working closely with West Midlands Police to identify other supporters involved in crowd disturbances in and around the stadium. Security had been heightened inside and outside Villa Park and both club and police were satisfied that the extra measures adopted ensured several threats to public order and safety inside the stadium were minimised.'

Graham Taylor speaking in the Daily Express March 5th 2003:

Football's not worth it if there's this much violence. We have to be strong enough to say it. I'm all for rivalry and banter between clubs, but a line has to be drawn.

Leicester City Vs Aston Villa Premier League
31st January 2004 Barracudas

Inter club rivalry between Villa and Blues has never been confined to when the two clubs meet on the pitch. We would clash regularly in the city-centre whether we had played or not. In the early to mid 80s it was always Blues looking for Villa. We turned that on its head when we formed the Villa Youth We often took it to Blues on what they then considered to be their home turf

As the 80s wore on and the nineties began we had gradually asserted more control over most of Birmingham city-centre. There were no no-go areas for us anymore in the town. At the height of the Hardcore, Birmingham were reduced to a small part of the city. Following a match against Leicester City a large group of us had returned to Birmingham on the train.

This is a police report of the disturbances which occurred that day:

Football disorder - Birmingham City Centre - 31/01/2004

At approximately 19-06 hours reports from railway staff that a group of fans were baiting a group of Newcastle United fans on one of the platforms at BIRMINGHAM NEW STREET. This group - 40 strong - were soon identified as the Aston Villa prominent group as they were followed turning left on to HILL STREET, BIRMINGHAM CITY CENTRE. Walking down they began raising hoods and scarves to conceal their identity. This group had not been seen all day either leaving BIRMINGHAM NEW STREET or in LEICESTER. Strongly suspected that group avoided NEW STREET station in the morning possibly travelling from intermediary station and then did not enter LEICESTER due to a number being on Crown Court bail possibly drinking in NARBOROUGH (To be confirmed). It is believed the group travelled into BIRMINGHAM NEW STREET on local train arriving shortly after the special train arrived from LEICESTER. This had about 375 ASTON VILLA fans on board with 6 BTP (British Transport Police) on board.

BTP spotters went forward ahead of the group as they approached the Queensway with approximately 6 more officers shadowing the group. As spotters reached BARRACUDAS public house, HURST STREET members of the BIRMINGHAM CITY prominent group were seen in both the window and doorway fully aware of the approaching group.

A charge was made by the VILLA group towards the bar - officers drew batons to stop the BIRMINGHAM CITY group from exiting but with the advancing VILLA group nearly on top of the officers, attention was made towards them - with this BIRMINGHAM CITY exited the bar - flares, bottles and glasses were thrown at the VILLA group for about a minute until officers forced the BIRMINGHAM CITY group back into the bar. Officers held the BIRMINGHAM CITY group at the doors. With this the VILLA group again advanced with officers attempting to force them back with batons. Then

235

another group of BIRMINGHAM CITY prominents appeared from PJ's public house - approximately 30 strong and charged the VILLA group - officers on scene, re-grouped and charged the advancing BIRMINGHAM CITY away.

A van of WEST MIDLANDS POLICE arrived and with this, both groups disappeared, with part of the VILLA group ending up in the CROWN public house, on STATION STREET adjacent to BIRMINGHAM NEW STREET.

Mark B: Blues shit themselves that night; they wouldn't come out to have a go at us when we landed. They left it all to the old bill to get rid of us.

Wattsy: We were walking through the station and I saw a Nose with his dog's bollocks hanging out over his shirt. I gave him a slap, and this Newcastle fan joined in and tried to help him. I gave him a smack as well. I was then, when we got to Barracudas absolutely hammered by a copper with his truncheon when they arrived. It was a bit of a mixed day really.

Charlton Athletic Vs Aston Villa Premier League 27th March 2004
Kings Cross

Fowler: A lot of us were on bans. The reason we went to London that day was because on the Monday we were all in court for Rocky Lane. It was supposed to be the last piss up before a few of us went away for a while. So we said, 'Fuck it lets all go down to London for the day!' As the day wore on we were in the Flying Scotsman in Kings Cross and someone said 'Luton are just coming out of the station down the road!' As they said this, the old bill suddenly came into the pub and barred the entrance. I thought 'Fuck this,' and I kicked open the emergency doors and walked down towards the Luton. The old bill were filming me as I walked down the road. There were about 60 Luton. There was just too many old bill. Luton probably didn't even know we were there. I turned round and we all met up at another pub up the road.

Screwdriver: I had been in the bookies all day. I was doing my bollocks as per usual. I left the bookies and was walking up a road back to the lads. Some old bill pulled me. 'You're banned from football,' they said. 'Yeah, I know, but I'm not at the football am I?' I replied. We were miles away from a ground so there was fuck all they could do. They knew we were there however and who we were.

Tucker: We'd been sitting in pubs all day. We were in another one. It was some Irish boozer in Kings Cross. I was bored. So I said to JP who was sitting next to me, 'Fuck

this, I'm going for a walk!' He joined me and we left the pub. We walked round Kings Cross. We spotted about 20 lads standing over the road. We walked over, 'Alright lads? Who are you lot?' 'We're Ipswich mate,' they replied. 'Well watch yourselves lads, there's loads of Villa round here,' I said smiling as I walked off. The next thing I knew I got a dig from behind. It wasn't the lads we had just talking to. They had scattered. It was another 15-20 lads who had come running up the road. We ran. They chased us. They were shouting at us. They were trying to kick our feet from under us. They were that close.

Fowler: We were sitting in this pub having a drink. JP came banging on the windows shouting, 'It's off! It's off!' We all ran out. Tucker was shouting, 'It's West Ham! It's West Ham!' I ran down the road towards him and as I turned a corner there was a firm there.

Screwdriver: We emptied out of the pub and ran round the corner, we spread across the road and there they were in front of us. We bashed them; we had them on their toes.

Fowler: They were Chelsea. They were standing in the middle of the road. I ran over to one at the front who was standing underneath some scaffolding. I chinned him and then Screwdriver also ran in. They were backing off. The old bill then appeared with batons and started shouting at us. They were going, 'Back off! Back off!' I'm thinking fuck this I'm in court Monday for Rocky Lane, so we did one onto the tube.

Tucker: The lads piled out of the pub and they destroyed Chelsea. We absolutely destroyed them. Chelsea realised too late what we'd got in the pub. As it emptied they realised and they got slaughtered.

Screwdriver: Chelsea ran. I chased some of them up the road. I caught up with some by the station. There was a curly haired geezer. He was saying, 'They're fucking mugs them Villa.' I just chinned him. I put him on his arse. 'Mugs are we mate?' I said as I left him there on the floor.

Fowler: We get on okay with Chelsea. We know a few of theirs and they know a few of ours. We ended back at the Worlds End pub on Baker Street. There was a couple of Chelsea there. One of them was going on at Liam. 'Fucking hell so and so ain't gonna be happy with this!' 'Fucking Fowler, who does he think he is?' I went walking over to them. I said, 'I'm Fowler, what's the fucking problem?' He shit it. 'Oh no! I didn't mean anything by it.' He said. 'I was just saying we shouldn't be fighting each other!' We were all dawn-raided for that night. We got jailed the following Monday for

Rocky Lane. I was given six months. I did that sentence. I was out on tag in a couple of months. I did six weeks in prison and six weeks on a tag. One week I'd forgotten to sign on. The old bill came and kicked my door in one morning. I said to them, 'What the fucks going on? This is a bit heavy for not signing on isn't it?' They laughed and said 'No it's nothing to do with that! You're being nicked for fighting in London!' They had nicked Screwdriver as well. He didn't live far from me. He was in the van when I was put in there. I got twelve months for that as well. They dealt with me and 19 others. They had dropped the charges on a lot of it. They had fuck all on me. I was standing under the scaffold and not on CCTV when I'd sparked the one. They'd got Screw bang to rights and they hadn't dropped his charge. They were doing him for Affray. Another one of ours was also bang to rights filmed wielding an iron bar. What they said to everyone else was, we'll drop the charges and put everyone on section 4 public order charges. We'll throw the charges out against two if Fowler pleads guilty to an affray charge. They had fuck all on me but were trying to pressure me to put my hands up by using the lads. They all had families and mortgages to pay for, what could I do? To be fair the lads were saying to me 'Fowl, it's up to you, don't put yourself in if they've got nothing on you!'

Everyone was around me talking. I told all their barristers to fuck off. My barrister came over to tell me to calm down. It seemed all they wanted was me. I said to him 'Fuck off. I ain't putting my hands up to fuck all!' They all got round and said to me, 'If we write down on a note to the judge that we'll plead guilty on the grounds that Mr Fowler did no more or no less than anyone else at the incident. Will you go guilty on these grounds? I thought fair enough if it helped the lads. The prosecution accepted it and I went guilty. I stood up in the dock. The Judge said, 'We'll deal with the affray charges first!' He continued, 'Stand up Mr Clark! Screw stood up. 'You, you are a disgrace to football! You will never learn your lesson! I sentence you to 12 months in Prison!' I thought you dirty bastards. They had conned me. I was up next, so I stood up. 'Mr Fowler!' I said 'What?' I knew what was coming. They'd had me in the net. 'You are a disgrace to football! You will never learn your lesson! I give you 12 months!' They had fuck all on me. I was conned into admitting something. I admitted to something which they had no proof of me doing. All they wanted was me the bastards.

We got shipped to HMP Pentonville. What a fucking place that was! What a nightmare. It was a real fucking horrible place, I've been in some prisons, Durham, Winson Green, Stafford, and Blakenhurst, but that fucking place was the worst. Screw got scabies not long after going in there. It was a different fucking world. There were so many different nationalities you'd think you were in a different country.

Screwdriver: I was sitting in a room on association in Pentonville. The room was ful of Nigerians who could hardly speak a word of English. All of a sudden these people entered the room. They were from the Home Office, they were immigration. They approached me. They came to me and said, 'We believe you are a New Zealand national?' 'Yeah I was born there but I have lived in this country since I was four,' I replied. They informed me they would be attempting to deport me and return me to New Zealand once my sentence had been served. They ignored everyone else present and left the room. I was amazed.

Simmo: I've got one thing to say about the Kings Cross incident. Two lads, Fowler and Screwdriver, they put their hands up to a more serious charge to get a few of us off the hook. That doesn't happen too often, people putting themselves on the line for others. It says a lot about Villa Hardcore. I'll never forget what they did.

From the Birmingham Evening Mail August 3rd 2005:

A notorious Birmingham football hooligan has been jailed and banned from football matches for ten years for his part in a street brawl.

Soccer thug Steven Fowler, 36 from Castle Vale was handed a 12 month sentence for affray over the violent clash in North London.

He was among 13 Aston Villa fans who admitted being involved in running battles on March 27th 2004.

Police rushed to the Kings Cross area as Villa fans clashed with Chelsea supporters in what officers described as a 'pre-planned brawl' that sent terrified passers-by scattering for cover.

Scotland Yard said a number of the men were armed with street furniture, bottles and glasses during the violent street brawl in Pentonville Road. Baton wielding officers took more than 30 minutes to bring it under control.

Villa fans had been on their way home after beating Charlton Athletic at the Valley, while Chelsea had beaten Wolves at Stamford Bridge. Fowler - tagged by the police as a hardcore category C hooligan leader at the time of the 1998 World Cup in France - was one of 5 Villa thugs jailed yesterday by Judge William Kennedy at London's Snaresbrook Crown court. He also received a six-month sentence at Birmingham Crown Court last year for his part in the 'Battle of Rocky Lane' between Villa and Blues fans that preceded a derby clash in 2002.

Chapter Eleven: Villa Hardcore.
Battle at the Uplands

West Bromwich Albion Vs Aston Villa Premier League
22nd August 2004

The two sides met again in August 2004. Most of the lads struggled to get tickets. Everyone met in the Rose Villa Tavern in Hockley in the heart of Birmingham's Jewellery Quarter. We met early in the morning as the match was a 1 o'clock kick-off. A few lads went to the game. The rest of us stayed in the Rose Villa to watch the match live on Sky Sports. The police had arrived outside the Rose Villa Tavern by now and were sat over the road in an unmarked car. They were filming whoever went in or out of the pub. They stayed there throughout the game and after the game we had a helicopter hovering overhead as some of our lads returned from the match.

Word had started coming through that Albion were going to land at the Uplands pub. The Uplands is about a mile from the Albion ground. It was decided everyone would go down there following the match.

Fowler: West Brom, I've never rated them. They don't bother me in the slightest. They're nothing to us. They think they are but they're not. I'm so bothered about West Brom that we played them once and I went to watch some boxing in Newcastle. That's how bothered I am about West Brom. I rate them on a par with Coventry, nothing special.

Jonesy: I was at home. I had received a number of phone calls throughout the afternoon. They were explaining that Albion were going to land at the Uplands. After the match I rang up a friend of mine to pick me up. I made my way to the Uplands. When I got there most of the lads were already there. They were congregating on the car park. More and more lads were arriving by car and private hire taxis. One of the lads received a phone call. It was from one of their lads. Albion were on their way and coming down to meet us. This was approximately two hours after the match had finished.

Tucker: When I arrived at the Rose Villa Tavern. I said to Fowler, 'D'you fancy going down the Uplands for a look?' We went down there. When we got there a few people were saying, 'Albion are coming!' Yeah whatever, I remember thinking. I didn'

think they would show up to be honest. Next thing I knew, people were shouting, 'They're here! They're here!' Albion were coming down the road towards the pub.

Jonesy: Some of our younger lot, who were with us, noticed a number of private hire cars pulling up and stopping in the distance on the brow of the hill. There were around 5-6 cars that had stopped. Unbeknown to the Albion lads, British Transport Police had been monitoring their movements and had followed them from the Royal Oak on the Soho Road. BTP then proceeded to film the events which followed. A small group of Villa fans ran up towards these taxis. Albion had begun to run down the hill towards us. There was then a fierce encounter around some bushes with hand to hand fighting. One Albion supporter, Cleary, pulled out an iron bar and caught Dino across the head. It split his head open. There was only a small number of Villa fans involved at first. Albion got the better of the earlier exchanges. We weren't organised at first and the younger element got a bit too excited.

Tucker: We ran up the road towards them. A few of ours and a few of theirs at the front ran into each other. The rest of the Albion weren't that keen to come down. Then someone shouted, 'It's the old bill, look there's old bill!' We could see the police filming at the top of the road. We started to walk back down. To the Albion it must've looked like we were backing off. They must've been thinking, 'Look, Villa are shitting it here.' You've got to remember a lot of us had only just got out of prison.

Jonesy: We realised we had our work cut out with what we'd advanced up the road with. At this time the rest of Villa's lads finally left the pub and ran up the road towards the melee to meet Albion's lads head on. This was Albion's main firm. The fight had advanced closer to the pub. Now that the main Villa firm left the pub and hit Albion head on. Fowler was pointing to some of their lads. He was shouting 'Look! There's a camera! The Old Bill are filming this!' He was close to Payne who ran at him while Fowler was pointing at the cameras. Fowler put him on his arse with one punch. What should be taken into consideration is a lot of Villa were already on banning orders. A lot were dubious about getting involved because they were aware that the police were filming it from a safe distance.

Dino: I was drinking in the Uplands. I heard a shout, 'West Brom are here!' I went out onto the car park to have a look. I could see them across the road. I thought I'm not letting them get to the car park. I ran towards them. I met them on the central reservation. The one Albion lad came towards me. He had a long leather coat on. I grabbed hold of it and swung him round and onto the floor. He landed against a steel barrier which ran alongside the road. Payne then came towards me. I chinned him and he went down. I'm having a battle with them. The next thing I knew, 'Bang!' I felt a blow to the head. I remember at the time I thought it was a snooker cue that had hit me. I kept on fighting. I could feel sweat rolling down my face as I was fighting; I was just brushing it away out of my eyes. I later found out it was blood. One of our lads grabbed me, he was in the army. He said to me 'Fuck me, you need to get to hospital with that!' I remember saying to him, 'Why what has happened?' I still didn't realise. He tried to drag me away but I was still trying to get stuck in. He took my tee-shirt off and he wrapped it round my head. I've got to give credit to the Albion lads that day. They were game and they kept coming back every time they were put on their arses. You can't knock them for that but we easily had the upper hand, even before our numbers were superior.

Jonesy: Fighting was taking place on both sides of the road. One of the older lot ran straight into the middle of the Albion. He was hit with an iron bar. He'd managed to put his arm up to protect his head which the bar was aimed for. He then took his leather belt off and started swinging it around in the air, indiscriminately catching a couple of Albion lads across the face. He later found out that his arm had been broken. It was then everyone seemed to get it together. We made a charge at the Albion. They started to back off and then they were run back up the road where they had come from. Then several more Albion arrived. They regrouped towards the top of the road. They then ran at us again. This time we were ready. More fighting then erupted across the whole road as both mobs were spread out. Several Albion ran straight into Villa and were duly despatched. One went straight down, I think he was Asian, he got a severe kicking. As more fighting ensued on the left hand side of the dual carriageway one of our lads lost his shirt. It was literally ripped off his back. It was then Tyson and Jez took it in turns throwing a bin back and forth between the two mobs. You couldn't really get near them. I was in the middle of the dual carriageway I tried to have a pop. I dodged a brick thrown by them. Apart from a few kamikaze dives into Villa by a couple of Albion most were keeping their distance. They were easily outnumbered by this point and they were backing off steadily. Another one of the older lot shouted 'Come on Villa! One last charge!' Judge Ross mentioned in the later court case, the 'Final charge' where we finally had them on the run and chased them up the road.

Tucker: If you look at the video we're pointing up the road going, 'There's old bill there's old bill,' but they still came down. It was one of those situations then, every time we ran at them they backed off, but they kept on coming back. Don't forget there was originally more of them coming. They got stopped, but they still came for it with what they had, fair play to them.

Jonesy: There was already a police helicopter hovering above. I later learned the helicopter was filming the whole thing. The police arrived in big numbers. They were in vans and proceeded to run down and baton charge us back towards the pub. Several Villa were arrested. A few Villa had escaped on foot and in cars. Some of our lads had scarves on throughout the whole thing. The friend who had dropped me off, who had stood watching the whole event, told me to get into the van and we got out of there. I went to the Old Crown and Cushion pub in Perry Barr. We were joined by a few other lads who had been present.

Dino: Then the police started to arrive and we all went back into the boozer. I had a look at the damage in the mirror. It was a gaping wound. That's when I realised how serious it was. We managed to get out of the pub and we tried to get away by sneaking out the back. We ran onto some allotments. The helicopter was overhead and they could see some of us escaping. We jumped out of the allotments onto the road. The police drove down and stopped me there. They saw the state of my head and radioed for an ambulance. They took me to hospital. I was taken straight into theatre. They put 22 stitches in my head wound. They didn't arrest me there and then. The police waited and took me home. They insisted that I stripped out of my clothes. They took my clothes with them saying they'd be in touch. I was then raided with all the other lads. They said in court I'd been hit with an iron bar. The consultant who operated on me disagreed. The way it was split cleanly indicated a bladed instrument. I was sentenced to 18 months in prison and received a 7 year banning order from football.

On Monday 23rd August the Birmingham Evening Mail reported:

FOOTBALL THUGS RUN RIOT
By Steve Johnson and Alex Valk

SCORES of football hooligans armed with baseball bats and iron bars battled with riot police in a Birmingham street after the Albion's clash with Aston Villa.

Eight supporters were injured and 12 fans arrested as up to 80 people confronted each other outside the Uplands pub in Oxhill Road, Handsworth.

The violence which police believe was pre-arranged happened two hours after yesterday afternoons 1-1 draw.

They said running battles between fans erupted outside the pub, with rival groups of thugs chasing each other along Oxhill Road, Sandwell Road and Island Road less than a mile from the Hawthorns. Thugs rampaged through the streets in a running battle lasting half an hour before riot police managed to regain control.

Jonesy: The next day I saw the incident widely reported in the press. A major police operation was launched to apprehend the people who were involved. In November a number of dawn raids were launched. A number of arrests were made. In December photo's of people they were looking for appeared in the local press. My picture was amongst those on the front of the Birmingham Evening Mail. It was that clear I was recognised by an elderly partially-sighted relative who had seen it while passing a paper shop! I had received phone calls that morning telling me that my mug was on the front of the paper. I decided to pop into a local shop and survey the situation which at best didn't look good. There I was, clear as day. David Blunkett could've picked me out. The game was up. All the lads at work knew it was me on the front of the paper. I decided to hand myself in that night. The investigating officers were not on duty. The station officer told me they'd contact me in the New Year. Just after New Year my phone rang. It was the police. They wanted to know when I could go in to be questioned. I asked if it would be wise to bring a solicitor. They said 'When you've seen the video you'll think it would be very wise to bring one with you.' I arranged to go in on the Wednesday with a solicitor. My solicitor went to view the tape. After he'd viewed it I asked him how it was looking. He replied 'Just say you were drunk, it's not looking very good at all.' I then went in to be formally interviewed on tape. I watched the video. I was on it a number of times. I was as clear as day. It was done with a graph system and they placed me taking part in various confrontations. After this they formally charged me with Violent Disorder.

Jez: I didn't get arrested on the day but I was raided a few months later. I got 22 months and a further ban. I had been banned for 5 years already for jumping on the pitch at Middlesbrough - football intelligence had rolled up at court with a thick folder and had asked for a bigger ban than usual because of the people I associated with. I got a further ban of 7 years.

Jonesy: We appeared at Birmingham Magistrates on two occasions. Due to the large number of us in court we were dealt with in an alphabetical order. We finally ended up in Crown Court in 7th July 2005. Four Albion fans had been sentenced the previous Friday. They received heavy sentences. Judge Ross was sitting for all of the cases. He seemed determined to make a name for himself by coming down hard on us. This was very much the case. A number of us had pleaded guilty before the hearing. There was no defence. We had been caught bang to rights on CCTV. The video was played in court. References regarding our work and social life were read by the Judge and dismissed. I was sentenced. I appeared in the dock and I received a sentence of 20 months with a 7 year banning order from football matches. This also includes certain areas of Birmingham which I am excluded from on match days. This seemed harsh and was a major loss of our freedom. However the events in London which unfolded throughout the day seemed to bring things into perspective. London was being bombed by suicide bombers. After all was said and done there were 50 odd people down South who would never return home at all. Here was me losing 5 or 6 months of my liberty in comparison. It brought things into perspective. I was shipped out to Winson Green prison, HMP Birmingham for the start of my sentence; I spent three months in the Green and was then moved to HMP Ashwell in Leicestershire. Some Albion lads were with me throughout my sentence. We all worked together in the kitchens at Winson Green. Banter took place but at the end of the day we were all in jail together. I came out of prison three days before Christmas on a 'HDC' a Home Detention Curfew, with a tag. I still follow the results and I am still in contact with a lot of the lads. The Villa and the social scene has always been a major part of my life and it still is. I made a couple of very close friendships with the lads I was jailed with. I also received major support while I was inside from the lads who hadn't been jailed. A support network was set up for me and some of the other lads so we wouldn't suffer financially too much. People think it's just mindless thugs fighting, but when you are sorted out like I was you realise it's a lot more than that.

Tucker: I got 21 months and a 7 year banning order. It doesn't matter how long it is when you've got a ban like that. I think my ban is up in 2012. I can apply for it to be discharged early in 2010 but I spoke to someone recently. He said anyone who the police know well, they will not give them an early discharge from their ban.

Jonesy: I've had some lucky escapes over the years following Aston Villa. I've been nicked a lot of times and have received three banning orders. One banning order I received for a Blues match in 1987. It was just as banning orders came out. In Leicester in 1995, I was banned again but I escaped being sent to prison. I had a young family and was always in full time employment. I think those two things were a factor in me not going to prison before the Uplands. Prison was an education in life. It opens your eyes. The only thing you have in there to look forward to is the gym. Working in prison is classed as a privilege. In some circumstances it enables you to have extra gym sessions. A lot of bollocks is said about the screws in prison. Some of them are genuinely okay. Once they know you're okay they treat you fairly. You have to remember we were football lads. We're not thieves, we're not muggers, and we're not scum. Yes we've had a tear up at a football match - in my experience the screws know that. They know that other than that we're hard working men with jobs, mortgages and families just like them. They treated the football lads a bit differently. They know we are grafters. I was working in the kitchens. There was always a chance to thieve. Contraband was stuff like coffee, biscuits, scones, cakes and milk, all manner of things. I knew this Blues fan in there. I was talking to him one day and he pulled a doughnut out of his pants and ate it. I couldn't believe it. I went to church the one morning. I was on 23 hour bang-up on K Wing at that point. I went just to get out of the cell. It was basically a meeting place so they could get tobacco. People were in there ripping pages out of the Bible to use as cigarette papers.

Fowler: I was inside for Chelsea at Kings Cross. They transferred me to Winson Green Prison in Birmingham because I was in Crown Court for the row with Albion at the Uplands. I was on a wing with Big Jim, one of our lads, and some Albion who had been convicted for their part at the Uplands. I went to court the one day for a remand hearing. When I returned back to prison one of the Albion lot came up to me. He asked how I'd got on. 'What have they got on you Steve?' he said. 'You can see me punching one of yours and the lad hitting the floor,' I said. 'Who was that?' he asked. 'I'm not too sure but I think it was Payne,' I replied. It was as simple as that. Now this fat twat went running straight to Payne, who is one of their lads. He said to Payne, 'Fowlers giving it large about putting you on your arse at the Uplands!' Apparently Payne was going, 'He didn't put me on my arse!' He got the needle about it. I didn't say it was him for definite, I just said I wasn't sure. It could've been him. This fat twat, who is a nobody at the Albion, was just trying to shit stir. He caused the trouble.

Big Jim and I were sharing a cell. We were there one day cleaning our cell. We were getting rid of the cockroaches the Green is plagued with. We had a bucket full of water near the door. Big Jim, the clumsy fucker, kicked it over. Water went everywhere, onto the landing and over the side. A screw called for a cleaner. The cleaner was Payne. He came up and was cleaning the water up. One of Albion's lads Clem was two doors down from me. I came out and Payne was standing there talking to Clem. Clem is a decent lad. Payne was asking him if I had been talking about him. I saw them talking and walked over. I was oblivious to what they'd been talking about. I didn't at this point realise what had been said. I walked up as he was asking Clem if I'd been talking about him. He had to say something to me then. Otherwise he'd have lost face in front of Clem. He started saying stuff to me. At first I didn't realise what he was talking about. He was going on about me saying this and that. I thought he was on about the bucket the big Irish fucker had kicked over. He said 'Did you say you'd put me on my arse?' It really didn't register. I thought he was moaning about the mess. I was thinking more bucket. He turned around and I realised what he was on about. 'Hey! You! Who the fuck d'you think you're talking to?' I asked him. He said 'Go to the recess. We'll so it out there!' I followed him to the recess area. He walked into the recess and I followed him in. Behind me was a mate of his, the cunt with the iron bar at the Uplands, Cleary. I've clocked him behind me. I turned and said, 'Look it's between me and him, don't bring it on top.' As I turned round. Payne was throwing hay-makers at me. He was proper wind milling. I grabbed him. I pulled him towards me and I nutted him. As he hit the floor Cleary grabbed me. As he grabbed me, Big Jim who had followed us grabbed him. 'Get your fucking man off me Fowler,' Cleary started shouting. 'It's between them two, it's a straightener,' said Big Jim. Payne was on the floor. There was blood everywhere. It was all over my trainers, the floor, it was everywhere. Payne's head was cut. Then a shout went up, 'The screws are coming!' Everyone had congregated where the fight was. Prison is like a school when there's a fight in there. Something is going on and they all want a look. There was this black lad, Russian, who was locked up with us. He said 'Fowler! Fowler! Quick get in here in the showers!' I walked up to the shower area. The screws walked in as Payne was getting up off the floor. They asked him what had happened. 'I fell over Boss,' he told them. They then walked up to the shower area and saw me. They clocked the blood on my trainers. 'What happened to you Fowler? They said. 'I picked him up Boss,' I told them. I went and washed my hands next to him as he was cleaning himself up. 'If I get nicked for this, if I lose time for this, I'm going to fucking do you,' I told him. 'It needed to be said Fowler,' he kept on repeating. Just shows you what damage gossip and bullshit can cause.

The fat twat who caused it all, he was fuck all. He was doing fuck all at the Uplands. He'd driven there in his car and was only walking down the road on the video. He put his hands up and got 18 months for that. It shows you what a fucking div he is. He caused it all and he spent the rest of his time in the Green in his cell shitting himself. I found out he had caused it. A few of the West Brom lads told me it had been him shit stirring. They said they didn't want trouble on the wing. They thought it was going to go off. Some lads were in there from the Vale. They were all going 'Let's fucking do them Fowl!' But we all wanted our tag, the Albion lads and us. They told me it was the fat twat. They said 'Don't worry Fowl we've sorted it with the fat cunt.' They'd gone into this clown's cell and they'd told him straight. 'If there's anymore trouble, if any of us lose our tag as a result of this, you're having it!' He was shitting it. Like I say he didn't come out of his cell unless he had to for the rest of the time he was there. He never said boo to me the whole time afterwards.

The screws came into see me the next day. They asked me if there was going to be any trouble between Villa and Albion on the wing. I told them it wasn't going to happen. It was all forgotten about. Someone put on the internet that I had moved wings after the fight with Payne. What they forgot to mention was, on the following Friday Payne and some other lads, Albion and Villa, got shipped out to Ashwell prison in Leicestershire.

A Villa lad we called Pitchfork from Worcester got me a job on D wing. I moved off that wing two weeks after Albion were shipped out to Ashwell. They can put whatever spin they like on it. Albion, I just don't rate them. They had some good lads that day but that was it. 15-20 good lads and that's it all they have. We landed at Albion once. It was a friendly match just after the Hardcore started. We got to the ground and found no Albion at all. There wasn't a sniff of them. There was this black geezer in the ground bouncing up and down. He was behind a fence looking at us as we were walking up the road to the away end. He was going, 'When we checking it? When we checking it Villa?' The silly cunt. Clinchy just gassed him.

According to the Birmingham Evening Mail 60 men in total were jailed for the disturbance, 38 Aston Villa supporters and 22 men from West Bromwich. Sentences totalled 80 years. According to the press the participants included a multi-millionaire company director, an ambulance driver, an Iraq war hero and a quantity surveyor. They claimed the disturbance went on for 7 minutes and that up to 80 people had been involved at one point.

From The Birmingham Evening Mail 5th December 2006:

THE THUGS WHO SHAMED A CITY
By Mark Cowan and Jasbir Authi

THEY appeared to be the height of respectability. A hard-working multi-millionaire company director, an ambulance driver, a hero soldier commended for bravery in Iraq. They appeared to be just the kind of people the community needs. But today they can be revealed as violent football thugs. They and more than 50 others - many with good jobs or involved in charity work where they live - have been sentenced over shameful football violence which brought terror to families in a Birmingham street.

It perplexed His Honour Judge Ross, at Birmingham Crown Court, who said. 'That is one of the great tragedies of this case. Man after man are mature family men, often doing good work for the communities, yet they became involved in this. It has been one of the features that family and friends are more than surprised by what some people who are otherwise respectable get involved in. I don't understand it and expect I never will.'

The Aston Villa and West Bromwich Albion yobs were involved in a pre planned pitched battle outside The Uplands family pub in Handsworth, two and-a-half hours after the 1-1 draw in August 2004. The Birmingham Mail can today finally name the 60 thugs after a court order gagging us from reporting their trials was lifted. Up to 80 men - fuelled by booze and some armed with iron bars, wooden posts, bricks, bottles and glasses - were captured by police cameras as they rampaged outside the Uplands pub, in Oxhill Road, as terrified passers-by, including a woman with two young children, cowered in fear.

Following extensive police inquiries, 60 men were charged and 58 of them received football banning orders. A handful of the jailed yobs had previous convictions for football hooliganism - including three men for the infamous 2002 'Battle of Rocky Lane' between Villa and Blues thugs on the eve of the teams' first top flight clash for 16 years. Police said hooligan groups attached to both clubs arranged their own 'fixture' of a different kind. What they didn't know was that one of the key thugs was being secretly taped by police. Police said a crowd of Villa hooligans, some already banned from football matches for hooliganism, had been drinking in the Rose Villa Tavern, in Highgate, just outside the two-mile cordon imposed by their banning order. Meanwhile, Albion fans were in the Royal Oak, in West Bromwich. A flurry of phone calls was exchanged between the two groups but police were secretly videoing a Baggies fan as he spoke to an unknown Villa counterpart.

'How many do you want?' he asked. 'How many's a good knock like? How many, 40-50?' After apparently spotting police he said: 'Old Bill got us now. See you later.' When police arrested him he dropped a pool ball under a hedge. Text messages were found on the mobile phones of two other fans. One read: 'Not going to match. Just going to smash town up.' The Villa group, their numbers buoyed by other so-called fans, left the Rose Villa Tavern for the Uplands Pub, in Oxhill Road, Handsworth. By a stroke of 'good fortune and good policing' as the trial judge said, police spotters were on the scene as they thugs clashed. They capture seven sickening minutes of violence which proved the crucial evidence that led to the thugs being brought to justice.

Notorious thug Steven Fowler - branded a committed football hooligan by the trial judge - was jailed for 20 months for his part in the brawl on August 22, 2004. Just weeks before, he was jailed for a year for his part in another violent clash between Villa fans and Chelsea supporters in London in March 2004.

Yesterday, a father-of-three from South Yardley became the last person to be sentenced for his part in the mass brawl, nearly two-and-a-half years ago. The assembler, who didn't throw a single punch but acted "a referee", received a 12-months prison sentence suspended for two years, a five-year football ban and was ordered to pay £500 in costs. After his conviction, Judge Martin Cardinal lifted the reporting restrictions. A West Midlands Police spokesman said: 'This was a lengthy investigation that resulted in 58 people being banned from football matches for a considerable period of time. If you go to football matches intent on causing trouble you will be arrested, put before the courts and banned from watching the game. It should be made clear that, while these people may claim to be football fans they are, in fact, criminals.'

West Bromwich Albion match day operations manager, Kevin Jennings, said: 'We are pleased that the leading police officers in this case have highlighted the role the club played in apprehending the offenders. At the start of the 2004/2005 season, the club provided the police with extra funds to enable the force to have evidence gatherers - officers with video cameras - in operation on match days. This proved crucial during this incident. Following the jail terms handed out by the courts in this case, we are hoping hooligans will think twice before causing trouble.'

Birmingham City Vs Aston Villa Premier League 9th March 2005 The Vine

GBV: We were in the Vine. There were about 200 lads in there. The old bill were all around the place. Fowler was in the corner with a few Hardcore lads and I had a good chat with Steff one of them who I know. The police stayed outside until about 7ish. There were probably 80 Villa lads still left in the boozer.

T: Someone got a phone call to say Blues were on their way. We didn't know it but they'd been drinking up the road at the Albion Vaults about a mile away. The phone call came and we left the pub. There must've been about 60 of us. I was with Oz and a lot of us were Youth. They said they were up the road so we headed up to meet them. We were strung out. We didn't expect to bump into them so soon. All of a sudden we met them by the Manor Tavern. There were around 40 of them. I think we were both surprised to see each other so soon. Some of ours were still coming out of the Vine so they had to sprint up the road as soon as the roar went up.

Stan: I was drinking in the Manor Tavern. I was with Big Swiggsy. Someone said to me that Blues were on their way down Lichfield Road. Swiggsy and I left the Manor. As we left the pub Blues were just walking past and meeting the Villa who had run up from the Vine. We steamed into them from the side and Swiggsy put one of them on his arse.

GBV: Suddenly someone received a phone call to say Blues were on their way down the Lichfield Road towards the Vine. Fowler then shouted, 'Right! Who the fuck is having it with me?' I and three of my mates went to the door to get ready. Fowler was shouting 'No-one leaves the pub until I say so right?'

We saw the Zulu's at the top of the road. Villa had flooded out of The Vine. Both firms started to run toward each other. They gave it their usual Zulu chant. We said fuck all we just wanted to get into them, never mind the war cry bollocks. Glasses were flying from both sides. Big Tony from the Adventurers was at the front. He banged a couple of lads straight out. A black lad came at me with a flying kick. I slipped out the way and banged him on the side of his head.

Big Tony: We clashed with them in the road. We outnumbered them and they backed off pretty much straight away. I put four of them on their arses. They reckon they did me. They didn't, not one of them managed to hit me.

Kas: Tony was all in white. Being black I was joking that he looked like an Irish version of a pint of Guinness. He stood out and he was slapping them around for fun.

T: As soon as we saw each other the missiles started to fly and both firms ran into each other. It was their younger lot. The fight spread out into the road. Big Tony was at the front and steaming into them and they were just bouncing off him. He laid a couple of them out cold. We got the better of them. The only two of theirs who stood were Duffy and Gorman. Well I say they stood. They had got trapped down by the Manor Tavern. They were separated from the rest of their mob. All the rest turned round and legged it up the road. As they started to run the old bill started landing. Blues say that they did one because the police were arriving but they were on their toes before that, barring to two lads already mentioned who were still having it while the police were landing. Blues were well on their way back to Small Heath and Villa started throwing bottles at the police and backed them off for a while. Then more police arrived and we were chased down the side streets of Aston. Some were arrested but most got away.

Stan: There was fighting in the road for a few minutes and then the police started to arrive. They were filming so everyone literally disappeared. We walked back into the Manor tavern and carried on drinking. Hamilton, our football intelligence officer, came in the pub about five minutes later. He came over to us and said to me, 'What's been happening then?' 'No idea,' I replied, 'I am merely an innocent bystander out for a quiet pint.' He grimaced at me and left.

GBV: The old bill appeared and I decided I was not hanging around to be filmed by them so I slipped down the side of the boozer. I met up with Oz and walked down to the Swan & Mitre. A few of the lads went back to Adventurers and we later met up with them there.

Big Tony: The old bill caught up with us at the Britannia pub just down the road a while later. A fight broke out inside and they kicked the door off the pub and searched and arrested sixteen of us inside. We were released on bail. We had to wait six months to hear that no further action was being taken.

Kas: They took all of our clothes for forensic analysis. They issued us with those white paper boiler suits. Tony is a big lad and his suit looked tiny on him. The sleeves were half way up his arms. It was hilarious looking at him wearing that, even more so when he bent over and split it up the crack of his arse. We were in pieces laughing at him.

Birmingham Evening Mail Monday 21st March 2005:

DERBY SHOWDOWN
SIXTEEN HELD AFTER VIOLENT STREET BRAWL
By Mark Cowan

SCORES of hooligans armed with bottles and pool balls clashed in a violent street brawl after the Second City derby.

Detectives said up to 200 yobs were involved in the confrontation in Lichfield Road, Aston last night. Sixteen people were arrested as the fighting spilled out across the road. The sickening violence happened around five hours after the match.

Detectives were today due to begin sifting through CCTV footage from cameras on Lichfield Road to identify those in the trouble at 7pm. Thugs rampaged through the street in a violent battle, hurling pool balls and bottles at each other until police swooped. Det Insp nick Murphy, from Queens Road CID, said further arrests could follow.

SPOTLIGHT

Mr Murphy also appealed to members of the public innocently caught up in the trouble to get in touch. 'This was a large scale incident where people were fighting in the street,' he said. 'There may have been people driving past who have seen the incident and I urge them to come forward.' The brawl has again thrown the spotlight on the mindless thugs bringing shame to genuine fans of the city's two top flight teams.

Chapter Twelve: Villa Hardcore. The End?

Fowler: I always get phone calls from Blues, mainly on a weekend when they've had a drink. It's normally just some joker acting the big guy in front of his pals, 'Oh look I've got Fowlers number, I'm in the loop!' It's pathetic. Sometimes though, they'll say, 'Where are you?' I'll usually be in the Skylark, a pub on the Vale. It's the only pub left open on the Vale now in fact. I'll tell them where I am, 'Right,' they'll go, 'we're landing!' Fine, I think, go for it. 'Yeah whatever,' I tell them, 'you carry on, I'll be here I'm not going anywhere.' There are Blues fans that drink in there and live on the Vale. They're good lads some of them, but it's the Vale first with a lot of people. If anyone ever came on the Vale they'd have the whole estate onto them and I mean the whole estate. Football is a mad Saturday thing with most people including me. Outside of a match-day it's 'Who the fuck do you think you are coming on our manor?' It's all talk at the end of the day. Talk is cheap especially when you've had a drink and are acting up in front of your mates. It is with a lot of people.

Reidy: I've read a lot of different firm's books where we always seem to get slagged? If nobody rates us, then why does nearly every firm talk about us? If nobody rates Fowler, then the same applies again. Why does he get mentioned in nearly all the books? The truth is, over the years Hardcore have turned up at all the top clubs. The chances of actually getting into a ruck with many of the top firms are pretty slim now because of the police intelligence nowadays. You haven't got a chance. All you can do is turn up and with a little bit of luck get something on. We have been trying to do that for years. That's what probably pissed the other firms off. How many firms out there, hand on heart, can turn round and say they've had a result against Villa Hardcore? The Cockneys are the best at it. They are always talking about the old days. Nearly every one of their top firm have took the Holte End. In all their books they mention this happened mid to late 70s. In those days the Holte held 28,000 so anybody with an IQ of that above an ant will know it would be impossible. They may have come in for 5 minutes and then got kicked out. In the early 70s a small group of Blues came to our ground and stood in the bottom right hand corner like a load of sheep waiting to be sheared. To be fair to them, the hatred was nothing then like it is today. They thought they could sit in some parts of our ground in the season they got back in the Premiership. They couldn't and they got slapped and fucked out. The days of any away fans sitting in any part of our ground apart from the away section has long gone.

Fowler: I don't hate Blues. I dislike em to an extent. I have two lads who are die-hard Blues fans that work for me. I don't hate them. I hate the club. I hate their firm but i the true sense of the word. I can't say I hate every single Blue-nose. When we play them I want to get in to their firm and prove we're number one, but I can't say I hate them. I even respect one or two of them. We hit the Sentinels pub once. It was run by ex-Blues player Steve Lynex. There were a few of them in there and we hit it. We totally trashed the place. We then went down to John Bright Street to another place where Blues used to drink. They saw us coming and we had a bit of a running battle with them. When did they do that to us? Once they did it at the Vine. Blues, they had a good mob when I was growing up. Fair play to them. For us, when we think of Blues we think of Gary Williams and his mob. I don't think he got much of a mention in their two books. That was wrong. Of all the battles we've had with Blues 99% of the time it's been Williams calling the shots for them. When we were in Scotland it was Williams and his mob that landed on us. He should've received more credit from his own.

GBV: Blues think we're scared of them. Some of them actually still think they are what they were in the mid 80s and they're not. We played them at Villa Park we ended up in town with about 30 lads in the Briar Rose. Oz and I fucked off to the Trocadero. I'd done quite a bit of the white stuff and was off my head. We were sectioned 60'd by the police outside the Trocadero. We decided to go to the Dubliner in Digbeth which is a notorious Blues pub. There were about ten black lads in there all of them Blues. Oz decided he was going to introduce himself. We had verbal for about three or four minutes. We were invited outside. On the way out one of the black lads pulled a blade which I grabbed but he slashed my hand. We were both knocked out, but we went and had it with ten of them. No Blues can say they've ever done that to us in one of our main boozers but we did it that night.

Fowler: When I got out of the prison I had to go and report to Queens Road Police Station. I think it was a couple of days after Blues had landed at the Vine. When I got there Hamilton our football intelligence officer was there. He took me into the back room. I said to him, 'Been busy lately haven't you? 'He went, 'Why Steve, what have you heard?' I said 'Listen mate, I hear about things long before you even get a sniff.' You could see him thinking about this. He turned round and said, 'Listen Fowler, you could make a lot of money out of stuff like this.' He was basically telling me he'd pay me for any information I could throw his way! I said, 'Are you fucking mad?' I laughed. 'Well Steve, the offer is always there!' he said. It just goes to show how keen they are to have lads as informers.

Baz: I have just had my ban lifted. My daughter is now twelve and she is pestering me to take her to a match. That will be my priority in the future. As far as the firm goes I feel that the police got the result they wanted and after the other events at the

Uplands and the Chelsea thing most lads are on lengthy bans. I don't think there will be any more days like Rocky Lane or the Uplands. There has always been some element of hooliganism at the Villa. I hope there always will be. All I can say to the lads is enjoy it while you can.

Fowler: One thing we had was organisation. We went to some places, Coventry for instance. I got our firm from Birmingham to Coventry. While the game was on we went into their main boozer. When Coventry came back we were in there! They were crying, they were that desperate to get us out, but we didn't shift. No-one, not even the police expected us to be in there after the match. Organisation is everything. It can turn a smaller firm into something that much larger numbers will struggle with. That's what we had with Villa Hardcore, brilliant organisation. I took us to places where some people would swerve going to. Millwall to look for Carlisle for instance, that took some bottle to even attempt but we did it. Organisation was something which set us apart from the rest. We'd land in places like Leicester without the old bill having a clue we were there. We'd then ring up Leicester and say 'We're here!' They ask us where we were. 'Here in your main boozer, come and shift us,' we'd reply. The main thing about the Hardcore was that it brought a lot of groups together. Lads from East Birmingham like the Stechford lot, South Birmingham like the Bartley Green Lads. West Birmingham was represented with lads like Palm, Young Ginge and the Weoley Castle lot. We had a good, very good set of lads from the Black Country. You had the lads from Aldridge and Brownhills and further a field. Don from Aldridge, he used to make me laugh whenever we had a row, he'd always get his head or something cut open. You could always tell if we'd been in a row or not by the state of Don's head. We even had a couple of lads from Hinckley, Leicestershire. Then you had the older lads like Luddy and his mob, Skinhead Neil people like that. They've been going down the Villa for years. All good lads, the Hardcore united a lot of different groups at Villa that's what people don't realise. The main thing is we are all mates, very good mates. We still are. No-one is above having the piss ripped out of them, no-one. Even though we are banned we still meet up and socialise. We go on holiday together. I know that I could call any of them, any of them no matter what time and they would be there. Hopefully this book will put a few things straight. People have written about me in the past and a lot of it has been untrue. One thing I stressed when I knew this book was being written is that we told the truth. There are always two sides to every story of course but this is the story how we saw it.

Young Ginge: I have grown up with football and around football lads. It became my life from an early age. It's been good and bad for me in a way. Growing up around football lads has taught me respect. I have never been out committing burglary. I've never attacked anyone for no reason. I have never stolen cars. I have never mugged anyone. I have never hung around with gangs on the streets. I have worked since I left school. I have paid tax. What money I have had left I have saved for the weekend. I saved my money for the football. I wanted to hang around with proper lads. Lads that aren't criminals like the muppets who hang around on the streets.

Jez: I am now 32 years of age. If I could turn back the clock to 15 or 16 I would not change a thing. Being involved with Villa Hardcore I have had some of the best times of my life. I have travelled to parts of the world I wouldn't have travelled to otherwise. I have made true friends who would stand with you to the death, not just with regards to football violence but in all aspects of life. If along the way I have had a few beatings, been arrested and spent a bit of time in prison, then so be it. Let me assure you that the fun and the laughs and the buzz far outweigh any minus points. You know the score, I am Villa Hardcore and I always will be.

Fowler: People ask me if I have any regrets. I wouldn't change a single thing. I've done a lot of jail for the Villa. Time wise I've probably done more than any of the lads. Four times I've been jailed for fighting for my club. You must understand I think all our lads are great, they're everything to me. I've met some great lads, people who I have now known for years and I will always remain friends with. We all go away together, we all socialise together. We had a photo-shoot which Luddy arranged and we had 200 lads turn up, just for a drink. We are all good mates.

Jonesy: I settled down too young really. I have drifted in and out of the scene for 25 years now. I have always gone to the matches. I drifted away from the social side of things to concentrate on my family. I always got a big adrenalin rush from the violence. Sometimes even if something didn't happen I would still be buzzing. Nine times out of ten nothing would happen. The buzz was still there regardless. In the 90s things changed. CCTV became more widespread. Filming by the police was commonplace. Sentences became longer. You have much more to lose now than ever before.

Fowler: I am not getting involved anymore. I can't afford to. When we started Villa on the pitch were going nowhere. Doug Ellis was in charge and he was happy with us being a mid-table club. We went everywhere the team played but we didn't always go to the matches. We'd stay in the pub. We'd have the crack with each other. That was what it was all about. One year we went to Forest. They made us pay in the game or they said they'd arrest us. We paid in to the game and walked straight out the other end of the stand. We went on the piss.

It's all over for me now. I was first nicked at football when I was 23. I have been banged up for the Villa on numerous occasions since then. When I first started getting into trouble you would get something like being bound-over to keep the peace. Now it is five-year bans and lengthy prison sentences. It's just not worth it any more. They'll never stop football hooliganism of course. There will always be young lads coming through wanting to test themselves against other teams. Then when they learn it's not worth it another generation will be coming through. Plus you will always have the older lads about on the fringes. The days of big mobs have also gone. You throw a punch on a night out in a city-centre now and you're nicked straight away with all the CCTV around. So the chances of you getting a firm of lads into a city-centre unnoticed are virtually non-existent.

Tucker: My life has always revolved around football. Even with a family I would try and arrange things so they didn't clash with the football. Holidays and weddings etc, I couldn't go if the Villa were playing someone. I honestly wouldn't change a thing. I have made some good lasting friendships with real people who wouldn't and haven't let me down. We're Godfathers to each others children, we all holiday together. I have made friends at other clubs through meeting people at certain incidents. People like Steve and Fletch from Sunderland. Fletch has gone out of his way to put us up when we have gone up there. Gilly from Wolves is a good lad. Another one is Spider from Man United, he is a brilliant lad who since I have known him has gone out of his way for me a couple of times. All top lads.

If I have one regret, it is the Uplands incident. Looking back it was a step too far. We were mostly all banned. We had only been out of jail for Rocky Lane for about 12 months. We had nothing to prove, especially against Albion. We should've kept out of it. I didn't actually do anything on the video. I was jailed for who I was and who I associated with rather than for what I actually did. When I went inside two lads, Liam and Fowler paid my mortgage so I wouldn't lose my house. Liam is a lad I have a lot of time for. Blues call him The Shadow. He is just so tall and thin. He has been a good friend to me and he has been very ill recently. When I was in trouble he was there I haven't forgotten that. Recently I was ill myself. I was going to the doctors and getting nowhere, when Fowler heard about it he told me he would pay for me to see someone privately. That's what a lot of people don't realise, how we all, especially Fowler, go out of our way for each other.

Fowler: It's when judges call me 'the scum of the earth' that gets me. I am a hard working employer. I employ people and give them work. I went out on a Saturday and got into fights with people who wanted to hurt me. I used to get scared, everybody gets scared in those situations, but the adrenalin rush was bigger than the fear. I'm not stupid, I'm not mad. I don't want to be one of these people who are considered mad

I'm not, far from it. It was confidence with me. I took Villa's firm over when I was 23. Name me one person who has done that. I had the confidence and everyone knew when it came to it I would be there.

I wanted to do this book because I want to be able to get it out when I'm old and have a reminder of what we all used to be involved in. We had something special. I don't want to be one of these celebrity hooligans. Have you seen the state of them? There was this book being written called Top Boys. Cass Pennant a West Ham celebrity hooligan was writing it. He got in touch with one of our lads, Spenna and asked him if I would like to be in it. I told the lad to tell him to piss off. He was going round the country making money off lads, he wasn't using me. Spenna then asked me if he could give him a bit of information about us for the book. I said he could but that he wasn't to mention anything we were up in court for, i.e. the Uplands against West Brom. Anyway Spenna gave him this interview and afterwards Pennant asked about the Uplands. Spenna told him a bit about what had happened but off the record. The next thing we knew it was in the book! Spenna and I were on trial together. Spenna's barrister is giving it all how his client was a law abiding citizen and the judge pulled out this Top Boys book! He said to the barrister that what he was saying contradicted what was said in the book. I felt like killing Spenna but it wasn't his fault. Pennant did not care who he dropped in the shit, he was just out to make money. I was in prison for Chelsea at Kings Cross. Bravo Television got hold of Tuckers number through one of the people featured on the show. They wanted to include Villa Hardcore on the series. They rang Tucker asking if we would appear on a programme about football hooligans. I was sat in jail and Tucker came up to visit me. He told me about the programme. I told him to tell them to piss off. He was surprised but I said to him I am not having any of our lads standing on television looking like mugs. You only have to see the programme to see what a mockery it made out of a lot of the lads featured. Look how it made Blues look. Running at the camera shouting Zulu! Did they think we would do that? If they did they thought wrong. It's not what we were about. I don't want fame or infamy out of it. I'm not going to stand on television looking like a plum while some reporter fires questions at me. I don't need the money for one, I'm quite comfortably off. For me it's all about dusting our book off in years to come and remembering the laughs we had. I m banned till 2015. I am glad I'm banned. If I was allowed down the Villa and omeone came down the road with a firm I would be in there. The last time I was in ourt a judge told me the next time I was in trouble they would start at five years. Five eas for a punch-up at the football? I don't want to risk everything I've worked for ver a punch at a football match. I've been there, and I've done a lot of things, for me 's all over.

Personally my days as a full-time active football hooligan were numbered in 2000. I had a work related accident which resulted in a hip replacement aged 36 and extensive knee surgery. Basically within a few months I lost everything. I'm not whining about it, it happened. I accepted it and moved on. The lads rallied round. People like Stickman and Archie came to see me regularly. Dandy and Big Paul came and terrorised me while I was in hospital. One of the first people to contact me after my accident was Fowler. He wanted to know how I was coping money-wise and informed me that he was paying for me to go to Greece with the lads on a holiday which had been planned. I knew about the holiday but had ruled it out as the money situation was bleak. He helped me for a number of months helping me get back on my feet. That is one of the things people don't realise when they see the headlines branding him scum. What they fail to realise is he is more than that. We are more than that. We are a family. We care about each other. If one of us is struggling we'll have a whip-round and sort them out as best we can. That will always be the case with us. We look after our own. Fowler was paying a few mortgages of the lads who were jailed. He hasn't mentioned it once while we were writing this book, although plenty of other lads have. He doesn't want recognition for it. It is just the way he is. He just says he could not sit in the same pub as people who have struggled financially knowing he could help them. He has been able to afford to do so, so he has helped people when he could. He someone, along with Dandy, Jonesy and the rest I am fortunate to count as friends. I know they'll always be there for me as I will always be here for them.

I wasn't actively involved at some incidents following my accident due to operations etc. When a lot of the lads started receiving jail sentences that's when I felt I could help. I badgered the other lads to write letters and to make contributions for their canteen etc while they were inside. Money was sent into them all in prison. Fowler, who certainly doesn't need the money, received the same as everyone else. One of the lads was struggling when his marriage broke up while he was inside. We organised a whip-round and a flat for him to live in when he came out. We also made sure the rent was paid for a couple o months so he didn't have to worry. We look after our own.

So is it the end for Villa Hardcore? It is as far as football violence goes fo the contributors to this book. Hopefully the name Villa Hardcore will carry o and always be associated with Aston Villa's support. If it doesn't it won' matter, we have left our mark on the history of the club and our city in one wa or another. The younger generation at the Villa certainly seem intent o carrying the name on. We don't mix with them as such there is a generatio gap, we certainly don't look down on them. As soon as they have proven themselves, they are Hardcore. It's as simple as that. As for the Hardcore, we still all socialise together. We holiday together. We are still as tight as a firm as we were when we were all allowed to go to the matches together. Lads work for each other and help each other out. For me that is what it is all about. Whether we'll see another Fowler appear, who knows? What I will say is that in my experience, over close to 30 years as a hooligan, I have never seen anyone who could come close to him. He had the lot. The charisma, personality, humour, aggression and he always led from the front. He made Villa a recognised name once more on the England scene. We operated in numbers other people wouldn't dream of taking and calling it on. That made us different. Whatever the numbers we let them know where we were and that we wanted it.

I don't regret being involved. I regret some of the things I have done over the years but you have to understand Villa's hooligan following has become a family to me. Hindsight is a wonderful thing and I can now see why I did everything I did. I found something which fulfilled some inner need in me. It's time for me to move on now. I don't feel the same way about getting involved anymore. I've matured finally I think. It was never planned with me, the violence. It was spontaneous - an incident during a game, a wrong word or someone turning up mob handed would cause me to want to hurt people. You cannot excuse that sort of behaviour in a civilised society, but as I have tried to show in this book, it is a fact of life for many men like me. We are products of our environment. If the conditions hadn't have existed to produce us then we wouldn't have existed either. They bred us for centuries to fight; suddenly we are surplus to requirements. I know a lot of people say ordinary people get caught up in it. The targets were never normal supporters; it was always about the other teams 'lads'. In my experience it was all part of the match-day thrill for the ordinary people. Those feelings have gone now and it has to be down to maturity. I still have a fire in my belly but it is about other things. I resent the way working-class people are so easily bracketed by the ruling elite and the imp wrested middle-class intelligentsia. I resent the way hard-working, tax paying football supporters can be labelled scum so easily by the establishment. How lads whose worst crime is having a punch up with other like minded adults on a Saturday afternoon can be treated worse than sex offenders or animals who batter the elderly. It is an interesting fact - especially in the light of Gary Glitters arrival back in Britain - that this country currently places travel restrictions on over 3000 football fans. At the same time only 6 paedophiles are prevented from travelling abroad to ply their evil trade. It says a lot to me about the sympathies of the ruling elite when you consider obvious discrepancies in justice such as these. Read about football lads receiving 2 years in prison for confrontation at a football match then read in the same papers that someone who has downloaded images of children has received 20 weeks in prison. That to me screams injustice and a rather warped sense of humanity from the ruling elite.

I think now I see the bigger picture about a lot of things and value certain things more than I ever have done. I certainly took my time but I got there. I am not however ashamed of my past. Fighting is in my blood. We were British warriors of the modern world. We are descendants of Harold Godwinson. We are sons of Brithnoth and we carry the spirit of Maldon. We were bred for battle and for battle's sake alone. Come swiftly to us, warriors to war.

He ordered each of his warriors his horse to loose

Far off to send it and forth to go,

To be mindful of his hands and of his high heart.

Then did Offa's Kinsman first know

That the Earl would not brook cowardice,

Then did Brithnoth begin his men to bestow -

He rode up and counselled them - his soldiers he taught

How they should stand, and their standing to keep,

And bade them their round shields rightly to hold

Fast to their forearms, that they flinch not at all.

A translation of the Battle of Maldon by Wilfred Berridge

I am proud to say I was one of the best of the best.
I was Hardcore. One of Aston Villa's Hardcore from Birmingham...

HARDCORE PHOTO SHOOT '08

HARDCORE PHOTO SHOOT '08

HARDCORE PHOTO SHOOT '08

HARDCORE PHOTO SHOOT '08

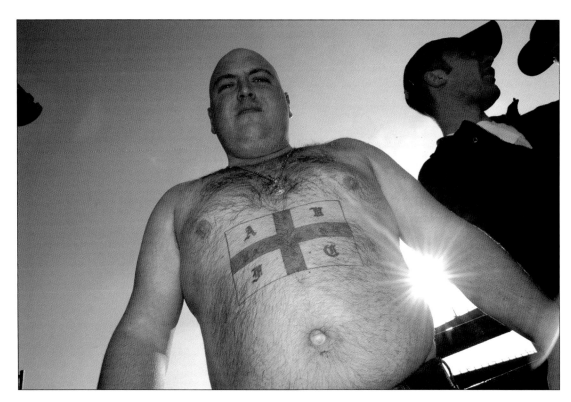

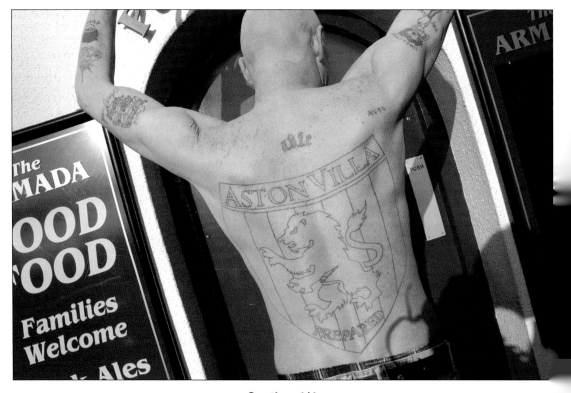

HARDCORE PHOTO SHOOT '08